Books by
Madelon DeVoe Talley

CAREER HANG GLIDING

THE PASSIONATE INVESTORS

The PASSIONATE INVESTORS

Secrets of Winning on Wall Street from Bernard Baruch to John Templeton

Madelon DeVoe Talley

Crown Publishers, Inc.
New York

The author and the publisher wish to acknowledge the following for permission to reprint the following material:

Jack J. Dreyfus for "Arithmetic Can Kill a Ghost" (from an advertisement used by Dreyfus & Co. on margin arithmetic); Talton R. Embry and Magten Asset Management, New York, for the chart on the power of compounding; T. Rowe Price Associates for the chart showing price-earnings ratio from quarterly report of the New Horizons Fund; The Insiders, $49 per year, published by The Institute for Econometric Research, 3741 North Federal Highway, Fort Lauderdale, Florida 33306, telephone 800-327-6720, for The Insiders Index; The Royal Economic Society for passages from *The Collected Writings of John Maynard Keynes* (vol. 12, pages 17–18, 38, 39, 51, 55, 64, 81, 106, 109); *Vogue,* for "Hiring a Broker," copyright © 1985 by the Condé Nast Publications Inc.; Curtis Brown on behalf of C. & T. Publications Ltd., copyright © 1976 C. & T. Publications for a passage from *Winston S. Churchill* (Vol 5, *1922–1939*) by Martin Gilbert.

Published by Crown Publishers, Inc.,
225 Park Avenue South, New York, New York 10003
and represented in Canada by the Canadian MANDA Group.
CROWN is a trademark of Crown Publishers, Inc.
Manufactured in the United States of America
Library of Congress Cataloging-in-Publication Data
Talley, Madelon DeVoe.
The passionate investors.
Includes index.
1. Stocks.   2. Investments.   I. Title.
HG4521.T29   1987   332.63'22   86-24281
ISBN 0-517-56563-3
10   9   8   7   6   5   4   3   2   1
First Edition

TO MY CHILDREN,
MELANIE, MACDONALD, AND MARINA TALLEY,
WHO GREW UP IN A HOME
PASSIONATE FOR THE BUSINESS OF
WALL STREET.

CONTENTS

INTRODUCTION

INVESTING RESEMBLES PAINTING; BOTH ARE creative endeavors. To become good at either, you have to do it. You have to paint, you have to invest. Yet simply doing it isn't enough, because learning solely by personal experience presents obstacles. You need time, which frustrates many, and you need objective, honest self-analysis, which is often elusive. So it is usually better to allow an apprenticeship period, during which the serious student works to comprehend the vision and the wisdom of those he admires in his field. Only by gaining such understanding can the individual responsibly earn the right to break away from the conventional, the accepted, and to venture into the unknown and untried, to emerge eventually with an original style of his own. With hard work and luck, a successful investor, a successful painter will be the result.

Yet, despite the originality of each of the investors' styles described here, the separate tales from these seemingly disparate people show an amazing continuity of thought. Taking the long view, Benjamin Graham's approach to successful investing is not very different from my sister-in-law Helen Sampson's. For, just as a painter works by continually shaping and paring, each successful investor meticulously tries to remove the excess, what hasn't worked, and to leave a few clear investing principles that he adheres to.

❦ 1 ❦
MAKING MONEY
Understanding
the Investment Mentality

INVESTING WELL AND MAKING MONEY IN THE market is a modern adventure. Successful investors are not unlike the Homeric heroes; their twentieth-century quest for profits is today's equivalent of the ancient search for the golden fleece. However, this is an intellectual quest, for fit argonauts who are willing to undertake a rough voyage. These argonaut-investors resemble Jason's band of legendary adventurers in single-minded pursuit, seizing opportunities, more than they do the later Romans and Greeks who conquered and stayed to govern.

These two distinct attitudes, particularly in terms of profits, are like the differences in modern times between an investor and an entrepreneur. An entrepreneur manages the growth and development of a company, a long-term proposition similar to the efforts of the Greco-Romans. The Homeric characters, on the other hand, like investors in the stock market, were interested in a good but quick return on their investment, a return, moreover, unsaddled with the problems of management.

Like Jason's search, today's voyage is strewn with obstacles that need clearing before the trip can proceed, dangerous debris that includes cloudy layers of misunderstanding and cynicism. There is first of all a perception that people who work in the investing field are fools and knaves, and this image is fueled daily even by insiders. My brother, Ray DeVoe, a stock market pundit, posed the question, "Is there intelligent life on Wall Street?" in one of his market letters, in an analysis of everyday Wall Street foibles. One day, a specialist on the floor of the stock exchange called to tell me a story going the rounds about what happened when Einstein went to heaven: He warmly greeted the first person he met when he arrived, asking immediately, "What is your IQ?" The man responded, "One hundred twenty." Einstein said, "Wonderful, we can discuss books and ideas." Then Einstein repeated his question to the next man he encountered: "What is your IQ?" On hearing that it was 160, Einstein was thrilled. "Wonderful," he said, "we can discuss nuclear relativity." At his third encounter, Einstein again asked his question and the third man answered, "Eighty." "Terrific," said Einstein. "What fun we're going to have! We can discuss the stock market."

Such ridicule of the profession is commonplace. And it's promulgated not only by insiders, but also in the most widely read and quoted investing literature. The most common conclusion, always summed up with resignation and a mocking undertone, is that investing is a game; investors can enjoy it and amuse themselves, but they must accept the fact that the odds favor the house. This point of view seems de rigueur for investment salesmen; possibly, too, it's comforting for an individual investor to know he is not the only fool in town. Why, after all, feel badly or try harder when it doesn't matter?

Accordingly, writers in their analyses will refer to investing as a gamble, implying to their public that it is simply a more sophisticated racetrack or Lotto window. And indeed, for some investors, it is. They look for a tip at cocktail parties or other outings and are quite willing to invest their money in any company that is spoken about enthusiastically. Their approach is the same as to any game of chance: Give me a name (or number); I can't win unless I have a ticket.

Another prevailing psychological attitude that is a significant detriment to successful investing is the desire for instant gratification. Everyone would like to find a route to riches without having to work for them—in fact, without embarking upon a quest at all. I was struck by this attitude one early afternoon in New York City, when the Newsweek building's neon weather indicator registered 95°. I looked at the line that had formed in front of the newspaper kiosk at Fifty-ninth Street and Madison Avenue. A polyglot group was patiently waiting there, reading to pass the time in that hot sun, in order to buy lottery tickets. As I passed, I saw the headline of the *New York Post:* "Lotto Prize Now $23 Million." I smiled. In fact, New York is only one of twenty-one states now actively promoting state-sponsored lotteries and off-track betting. A $10-billion-a-year industry has been created to meet the needs of people intent on their Cinderella dream.

Such dreams have even taken over the intellectual world. The MacArthur Foundation annually gives "genius" awards to winners chosen by a mysterious board in what seems a random manner from candidates assembled by a team of foundation spies around the country. The chosen few are notified by telephone of their selection. In the beginning, the winners expressed disbelief: Was there really such a magical financial prize, with no strings attached? Now, there isn't an intellectual in a garret anywhere who does not hope for this generous award. But, unlike the lottery, this is a contest for which there is no queuing up. An intellectual can only hope that a "genius scout" somewhere in his territory will discover him.

Whether the quest is for a dream Lotto number or being dubbed a MacArthur genius, the odds of winning a Cinderella prize are minuscule. No matter, the dream of these rewards continues for many to be a worthwhile fantasy, while the requirements for accumulating a treasure over a period of time frequently may be neglected. Perhaps this is so because the qualities needed for success with a long-term objective are considered mundane in a fast-track world. Perseverance and patience are the two most necessary. Yet, being realistic once you have considered the odds can be the start of a genuine treasure odyssey. Once the psychological blanket that encourages intellectual laziness is lifted, the clouds that obscure the possibility that intelligence pays off in Wall Street can readily be dispersed.

Fortunately, the chances of making money in the market are far superior to the chances at any gambling table or lottery window in the world. But success does require some study and a flexible attitude. Baron Guy de Rothschild once discussed with me the reasons for the difficulties some people have with investing. He felt their culture impeded their efforts, particularly their risk-taking abilities. In Europe, he explained, particularly in strongly Catholic countries, it has been difficult for people to embrace the idea of making money with money, because, until recently, most of the fortunes of any size were rooted in land estates. The borrowing and lending of money were often considered vulgar or sinful, and originally, this attitude left a vacuum that the Rothschilds could fill. Moreover, the baron said, this conservatism prevented businesses in Europe, even to this day, from being as aggressive as they should be with their investments. An open yet positive attitude has to be the first step before embarking on a treasure hunt.

Many people also believe, like those early Greek and Roman entrepreneurs, that it is far easier to make money building a business than investing in the market. "Not true," would say the seven out of eight business owners who start up a business and, within a year, close their doors, usually with all of their capital investment lost. Helping to perpetuate this belief in entrepreneurship is the "*Forbes* 400" list. Every year, *Forbes* magazine publishes thumbnail sketches of the four hundred individuals and families with the greatest net worth in the country. In 1984, only about twelve of the listed fortunes, or 3%, derive from investing, and this category includes the Allens, Loebs and Dillons, families that have established investment banking firms. Obviously, the success of these firms contributed to the families' megafortunes, although the central figures in the firms were known originally for their investing acumen.

The *Forbes* 1986 list reflects the changes in American business over the last two years. Real estate and investing fortunes have increased, while fortunes derived from oil and gas as well as manufacturing have decreased. Familiar Wall Street names were added: Michael Milken, William Simon and his partner Ray Chambers, Irwin Jacobs, Saul Steinberg and the Kohlberg, Kravis and Roberts leverage buyout group.

The listed fortunes derived from Wall Street have doubled in two years, though they are still small as a percentage of the 400. Wall Street also drives many of the *Forbes* fortunes by changing the market value of their stocks. Wal-Mart's stock increased 60% in 1986, adding $1.7 billion to founder Sam Moore Walton's fortune.

The *Forbes* annual list should be required reading for any investor, since it gives an overview of the ways in which money was made in different fields.

Not everyone in the world has the energy to develop and nurture a company, but everyone can develop the insight to spot a company that is ripe for future growth. An investor can target any area of the economy that interests him and focus his investments where significant changes are taking place, the same changes that benefit those entrepreneurial millionaires.

How then does an investor take advantage of the opportunities that abound in a growing American economy and avoid getting on a losers' list? Once we have checked our approach and are convinced that it will work, the next step is to remove some of those dense clouds that prevent clear vision—the debris that makes so many investors feel like Christina, blind and groping, reaching out for help in Andrew Wyeth's famous painting "Christina's World."

The most common problems investors experience that

make them feel that they are not doing well with their investments are:

Insecurity

One summer evening at a dinner party, I found myself laughing over an investing story. A Wall Street insider, a member of the New York Stock Exchange, told me that in the spring of 1983, he'd put $100,000 into a mutual fund, a first for him. He'd known the Fidelity Group well for years and when they created their Mercury Fund, an aggressive one, he concluded that this was the one for him. Before he knew it, his investment had fallen 30%. The night of the dinner, when it had recovered and was close to where he had started, he said, "I'm watching the market and the fund's price every day in case it looks as if small companies are going in the tank again." To be ready, he'd had his secretary type out the fund's telephone numbers on a card so that, just in case he got nervous, he could call to sell the shares.

I had started to laugh in the middle of his tale because I had done a similar thing. In the spring of 1983, one of my best friends had asked me to recommend two aggressive mutual funds for her. The new Fidelity Mercury Fund was one of my recommendations; I had chosen both funds based on the records of their money managers. Their common objective was to invest in aggressive, small-company stocks, an aim my friend had requested since most of her money was being managed conservatively. Then, a problem arose: The market shifted to favor stocks with solid fundamentals, after a nine-month heyday for small, growth stocks. An investor's only clue to the coming of the sea change might have been the offering of a new, aggressive fund. Such funds cannot be marketed unless there is a feeling of euphoria about the unlimited possibilities of small stocks.

In the fall of 1984, my friend asked me again to research the funds she had bought to see if she should get out of them; she thought now that they might be too aggressive for her and that perhaps she should try a money market fund. I delayed this research. One day I admitted to her that I was deliberately stalling, because her nervousness showed that she should wait; the market was bottoming, and when it turned again, these funds would respond. Then she could review their appropriateness.

Timing, the moment we choose to take action, is always significant. When we feel euphoric about an investment, it is usually at its top in the market. And when we are doubtful and hesitant, it is near its low. Perfection would be to step up to the plate when we feel conservative, but to wait until the next morning for our heads to clear, when we hear those champagne corks popping.

The investors in both of these tales had selected their funds for sound reasons and could afford to have a portion of their assets invested aggressively. Their problems arose because they had trouble living with downside volatility, especially when it followed immediately after their purchases. Investing in a mutual fund should always be a long-term commitment. That's the only way people have made money in them. Rather than panicking, an investor should add money, to benefit from dollar cost averaging. Howard Stein, chairman of the Dreyfus Corporation, once put it well: "Try to add just a little at first, when you don't feel like it."

Though one investor does not realize it when he is suffering, people tend to react in the same ways in the market. In 1984 the assets of money market funds exploded from $163 billion to $213 billion. Thirty billion dollars, 60% of that increase, was invested during the last quarter of 1984, precisely the period when my friend wanted to sell her speculative fund and move into money market funds. Other investors, feeling nervous, were selling equity funds and parking their money just before the stock market moved up. Their nervousness was costly. The first five weeks of 1985, the average equity fund was up 8%, and small-company growth funds showed an average increase of 17% (for that five weeks, the return was equivalent to one to two years' interest in a money market fund.)

Naïveté

At that same dinner, a former United States ambassador told his investing horror story over coffee in tones of shocked disbelief. Fifty-five years ago, his grandmother had left him a small trust of $20,000 at what is now called Citibank. Over the years, he had requested information from the bank. Why had bonds been chosen as the original investment? Could he remove the funds from the bank's custody? After being told for years that the funds were restricted, he discovered they were not, that all along he could have been investing in stocks. So the bank agreed to change its investment policy for his account and bought stocks. As soon as they were bought, the stocks went down. Now, the bank had told him, he could remove the money from the bank if he got the approval of his son, who is the ultimate beneficiary. When he asked his account officer why over the years he had been given incorrect information, he was told, "I don't know what past policy was. I can only tell you what we think today." The former ambassador asked the value of the account and was shocked to find that, after all that time, it was $19,600.

No sum in trust can appreciate in value if it is invested for income, and the income is spent. Yearly interest payments must be reinvested, rather than paid out, to get capital appreciation. Trusts often do have legal restrictions on their investment instruments; sometimes banks suggest prudent guidelines when they are set up. Remember, when the former ambassador's trust was established in the era of the stock market crash and the Depression, investment goals were different; the primary consideration then was preserving the principal for the next generation, rather than protecting it against the inroads of inflation by speculating, a much more recent objective. Today's investing formula for such a trust might assign 50% to fixed income instruments (to preserve principal) and 50% to stocks (to preserve purchasing power).

There will always be friction over trusts, their restrictions and over the bank chosen by the benefactor. The former ambassador's tale, with small variations, is unfortunately a common one. A trust document has to be read for you by your lawyer. Don't depend on either a bank's trust department or your ever-changing account officer for interpretation. Legal documents are subtly written and many things are permissible. It is in your interest to find the truth and to review your status periodically. Don't be surprised fifty-five years later.

Susceptibility to Hot Tips

The trouble with investing in someone else's confidential tip is that the investor does not have the slightest idea of what profit or loss to expect. The ride in a stock tip can be as steep as the Coney Island roller coaster's descent. Usually there is no one to question about it two months after your purchase. If you know the originator of the idea, chances are he will say, "You're still in that? I took my profits and got out long ago!" Profits, the investor moans inwardly.

Some ideas, though, are like catnip and everyone leaps at them. One confidential tip I remember well: "Sloan-Kettering is sponsoring a certain company's cancer test. Mr. X (a well-known and successful entrepreneur) has just bought a million shares." I fell for the story, bought the stock and the domino syndrome took over. More people bought the stock when they heard that I had bought it. A few months later, it was selling at 10% of its previous value and no one knows what that "smart investor" did with his shares or whether Sloan-Kettering ever really reviewed the cancer test. (I sold my stock and took the loss.)

Short-term Investment Orientation

If an investor is not realistic about possible profits, he will follow any fad that appears attractive. One such investor put all his money into municipal (tax-free) bonds, then a year later told his adviser that he wanted to move all that money into inflation hedges, such as oil and gold stocks.

His municipal portfolio had depreciated because interest rates had risen, so this investor took the losses and reinvested the remainder in oil and gold stocks. They, too, did well for a short time and then went down in value. Our Mr. Fad then insisted on switching to small technology stocks, the wave of America's future. It is better to end this saga here. Why, you might ask, did the investment adviser go along with these changes? Well, his client was paying both an advisory fee and brokerage commissions. To many people in the business, "What the client wants, the client gets" is a Wall Street self-preservation principle.

Unrealistic Expectations

One part of our lives must be based on realistic expectations, and that's when we try to make money with money. In our careers or love lives, we can dream on and on, and if we are lucky, some of these fantasies will come true. In these areas, dreams aren't expensive.

My past naïveté amply demonstrates the problem of unrealistic expectations. At the beginning of my career as a security analyst at the Dreyfus Corporation, I was asked to look at IBM to decide if it was a hold or a sale for one of our portfolios. After smothering it with analysis, I reported that, based on the fundamentals, it was definitely a sale. I could see only a 30% return in the next year for IBM. Now, a 30% return is a superb return in one year for any stock, but my expectations were in cloud-cuckoo-land and no one had reviewed typical returns with me. For the last fifty years, the average annual return has been 9% on the Standard and Poor's Index. So, if you are averaging better than that, you're not doing badly. Professional money managers who are able to outperform the index by 2% to 3% every year are considered the top in their field. In one exceptional year in the stock market, 1985, the Standard and Poor's Index was up 31.8%. Returns during the boom from 1982 to 1985 averaged just under 20%, and even during the last ten years the average return has been 14%. Perhaps recent history has raised expectations beyond what is attainable in the future. (If you add 2% or 3% to the Standard and Poor's average, you can find what would be considered good performance. Perhaps you're doing better than you think.)

Frauds, and Falling for Confidence Men

Familiarity with realistic returns helps you to analyze a promised result. One winter in Switzerland, I had a long discussion with a man who had come to Geneva, he said, to find his money. He was an American Indian who had made good, had started a firm, developed it and sold it to General Mills. With the resulting millions, he accepted the invitation of a man in La Jolla, California, to receive a 40% annual tax-free return on his money through international currency trading with no risk involved. I asked this successful businessman if he hadn't questioned that return, knowing from his own experience how large a promise it was. And he said, no, the man had delivered the 40% the first year. "Ah, but that was on paper," I pointed out.

The saga I'm referring to turned out to be the J. David Dominelli swindle that finally pushed its way to the front pages of our newspapers. Supposedly, $112 million was being held by European banks, but no one could find the money (not even my Indian tracker). And no wonder, since Dominelli spent the money instead of investing it. Dominelli involved fifteen hundred investors in his Ponzi scheme, many of whom were intrigued by the promise of avoiding United States taxes. Now they are reluctant to come forth. Still, I am sure the list of names includes the elite of La Jolla, California.

A promised 40% return in foreign currency trading is a lottery. The best equity manager ever made a 40% yearly return, but only for a few years. That's rare (and he never promised or guaranteed such a return). Clearly, then, understanding the odds of success and knowing realistic rates of return is the start of becoming a sensible (and profitable) investor.

Avoiding con men should be paramount. This is doubly

important if the investment is nonmarketable (meaning, you cannot get out of it the next day). Is there any way to spot one of these charming menaces? As the old adage goes, a leopard never changes its spots. Bankers know that they simply have to look back far enough to find the character traits they are seeking. Unfortunately, too few investors check out the people they buy from. They may fear they will miss a great opportunity if they do not act fast. And these leopards are seductive. They know how to sell. Often they are the very ones saying, "Get in fast."

Conveniently, the person selling these ideas is usually great at golf, tennis, squash or poker. He's in the in-group, his wife is usually a civic leader, he seems successful, but no one is sure what he has done in the past or is doing now. I have one self-protective rule called "The Three-Step, Slow-Speed Club Rule." Never buy into an investment offered to you at a club—and that covers all social and business associations—without first having your accountant, your lawyer and an expert in that field each check it. Needless to say, the kinds of deals you want to get into are hard to come by. They are rarely found loose in social settings. In fact, if you should discover one, you would almost have to force your way into it.

So, if you have made an investment and feel nervous about it, investigate immediately. If it is nonmarketable, your chances of losses are greater, an even better reason to make yourself question its validity immediately.

Acting fast makes a difference. A former acquaintance was sent to me when I worked at Rothschild. Nervous and slightly embarrassed, she explained that she had switched from a conservative adviser to one who was doing a great job, he was really making money for her, and, of course, that was why she had gone to him. The only problem was that he made her nervous. One of my colleagues reviewed the investment materials she'd brought, and after a few meetings, we knew something was seriously wrong. Her new adviser had her on margin with three different brokerage firms, she was totally invested in large positions in technology stocks, and, on top of that, her account figures did not jibe. Rarely does one investment adviser attack another, but this time we told her that she had a serious problem. I had her call her accountant from my office to make an immediate appointment. His findings turned out to be as bad as we had expected, but still, since the stocks were liquid, she was able to get out in time to salvage her capital. She was lucky that we had taken the time to help her, but she was smart, too, to have found someone to ask, despite her embarrassment when she realized that something was amiss. The fear of being considered either stupid or foolish should be the last worry in cases like this.

Laziness

This last investor's problem covers whatever the other headings didn't. It concerns the "should" factor—"I should change banks (or advisers)," "I should do something," "I should learn more about investments." Laziness increases that blind, helpless state. Try hard to do what you know you should.

THE ART OF MANAGING MONEY

Money managers with decent reputations have annual earnings like those of rock singers or baseball stars. What could better describe how rare and how valued such talent is? At Rothschild, my boss once asked me some questions about the art of managing money. I told him that being successful at investing required as subtle a technique as producing a great wine like Chateau Lafite Rothschild, and that basically many of the same criteria must be met. To produce a premier growth Bordeaux, such as Chateau Lafite, you need good soil, attention to many minute details and luck. The sun has to shine at the appropriate time or the current year will be adversely affected. Similarly, to make money in the market, you need good advice, attention to minute details (research and facts) and luck. You have to invest at the appropriate time or your return that year will be hurt.

Gilbert Highet, the Columbia University classicist and teacher, discussed in his book *The Immortal Profession* the development of wholeness of the mind. This can only be achieved, he felt, by assimilating other people's thoughts in order to form our own ideas. Such a process is a form of apprenticeship that creative people have undergone in the past. Similarly, the best way to improve your investing results is by studying the activities and the thinking of exceptionally good investors. Why start out without knowing their unwritten rules? No one begins to drive without knowing the rules of the road.

One of the younger investors I interviewed described his growth, learning and investment training thus: "I think very few people who are in the stock market have the opportunity to work for outstandingly successful people in their field. I'm sure somebody working for David Ogilvy on advertising campaigns is going to be better at writing campaigns and thinking about problems and addressing clients' needs than somebody who, for his entire career, works for average people. I had the opportunity to work with and for outstanding people and I met many of the great investors. I mean, those who've been great over twenty years, not those who've been great over two years. And all this gave me a chance to soak up a lot of information about how excellent investors think about things. As a result, I incorporated little bits of each one into myself, and I was able to enhance the ability I had."

By meeting some of these investors and by soaking up their thoughts, I think anyone can enhance his or her investing ability.

2

THE ENDURING OLYMPIANS

Bernard Baruch,
John Maynard Keynes and
Benjamin Graham

TO ME, THE ENDURING OLYMPIANS ARE THOSE whose memories have stayed vividly alive in investing lore. The three I have chosen, John Maynard Keynes, Benjamin Graham and Bernard Baruch, operated successfully in the early security markets of the twentieth century. Their investing exploits are common knowledge to anyone in the field. Our perceptions of their investing wisdom come from their writings.

Bernard Baruch, one of four sons of a country doctor, was born in South Carolina in 1870 and spent the first ten years of his life in the South, barefoot and happy in the Reconstruction years following the Civil War. Then his family moved to New York City, where Baruch went to public school and then studied for five years at City College of New York. He fell into Wall Street by chance. Unconvinced that following his father into medicine was right for her son, Baruch's mother consulted a phrenologist, who recommended that Bernard go into "big things," for instance, finance and politics. In 1889, after graduating from City College, Baruch started to read medicine with the idea of entering medical school in the fall. Baruch's father's dream that he become a doctor started to fade when his mother would remind them what the phrenologist had said. Soon afterward, she happened to meet a man, on the train from Long Branch, New Jersey, to New York (the Baruchs now had a summer home in Long Branch), who told her that he was looking for a young man to work for him. She arranged for Bernard to meet with that man the next day. (She preferred to take direct action and see that he was gainfully employed rather than scold him for his recent youthful escapade visiting a New Jersey "gambling hell.")

It was his mother's intuitiveness and instinct that got Bernard Baruch his start in Wall Street, as an office boy and runner. And, it didn't take him long to observe that money could be made using the differentials in stock prices quoted.

He became fascinated with the intricacies of classic arbitrage: Securities, then, could be quoted at different prices in New York, London or Amsterdam. (All arbitrage has been given a bad name by Ivan Boesky's recent exploits. Its classic meaning is what Baruch did. He looked for price differentials in a security, an activity carried on today in a modern version by the program traders rather than risk arbitrageurs.) Baruch went on to pyramid money for himself in the years ahead, learning as he went along, with what in retrospect seem to be multifaceted financial talents in arbitrage, investment banking and venture capital, as well as in aggressive shorting of securities. Eventually, Baruch's talents led him beyond Wall Street into the political arena, as an adviser to American presidents. One wonders if there is a successor today, near the old John Wanamaker store, to replace Mrs. Baruch's phrenologist.

John Maynard Keynes turned out to be a man of action as well as of thought. He entered Kings College at Cambridge and soon became prominent as a debater and scholar. Since his interests were more political than mathematical, he wondered about his future as an economist. By graduation he was still indecisive. The civil service appealed to him because, in the England of his day, it offered influence, public position and financial compensation. As he was without independent income and had done well but not brilliantly in mathematics while at Cambridge, Keynes decided to take the examination for the administrative grade at Whitehall. He placed second, and so he chose what he considered the second-best position, in the India office. The first-place winner went to the British Treasury. (Although Keynes was later to end up in the Treasury, his worst marks on the examination were in economics. This did not for a moment deter him from believing that he knew more than the testers.) Investing, then, became an additional activity for him in his already active life in the academic and intellectual community.

Benjamin Graham was born in 1894 in London, and a year later, he moved with his family to New York. His father continued to earn a living by importing china from Austria and Germany, while Ben attended public school at 117th Street and Saint Nicholas Avenue, and later graduated near the top of his class at Boys High School in Brooklyn. He had won a scholarship to Columbia University, but after his father's death, Ben had to help support his family, so he took evening classes and worked during the day with United States Express. Despite this double schedule, he graduated second in the class of 1914 at Columbia, which then offered him teaching jobs in the English, math and philosophy departments. (Graham never studied economics at Columbia.) The dean recommended him to a member of the New York Stock Exchange who had consulted him about his own son's progress at college. So Benjamin Graham ended on Wall Street in an investing career.

There has been nothing like the stock market crash of 1929 to the generation that lived through it and the

Depression that followed. Forever afterward, people defined their status and financial well-being by what happened on that date. In a way, the crash was the emotional equivalent of Vietnam to the generation of the 1960s. Life was no longer beautiful. People's expectations changed, their world darkened and their possibilities were forever limited. Most individual investors were wiped out in 1929 and the ensuing years. In an early advertisement for his financial firm, Jack Dreyfus remarked that, though one heard much about the billions lost in the market of 1929, people never mentioned the fact that billions were made in the markets of 1927, 1928 and 1929. It was the irresponsible use of credit that caused both those heights and the subsequent depths. Margins (the amount of security required on total investment) ranged from 25% to only 10%, and, Dreyfus added, where an individual's credit was good, no margin at all was required. Speculation had been rampant.

Not only was credit extended for speculation, but also investment decisions were made with very little research. In fact, investors were called speculators in the early part of the twentieth century precisely because so little information was available to the public. Financial reporting was almost nonexistent. Railroad companies did publish figures, but industrials were capricious. In 1899, when Amalgamated Copper went public, the only information it revealed about itself appeared in an eleven-line newspaper advertisement. Figures were jealously hidden, lest a competitor learn them. The stockholders of an industrial company often had nothing to rely on but a few words from management.

The stock exchange finally, in early 1933 after the crash, required listed companies to divulge financial information in an annual report that had been independently audited.

That was the world in which our three Olympians actively managed money. Graham was thirty-five years old, Keynes forty-six and Baruch fifty-nine at the time of the crash. None of them anticipated the extent of the decline and all were invested on margin at its onset. Keynes and Graham lost 60% to 70% of their assets, but Baruch, selling heavily at the start, had to have done better, perhaps because he was older and more experienced. They were the lucky ones who survived and came back strong in the markets.

Bernard Baruch tells a story in his autobiography about a boxing match he had in Woods's gym with a red-haired policeman whose beat went along Fifth Avenue. The policeman, a good boxer, batted Baruch around so that soon he was bleeding and attempting every boxing trick he had been taught. His senses were beginning to swim when his opponent uncovered. Baruch pounced, slamming him in the stomach and jaw. As the policeman fell to the ground, no one was more surprised than Bernard Baruch. One of the pros came over and slapped him on the back, saying to him, "You were getting a licking, but you hung on. You see, to be a champion you have to learn to take it or you can't give it." Baruch says that he tried to apply this lesson later in life: "To reach the top in any endeavor, you must learn to take the bitter with the sweet—the ridicule and taunts of other boys, the sneers, threats and sleepless opposition of other men, and the anguish of your own disappointments." And, he might have added, to be a champion investor, you have to take the downs along with the ups, and, at all costs, not get wiped out.

Winston Churchill witnessed the collapse of the New York stock market while traveling around the United States. Baruch sent his private railroad car to pick up Churchill in Chicago and bring him to New York.

He arrived the night of Blue Thursday and dined with Baruch on Fifth Avenue. Later, Churchill wrote about eating dinner that night with forty of the leading giants of finance in New York. One of the financiers gave a toast, first to Churchill's health and then, to the group he addressed as friends and former millionaires. Churchill describes his impressions of Wall Street the day after that dinner.

> I happened to be walking down Wall Street at the worst moment of the panic, and a perfect stranger who recognised me invited me to enter the gallery of

the Stock Exchange. I expected to see pandemonium; but the spectacle that met my eyes was one of surprising calm and orderliness. There are only 1,200 members of the New York Stock Exchange, each of whom has paid over £100,000 for his ticket. These gentlemen are precluded by the strongest rules from running or raising their voices unduly. So there they were, walking to and fro like a slow-motion picture of a disturbed ant heap, offering each other enormous blocks of securities at a third of their old prices and half their present value, and for many minutes together finding no one strong enough to pick up the sure fortunes they were compelled to offer.

It was refreshing to exchange this scene of sombre and for the moment, almost helpless liquidation for a window high in a titanic building. The autumn afternoon was bright and clear, and the noble scene stretched to far horizons. Below lay the Hudson and the North Rivers, dotted with numerous tugs and shipping of all kinds, and traversed by the ocean steamers from all over the world moving in and out of the endless rows of docks. Beyond lay all the cities and workshops of the New Jersey shore, pouring out their clouds of smoke and steam. Around towered the mighty buildings of New York, with here and there glimpses far below of streets swarming with human life.

No one who gazed on such a scene could doubt that this financial disaster, huge as it is, cruel as it is to thousands, is only a passing episode in the march of a valiant and serviceable people who by fierce experiment are hewing new paths for man, and showing to all nations much that they should attempt and much that they should avoid.

Churchill was on a three-month trip to the United States and Canada, visiting places he had been to in 1900, seeing the West Coast for the first time, promoting his book *The Aftermath*, lecturing and gathering materials for articles for Lord Camrose's paper. From the West Coast he traveled to Chicago, leaving there October 5 with Baruch. Churchill stayed with Baruch on Fifth Avenue during the crash, and later with Percy Rockefeller.

Were our three Olympians, Baruch, Keynes and Graham, good investors? Certainly they were the very best of their time, and their time was much more difficult for money managers. A game without rules creates bold and adventuresome participants, but few people can thrive with limitless freedom on the one hand and, on the other, no past knowledge to learn from. The slate is clean, everything is newly writ and being tried for the first time.

Our Olympians are like earlier athletes, as opposed to today's champions. These days, new records are set continually in some sport and old records broken. It looks so easy, too. One has to ask why this is so. Well, for one thing, athletes train more today in order to do better, and for another, their trainers use what they have learned from the experiences of others in past races, matches and meets. Then these trainers build their programs around this knowledge. In addition, athletes today come from a broader spectrum of society, and there are more of them competing to break those early records. Today's investors, too, have more knowledge of markets and specific securities, they build on the wisdom of the early investors or speculators and they are more highly educated before they arrive on Wall Street. So, like today's athletes, is it any wonder that a few are able to set records of their own?

Furthermore, investors also share with most athletes a single-minded pursuit of excellence; they know their achievement depends on their own efforts. Investors are probably the most competitive of intellectuals, yet, like athletes, they work alone to improve yesterday's score. Needless to say, such competitiveness creates jealousies; even the best tend to downplay another's performance and competence. A man of John Templeton's stature, for instance, may raise the issue of whether Lord Keynes was a good investor or not; another asked me if I would classify George Soros as an investor at all. ("What else," I responded, "since he makes money with money?") Yet another told me that although Graham was a good teacher, he got burned out as an investor, and didn't I know that Baruch really didn't avoid the crash? All these remarks are part of a psychological virus that I have come to associate with investing. It is a champions' disease, serving to raise their blood pressures and urge them back into the investment battle.

The wisdom of the Olympians has a contemporary ring to it. None of the three was timid or conservative. All were attracted to arbitrage, used leverage and made mistakes that cost money in their first investing attempts. Yet their friends continued to beg them to manage their money. Baruch once commented that he turned away money that was coming in over the transom, because of his belief that a speculator should act alone. What makes these men's experiences and thoughts so contemporary is the continuity of their evolution as investors. This flow of thinking has been followed and supplemented by the exceptional, successful investors who came after them.

BERNARD BARUCH—THE SUCCESSFUL SPECULATOR

Benjamin Graham described Bernard Baruch as "perhaps the only continuously successful speculator" of his time. Graham drew the line between speculators and investors by defining the former as those who anticipate and profit from market fluctuations, and the latter as primarily interested in acquiring and holding suitable securities at suitable prices. Baruch, on the other hand, said, "The simple truth is that there are no 'sure' things in the market," and that, therefore, he disagreed with such minute distinctions. A speculator to him was a man who acts before an event occurs (in fact, the word derives from the Latin *speculari*, meaning "to spy out and observe"). Baruch felt that such an ability was invaluable. To succeed, he found, he first needed the facts of the situation, then he formed a judgment based on those facts and finally, he had to act at the right time on the judgment he had made. (The last is definitely the hardest for investors to do. Baruch said that he had seen many men become powerless to act on their own behalf in the market.) But many people still associated the word *speculator* with gambling. In fact, Baruch once mentioned *gamble* in proposing an investment to J. P. Morgan and was ushered abruptly out of his office. The investment proposed was the embryo of what eventually became the profitable Texas Gulf. Lord Keynes confused the whole debate with his definition: "A speculator is one who runs risks of which he is aware and an investor is one who runs risks of which he is unaware."

Rule 1:   All good investors have to research the facts of a situation, make a judgment based on those facts and act swiftly to benefit from the situation.

In his autobiography, Baruch tells about the first time he was confronted with a great investment opportunity. On Sunday night before the Fourth of July, 1898, he received a telephone call from his boss, Arthur Housman, at his parents' summer home in Long Branch, New Jersey. Housman had heard from a newspaper reporter that the Spanish fleet had been destroyed at Santiago, Cuba. This news could mean the end of the Spanish-American War. Since the next day was a holiday, the market in America would be closed, but if the firm could buy American stocks on the London exchange, its customers could make big profits. The problem for Baruch—then twenty-eight years old—was how to get to New York from Long Branch fast and send off cables that would reach the market when it opened, on London time. No train was scheduled, so Baruch hired a locomotive and car to take him and a few others to the ferry on the New Jersey side of the Hudson River. Arriving in time, Baruch placed the orders in London while Housman called their customers. It was a great coup for the firm, which made immediate profits for its delighted clients when the American markets opened the next day.

Rule 2: Investors must remember the basic economic rule of supply and demand.

Baruch believed that he had become rich because he had remembered an observation of one of his professors, George B. Newcomb, at City College: "When prices go up, two processes will set in—an increased production and a decreased consumption. The effect will be a gradual fall in prices. If prices get too low, two processes will set in— decreased production because a man will not continue to produce at a loss and, second, increased consumption. These two forces will tend to establish the normal balance."

In 1901, a knowledgeable coffee merchant, Herman Sielcken, convinced Baruch that the copper market was becoming glutted because the metal was overpriced. Mr. Sielcken pointed out that Amalgamated Copper's plan to raise prices would fail, citing the collapse of an attempt to corner copper in France a few years before. Baruch investigated the situation, knowing that the stock had been pushed from·100 to 130 as the organizers tried to control the world's copper supply after they first overcapitalized the company and then overpromoted it. Baruch decided to short Amalgamated during the week of President William McKinley's death and funeral. The markets were nervous after the president's assassination and they closed for his funeral on Friday, September 20th. The directors of Amalgamated met that day and cut the dividend from $8 to $6. In the short Saturday session then at the exchange, the stock fell about 7 points. Baruch knew there would be significant action in his position on Monday. But Monday was Yom Kippur, and he stayed home, at his mother's request, on this holiest day in the Jewish religion. He always felt he had benefited financially from not being on the floor that day. For he would have sold the stock with a small profit, rather than letting it drop to 60, where he eventually closed out his position.

Rule 3: Analyze your investing losses to find out where you are making mistakes.

The first few years of Baruch's investing career were spent learning from his experiences. In that era—almost 100 years ago—an investor had to put up only 10% to 20% (margin) of the purchase price; the broker would carry the other 80% or 90% of the cost, using the stock as collateral. If the stock went down, the broker would ask for additional margin; if the investor couldn't come up with it, the stock would be sold. In the beginning, Baruch had no capital, so he put up only small amounts of money. He recounts that he would sometimes make a profit in one of these leveraged positions and then be cleaned out in the next one (it really was a trial-and-error way to learn, and a good one). In fact, at one point Baruch lost some of his father's savings. Yet when Baruch's mother told his father their son hesitated to approach him again, he produced a $500 check for another investment. That one gesture by his father demonstrably increased Baruch's self-confidence.

Baruch says that his early investing experiences made him determined to identify what he believed were his amateur mistakes. The most common mistake, he decided, is to know too little about the security being purchased, and the second most common is to try to make money too fast by trading beyond one's own financial resources. Soon, by analyzing his setbacks, he learned to work harder before he made a move and to take a cautious but opportunistic approach.

By the time Baruch was thirty-two years old and ten years on the Street, he had made $3.2 million in cash, but his success did not come until the second five years, after a five-year roller coaster ride.

Baruch carefully estimated who would benefit once the Depression was over. The market panic of 1893 was followed by a depression, a period when most investors despaired that conditions would improve. The nation's railroads had been overbuilt. In fact, at one point 60% of the companies listed on the big board were railroads; they had become the largest business in America. The trick for Baruch (which he accomplished) was to try to find the survivors—which railroads would be consolidated successfully and which industrial companies would pay out on their defaulted securities once good management could take advantage of a recovering economy. His race on the hired mini-train to take advantage of the open London market on that Fourth of July Monday in 1898 helped him, too.

At another time, his firm, A. A. Housman, got wind of a tobacco war building between two titans, tobacco magnate James Duke and financier Thomas Fortune Ryan. Baruch acted as an agent for Ryan. Union Tobacco was planning to buy Liggett & Myers, the only remaining independent tobacco company. This would make Union a strong rival to James Duke's American Tobacco Co. (It is amazing to think that then we were a nation of chewers and if we smoked anything it was a cigar or pipe.) The Union syndicate headed by Ryan sent Baruch as their agent out to St. Louis to buy up all available shares. Duke sent his own agents for the same purpose. It was the 1898 version of today's merger mania with the raider's agents soliciting the stock individually. Baruch, representing Union, won and came back with an option on more than half of the capital stock for $6.6 million. Duke ended up the winner, though, when Ryan then sold him all of Union Tobacco at a large profit as well as future entrée to Duke's inner circle of friends. The firm's commission, a decent one based on the work Baruch did on Liggett & Myers, of $150,000 enhanced its reputation. This transaction was the beginning for Baruch of a profitable long-term business relationship with Thomas Ryan, one of the financial titans of the period.

Baruch now received one third rather than one eighth of his firm's profits. By this time in his career, he had learned to hold some capital in reserve and not overcommit initially in his trading. This prevented his position from being sold out. He also knew the value of doing his own research before purchasing a situation. He began this in 1897, early in his career, when he'd done a study of the prospects of American Sugar Refinery. This transaction was an important turning point in his new approach to speculation. On the basis of what he learned, he leveraged his initial 100 shares and netted $60,000.

Rule 4:   Rely on your own cold and detached judgment of the facts of an investment.

Baruch became disdainful of tips and so-called inside information. He believed that, whether it was manufactured or merely exaggerated, someone was always misled by it. He even thought insiders in a company made blunders themselves based on such information, since it made them feel they were so much smarter than everyone else that they could ignore what was obvious to other investors.

After he profited from a venture with Daniel Guggenheim for American Smelting and Refining Company, Baruch naturally followed closely the action in the stock. The shares (called Smelters) had risen from the 80s to over 120. Baruch thought the rise was unhealthy and wanted to tell friends to whom he had recommended it. He went to the Guggenheims and explained his fears, advising them to sell. The family did not like this news and disagreed that their stock had risen too high. Baruch sold out, and Smelters continued to climb, so that in November of 1905 it was over 157. Eventually, it topped 200 and then started down. A story spread that Baruch had raided the stock, though he hadn't, but he had to buy Smelters to turn it around and stop the rumor. To Baruch it was clear that businessmen like the Guggenheims may have understood mining, but they lost their judgment when it came to the stock market.

Rule 5:   Try to avoid the psychology of crowds.

After observing swings of mood in the stock market, from wild hope to unlimited despair, Baruch found a book published in 1841 by the writer Charles Mackay. His *Extraordinary Popular Delusions and the Madness of Crowds* chronicled the investing frenzies that had gripped mankind through history. Baruch was fascinated by the repetitive patterns of the Tulip Craze or the Mississippi and South Sea Bubbles in their respective countries. He wrote the foreword for a 1932 reprinted edition of the book, and posed this idea: What if, during the dizzying markets of 1928 and 1929, investors had continually repeated, "Two and two still make four"? Would they perhaps have avoided the debacle? For readers of the new edition who wondered if the decline in the markets would ever end, he suggested that the appropriate "abracadabra" might be, "They always did."

Rule 6:   Retreat from the field of battle to study your investing mistakes and successes.

This is the most famous of Baruch's axioms. Sometimes he would sell his investments and go on a trip, thinking that when he returned, his mind would be fresh and his reserves available for new commitments. He did this for the first time in 1902; when he felt the market was high, he turned most of his holdings into cash and went to Europe. These funds enabled him to help his partner, Arthur Housman, after two of Housman's main investments suffered sharp drops during Baruch's absence. During the dizzying market of August 1929, Baruch was in Scotland grouse hunting. While waiting in London to return home, he cabled buy orders to New York, only to sell the following day. Then, having reached a conviction while returning on the boat, he sold more securities and continued selling on his arrival in New York.

Baruch listed in his autobiography some rules or guidelines for others, based on his experiences, though he remained skeptical of investors' emotional self-discipline. He realized that people had to learn for themselves, that it was part of human nature to think they could beat the game and outsmart the other players. Like them, he had arrived on Wall Street without a financial background or contacts of any kind and had learned by trial, error and observation. His list is admirable. Its commonsense quality is as relevant to followers of Warren Buffett's reliance on fundamental value as to those who admire George Soros's more flamboyant abilities, although Soros is closer to Baruch in his opportunistic, eclectic investing style. Each morning, Baruch's first stop was at the arbitrage wall of the stock exchange, to ask, "How's London?" Then he would buy in one market and sell in the other, depending on the spreads, an investing routine that would please Soros. He would recognize, too, that Baruch shared with him the vision and mentality of a venture capitalist or investment banker, who aggressively buys long and sells short, borrowing to make the most of his investments.

Bernard Baruch's Investing Rules

1. Don't speculate unless you can make it a full-time job.

2. Beware of barbers, beauticians, waiters—of anyone —bringing gifts of inside information or tips.

3. Before you buy a security, find out everything you can about the company, its management and competitors, its earnings and possibilities for growth.

4. Don't try to buy at the bottom and sell at the top. This can't be done—except by liars.

5. Learn how to take your losses quickly and cleanly. Don't expect to be right all the time. If you have made a mistake, cut your losses as quickly as possible.

6. Don't buy too many different securities. Better have only a few investments that can be watched.

7. Make a periodic reappraisal of all your investments to see whether changing developments have altered their prospects.

8. Study your tax position to know when you can sell to greatest advantage.

9. Always keep a good part of your capital in a cash reserve. Never invest all your funds.

10. Don't try to be a jack-of-all-investments. Stick to the field you know best.

JOHN MAYNARD KEYNES—THE ECONOMIC THEORETICIAN AND INVESTMENT PRACTITIONER

John Maynard Keynes has gone down in history as one of the great economic theoreticians of the twentieth century. Yet his friends and peers in the investing community of his day knew also of his active role as an investor, both for himself, and as bursar for Kings College, Cambridge. In both fields he excelled, a rare combination: a man capable of developing new economic theories who is also able to deal in the everyday world of making money with money. In fact, the income Keynes received from his investing activities after 1920 formed a significant part of his yearly earnings and augmented his writing fees and academic activities. Yet his genuine abilities as an investor were not well documented until 1983, when Donald Moggridge edited Volume XII of Keynes's letters on economics. Keynes had kept extensive notebooks recording his investments and the associated correspondence, which revealed his thoughts on investing as well as his techniques and the performance of the money he managed.

Secure in his prestigious job as editor of the *Economic Journal,* won in 1911 when he was twenty-eight, Keynes started investing in a special fund a few years later with money he saved from birthday gifts and various academic prizes. He concentrated on the foreign exchange market, where Keynes would short the futures of the currencies of France, Italy, Holland and, after March 1920, Germany, while going long such currencies as U.S. dollars, Norwegian and Danish kroner and Indian rupees. In the beginning, his speculation was successful, so he formed a syndicate with more investors and more money. This syndicate began well, but the denouement came fast. When Keynes closed it out, every currency dealt in showed a loss, for a grand total of $93,412. But Keynes rebuilt his fortune the same way he lost it, by using capital and investing again in the currency markets.

He wrote to Sir Ernest Cassel, a financier who had asked Keynes to inform him of investing opportunities. Keynes's letter explaining the investing climate and the opportunity he saw, combined with his humility in explaining past losses, was so honest and convincing that Cassel sent money immediately. This loan, along with an advance on his book, *The Economic Consequences of Peace,* got Keynes back in the investing game. He then worked off $35,638 in debts and ended $89,785 ahead by 1922.

Donald Moggridge, comparing Keynes's results with the Bankers Magazine Index, observed that in five out of the seven years during the period from 1922 to 1929, Keynes outperformed the index, and that after 1929 his investments cumulatively outperformed the market by an even larger margin than before (sounds pretty uniformly good to me). As an aggressive, highly leveraged investor concentrating on a small number of stocks, Keynes did well in rising markets. This is not surprising, considering his tactical methods; anyone so highly leveraged always magnifies his results. But Keynes's continued investing success is even more extraordinary for its time. The Thirties were not an easy period in which to make money. Many investors were either forced or chose to stay on the sidelines, tending their financial wounds. But Keynes was self-taught. He believed in going contrary to general opinion, and he multiplied his net worth handsomely during the Thirties, surviving the crash and the ensuing two depressions. His own portfolio grew from £7,815 in 1930 to £411,238 in 1945. In an article on Keynes ("The Original Contrarian," *Forbes,* September 26, 1983), Lawrence Minard, the author, estimates that the value of Keynes's portfolio in 1945 would be $10 million in 1983 purchasing power and that his 13% compounded return was indeed something to be proud of.

**Abbreviated Summary of
Keynes's Investment Performance**

	Keynes	Kings College Chest	London Industrials	N.Y. Common Stocks
1920	100	100	100	100
1929	36	228	105	326
1930	58	154	85	264
1936	2,350	680	140	195
1937	998	738	115	193
1945	1,908	1,124	160	190

In spite of dramatic declines in 1929 and 1937 in his personal account, Keynes was able to multiply his money 19 times since 1920, and the Kings College Chest fund 11 times, while the London and New York securities markets failed even to double.

Some of Keynes's thoughts and investing rules:

Rule 1: Rather than to buy or sell, "to be quiet" can sometimes be the best policy for an investor.

In a memo on the investing climate in 1931 to the board of the National Mutual Life Assurance Society, Keynes suggested that "To Be Quiet" was the best policy.

There is a great deal of fear psychology about just now. Prices bear very little relationship to ultimate values or even to reasonable forecasts of ultimate values. They are determined by indefinite anxieties, chance market conditions, and whether some urgent selling comes on a market bare of buyers. Just as many people were quite willing in the boom, not only to value shares on the basis of a single year's earnings, but to assume that increases in earnings would continue geometrically, so now they are ready to estimate capital values on today's earnings and to assume that decreases will continue geometrically. In the midst of one of the greatest slumps in history, it would be absurd to say that fears and anxieties are baseless. . . . But I do not draw from this conclusion that a responsible investing body should every week cast panic glances over its list of securities to find one more victim to fling to the bears. Both interest and duty point the other way.

And later, in 1938 in a letter to F. N. Curzon, Keynes said:

I feel no shame at being found still owning a share when the bottom of the market comes. I do not think it is the business, far less the duty, of an institutional or any other serious investor to be constantly considering whether he should cut and run on a falling market, or to feel himself open to blame if shares depreciate on his hands.

Rule 2: If one deals in equities, then it is normal to expect large fluctuations.

Keynes expected that in bad times some part of paper profits would disappear. "Results must be judged by what one does on the round journey." The other choices he found even less attractive: to invest in debt instruments for a sure but low rate of return or in real or other property where the risks were unpredictable.

Rule 3: Concentrate your investments, putting large sums into enterprises that you think you know something about.

Because Keynes recognized that an investor's knowledge and experience are limited, he put his full confidence in only two or three enterprises at any time. He believed that he made the most money from these pet investments, that nobody ever made much out of a mixed bag.

Rule 4: It is safe to bet that the extremes of misfortune will never occur.

Keynes made this comment in a letter to P. C. Scott in 1933, when, in discussing the future of America, he said he felt that general disaster for a great country like the United States is far less likely than disaster for a particular firm or industry. Nine times out of ten, he went on, "it is safe to bet that the extremes of misfortune will not occur." (It is interesting to reflect on Keynes's comment in view of recent market worries about the federal deficit or the international debt crisis. Of course, there's always that one-in-ten chance.)

Rule 5: The question of yield should not be overlooked.

Modern investors concentrate too much on monthly valuations and capital appreciation or depreciation, Keynes thought, and not enough on yields, future prospects and intrinsic worth. He said, "I consider capital profits and accruing income as the measure of success."

Rule 6: Pick the right shares.

Keynes, the man who wrote *The General Theory* and who invented what he called credit-cycle investment, was to say that, after twenty years of observing, he had not seen a single successful instance of credit-cycle investing, buying shares in slumps and disposing of them in booms—today's market timing. In a 1934 memorandum, Keynes said that he believed successful investing depended on three principles:

a. a careful selection of a few investments having regard to their cheapness in relation to their probable actual and potential intrinsic value over a period of years ahead and in relation to alternative investments at the time.

b. a steadfast holding of these in fairly large units through thick and thin, perhaps for several years until they've fulfilled their promise or it is evident that they were purchased on a mistake.

c. a balanced investment position (a variety of risks in spite of individual holdings being large) and if possible opposed risks . . . holding gold shares amongst other equities (as they move in opposite directions during fluctuations).

Another important rule, he added, is the avoidance of second-class, so-called safe investments, none of which can go up and a few of which are sure to go down. Keynes felt that this was the biggest mistake investors make. An ideal portfolio, he thought, should be divided between secure future income earned by interest and equities where one believes there is large potential in order to make up for the equities that are bound to disappoint.

In the postmortems he so often wrote about investing results, Keynes tried to analyze what had taken place in the economic world that neither he nor others had foreseen. In these memos he admits his inability to predict the large economic shifts of markets. His humility should humble all of today's market timers who still believe that investors can successfully move in at the bottom and out at the top of an economic cycle. Keynes remained leveraged in 1930, when his assets declined to one quarter of what they were in 1928, and he was margined as well in 1937–38, when his net assets fell by two thirds—substantial losses in his net worth, which he explained economically in hindsight. He relied on his maxim, "Investing results should be judged by what is done on the round journey." He died on Easter in 1946. His successful investing record continues to speak for itself.

BENJAMIN GRAHAM—THE FATHER OF
SECURITY AND VALUE ANALYSIS

Benjamin Graham has to be one of the great teachers of all time, if teaching performance is measured first by the influence of teachers on their field and, second, by their students who go into the world molded forever by that learning experience. Imagining security analysis without Graham is as impossible as imagining psychoanalysis without Sigmund Freud. In reading of Graham's long teaching career in New York, I regret that I did not fall into his orbit during one of the periods he taught at the New York Institute of Finance (a school started by the New York Stock Exchange), or in his usual classes at Columbia University. The institute is where thousands of us fledglings in the securities business took our introductory courses. I have often wondered what would have happened to me if I had had such a teacher in my early days. Instead, my classmates and I worked through Graham and David Dodd's book *Security Analysis,* chapter by chapter—learning by rote with a tired, dull teacher—rather than absorbing insight and stories from the master himself. *Security Analysis* is the bible of the financial analysis field, but it often seems hopelessly long and dry, certainly impossible to read from cover to cover. Graham himself recommended instead his *The Intelligent Investor* for young analysts.

Everything Graham learned from his career in Wall Street between 1915 and 1956 he dissected, developing theories of what does and what does not work in evaluating investments. Some of the experiences that helped to form his theories were:

Margins

Graham first realized what leverage could do in 1907 when, at thirteen, he saw his mother's margined U.S. Steel investment wiped out in the panic of that year. She had just been widowed, and this loss further diminished her resources. In 1917, Graham himself leveraged $10,000 a friend had given him to invest in a trading account, in which they shared the gains and losses. The account did well at its start, but toppled after America went into the war. Their investments were obscure, nonmarketable issues that were difficult to sell to meet margin calls. They suffered considerable losses, but eventually the account came back. Later, in 1926, Graham formed the Benjamin Graham Joint Account, again with capital contributed by friends. In the three years before 1929, the account appreciated from $450,000 to $2.5 million.

But, like so many other smart investors during that period, Graham had not learned the lessons about margin. In spite of his earlier experiences, he failed to anticipate how quickly borrowed funds could be affected by severe declines. Between 1929 and 1932, the joint account was down 70%, falling between the broad-market Standard and Poor's decline of 64% and the Dow's decline of 74%. Many who were investing on their own lost everything, wiped out by margin calls. As a result, they had no capital to stake on the comeback that eventually took place, unlike Graham. Since the joint account was margined 45% at the start of the crash, keeping its decline to the levels of the market averages was a feat equivalent to keeping a sailboat afloat in a hurricane.

It is no wonder that later, in *The Intelligent Investor*, Graham says that an individual investor should realize that when he operates on margin, he is speculating, just as he does when he buys hot stocks. Speculation can be fun, but it is not investing. He advised setting aside a small amount of capital in another type of fund.

The Evolution of His Style

Graham's start as an investor was a natural one for the period before 1920 when he joined Newburger, Henderson and Loeb as an assistant in the bond department. But his first big investment success was unusual—a value analysis of an arbitrage opportunity in a plan for the dissolution of the Guggenheim Exploration Company. The company held mining stocks in its portfolio, and Graham estimated that the market value of distributing these holdings to shareholders would be $76.23 per share versus the $68.82 market value of the holding company itself. Respect and profits were his rewards after the dissolution, when his firm made money in the arbitrage position he had recommended.

Another investment showed Graham that though statistics are important, management is vital. He compared the data for rubber and tire stocks and concluded that Ajax Tire was the most attractive. Graham met the president of the company only after the recommendation had been issued. And as the company eventually ended up in bankruptcy, he wished that the meeting had taken place earlier. Ajax statistically was the most attractive choice but perhaps interviewing management about the company's future might have made him wary of such a recommendation. The future plans of a management can quickly destroy a company's past record.

After the crash and twenty years of experience in Wall Street, with some resulting scars as well as admiration from friends and peers, Benjamin Graham, with David Dodd, wrote his classic textbook. Certainly, in 1932, his approach to investing was colored by the volatile ups and downs he had experienced: After that time, he focused on undervalued or special situations, though originally he was known for his arbitrage and hedging talents. His greatest investing coup came during this later focus on value. In 1948, Graham-Newman (his company, formed with a partner, that grew out of the joint account) purchased half of Geico (Government Employees Insurance Company) at a cost of approximately $720,000, a sum that amounted to 25% of Graham-Newman's assets. Graham made a greater profit on this investment than on any other. Simplified, 1.08 shares of Geico in the Graham-Newman portfolio had an original market value of $27. After distributions of dividends plus interest in three Geico affiliates, a share at its high in 1972 was worth

$16,349. Even after competition in the automobile in-
surance industry forced the stock down, each share in
1976 was worth $2,407 (90 times as much). The Geico
investment was a good example of Ben Graham's
talents, focused now on what had, for him, proved successful in the past. He never repeated the error of borrowing and being leveraged, although Graham felt he had
forgotten some of his principles when Geico went to great
heights.

Management of Fees

When Hartman T. Butter, Jr., interviewed him in 1976,
Graham told how his company, Graham-Newman, had
limited itself to a maximum of $15 million to manage,
which seems small in today's world. But he expected to
earn the greatest percentage possible on it per year. His
fee for new accounts was a 20% share in the profits after a
6% return to the investors, and originally he had earned a
$10,000 salary besides the profit-sharing arrangement. It
is easy to imagine that the later hedge funds and private
partnerships took their fee formulas from Graham's
model. In the Twenties bull market, some customer's men,
the old-fashioned name for brokers, ran accounts in which
they would split profits but not losses with their clients.
Brokers then often were teased with the question of where
were the customers' yachts, but probably "the customer's
men's yachts" would have been more to the point. The
fees of the "Benjamin Graham Joint Account" were high
when it was formed. It was scaled upward so that Graham
took 13% of the first 50% in profits and 50% of any profits
after that. This all looked sensational when the joint account appreciated from $450,000 to $2.5 million in the
three years before 1929. But since the fees were earned
only on profits, he and his partner went for years without
earning anything when the market decline came along.
In 1934, he made a new fee arrangement at a straight
20%.

Managing a Career

During his early years as an investor, friends would ask Graham to manage their money. Apparently he exuded not only intelligence but the assured confidence of someone who knows what he is doing, leading others to place their confidence in him. Graham had recommended securities to Bernard Baruch over the years, which encouraged Baruch to invite him to be his junior partner in 1929. Graham refused this clearly ego-building offer, for 1928 had been a profitable year for him. He had earned $600,000 with that golden fee arrangement when the joint account was up 60% after fees, compared with a 51% increase in the Dow. In the ensuing stormy market, Graham may have wished he had accepted Baruch's offer.

In his new introduction to the fourth edition of Graham's *The Intelligent Investor,* Warren Buffett, Graham's most famous pupil and disciple, said that Graham's writings "brought structure and logic to a disorderly and confused activity." And they did. Before Graham's *Security Analysis,* there were no principles to follow, only whispers about either a company's operations or what the stock market pools were buying and selling. Graham created a discipline for evaluating securities and left some sound investing precepts for us to consider. Many are explained in *The Intelligent Investor.*

Every investor, Graham says there, has to decide which category he falls into: Is he an enterprising or a passive investor? There are only two choices. Any attempt to fall somewhere between represents a search for a compromise that is bound to fail. Graham identifies the aggressive and enterprising investor as one who views his investments as he would a business enterprise, and few people can qualify for this category. Most investors should choose the defensive-passive strategy, since they do not have the interest, time or determination needed to become enterprising investors. All investments should be looked at from time to time, because businesses change periodically. And the rate of return an investor wants cannot be determined by the amount of risk he's willing to assume (conventional Wall Street wisdom), but rather by the effort and intelligence he brings to the task.

> *"The minimum return goes to our passive investor, who wants both safety and freedom from concern. The maximum return would be realized by the alert and enterprising investor who exercises maximum intelligence and skill."*

Investors have to choose policies that are unpopular in Wall Street, if they want to achieve better than average results. Prices of all securities fluctuate, and aggressive investors should search for companies that have become bargains because they are unpopular. Graham observed that enterprising investors concentrated on growth stocks, special situations, or undervalued issues, or they tried to be market timers, buying when the market was low and selling as it got high. He points out that it is much too difficult for investors either to time the market or to buy and hold a large position in a growth stock. His favorite example of the latter strategy was IBM, the daddy of all growth stocks. IBM fell from 607 to 300 in a period of six months in the early Sixties, and then again by 42% in 1970. Graham reasons that most investors would have sold from nervousness along the way, even after the decline, to lock up some kind of profit, but that they would not get the maximum possible gain. Fortunes can be made by people who buy positions in a company early on and hold the stock patiently through the company's vicissitudes. But only when an investor has a close relationship with the company, Graham says, would he be able to hold on over a period of time and ignore the temptation to sell.

Of all the investment methods that Graham studied in his search for something that worked, he found two that brought good results. The first was buying important companies selling at low price-to-earnings ratios, although this method, he observed, didn't work in the period from 1968 to 1971 (a period when growth stocks with high multiples did well in the stock market). The second was searching for a diversified group of stocks selling under their net current asset value or working capital value (there are periods when these opportunities too disappear). This approach is often taken by value investors, some who today follow Graham's habit of searching through the Standard and Poor's stock guide with its 5,000 company listings and a plethora of statistics on their stocks.

Chris Browne, of Tweedy Browne Inc. (the firm known as a Graham follower), searches out values today this way. He calls it an arithmetic approach to investment analysis: By buying stocks at two thirds of net current assets, an investor can fix his costs far below the value of the company itself. "Who knows why?" he added. "It just works out. They get discovered, they get taken over, they go private. Something happens." Browne compared net current investment to the development of an insurance portfolio, which excludes the extremes of the best and the worst. If, for example, a company will only insure drivers between the ages of thirty-five and forty-five who are married, with three children and a low-powered car for use around town, statistically it will have good results. An investor sets up the same odds by buying only companies that sell at a discount to their net current assets or working capital.

Analysts find these discounts, Browne said, by finding a company's current assets in a stock guide and deducting current liabilities, long-term debt and preferred stock. They divide this sum by the number of shares outstanding to get the net current assets per share. If the market price of the stock is two thirds of that figure, then it is a buy, because it sells for less than it is worth.

According to Warren Buffett, also a value buyer, says Browne, Tweedy Browne's rule that it will put no more than 3% of its assets in one position makes it a junk collector. Buffett prefers more concentrated investments. Graham, the father of value investing, would enjoy the subtle variations of analysis he has spawned. In that 1976 interview with Hartman Butter, Graham remarked that he had lost interest in the details of security analysis that had been important to him for so long. He felt he was moving away from the rest of the profession, which continually seeks formulas, framework and answers, and that only a few techniques and principles were needed. "The main point is to have the right general principles and the character to stick to them."

3

THE LIVING
LEGENDS

*The Contemporary Wisdom of
Roy Neuberger, Jack Dreyfus,
George Soros, Warren Buffett,
John Templeton and
Jacob Rothschild*

THE LIVING LEGENDS ARE SOME OF THE EXCEP-
tional winners in the world of money managers, men who
stand apart by their proven talent for making money with
money, not only for themselves but for their clients, partners or shareholders. My selection of six is purely subjective, but all these men have used a variety of techniques to
master the stock market and, for a period of time, to hold
it in bondage.

Roy Neuberger, today chairman of Neuberger Berman
and Company, decided in Paris in the late Twenties that
he wanted to buy the work of living artists and therefore
he needed a fortune. He joined a Wall Street brokerage
firm, Halle and Stieglitz, in 1929, as a runner and factotum

and, during the panic in the market, found himself in purchase and sales, where in those precomputer days everything was written out. Since then, Neuberger has spent fifty-six years in Wall Street, eleven years at Halle and Stieglitz and forty-five at his own firm. He has always analyzed stocks himself to determine the long-term outlook of a company. His vision is so clear that peers think his greatest analytical ability lies in eliminating puffery, and that this ability enables him to be exceptionally good at shorting stocks—in other words, at betting on their overvaluation in the marketplace. Jimmy Rogers, an apprentice who worked closely with Neuberger, was impressed by his timing in both buying and selling securities: "What I learned when I sat at Roy Neuberger's feet in 1969 and 1970 was that he was a superb trader. You buy 'em, mark them up a bit and sell them. If you hold them . . . you're going to lose." Rogers says Neuberger learned his market attitude in the clothing business, then took the lessons of merchandising into Wall Street with him. Moreover, he started on the Street in 1929, when staying too long in any security was dangerous. Neuberger also taught Rogers that it was not enough to research and analyze, that watching the tape was a way to understand other people's perceptions. Neuberger understood the tape so well, Rogers said, that he knew what General Foods was doing, even if he was in another room. He has concluded that today's tape is distorted by institutional activity and no longer is a meaningful tool; now his firm uses computerized charts. The conclusive fact is that Neuberger made the fortune he wanted many years ago in Paris. His art collection is highly valued, and Neuberger Berman, where he has a significant partnership stake, would be worth a minimum of several hundred million dollars.

Jack Dreyfus, now chairman of the Dreyfus Medical Foundation, feels that good luck and fortunate circumstances in his life set its direction. Nothing he did happened purely out of ambition but resulted from where he found himself. His Wall Street adventure simply happened, and what an adventure it was. As one of the early leaders in the mutual fund industry, he developed and marketed a new way for individuals to invest. In its early years, his fund had a better record than any other from 1953 to 1965, up 604%, 102 points ahead of second place and far superior to the Dow's 346%. Dreyfus first worked in Wall Street for a chart specialist, so technical analysis always came first for him. He admits that he had to use what he understood best and that he always was too shy to call up managements of companies and ask them questions. Yet he spotted Polaroid early and made a large investment in the company. It was one of the best investments of all times; Dreyfus held it as it split forty times. In the Wall Street caste system, technicians are counted, but not esteemed, the saying being, "I've never met a technician who's made money." But Jack Dreyfus did—and no one can read a chart the way he can.

John Templeton, who worked his way through Yale and won a Rhodes scholarship to Oxford, has far surpassed his boyhood dreams in Tennessee. The $6 billion in assets he manages today are invested worldwide. Templeton told me that when he took a night course to study with Benjamin Graham in the late 1930s, practically no one was doing quantitative security analysis. In fact, when John became a security analyst in 1937, there were only seventeen members of the New York Society of Security Analysts, and they were all called statisticians. They could report that a company had good management and a brilliant future, but would have no opinion about what it was worth. Today, value analysis, what Graham taught both Templeton and Buffett, has become quite popular, but, Templeton said, it is not widely used because it requires hard work and a big organization of experts. If value analysis has greatly narrowed the stock choices in America, it has hardly touched the field outside America because few people do it around the world. "Companies outside America are looked at in the same way they were when I went into Wall Street forty years ago," Templeton says. "Rumors, what other people know, what inside information there is, what the dividends are, who's going to split the stock . . . a sort of haphazard approach," but one that leaves elbow room for Templeton. It offers opportunities to those who search worldwide for bargains.

Warren Buffett. Everyone's choice as Mr. Investor, Buffett has carefully looked for and found a niche where he reigns as king. Painstakingly searching for superior companies when they are selling at bargain prices, he shuns the lures of wily brokers by sticking to his base in Omaha, Nebraska. Buffett believes that investors don't have to listen to every pitch. Instead, they should wait until the right one comes along, one with their fingerprints on it. This is the practice he has followed since starting a private partnership in 1956, and he has been so successful at finding a few undervalued bargains in which he can buy large positions, that many younger people in Wall Street today cannot imagine investing any other way.

George Soros, still a puzzle to the investing community, has been called by *Institutional Investor* the greatest money manager ever. In 1981 the magazine estimated that Soros would personally make over $100 million in his offshore investment partnership. His seventeen-year record of 35% compounded annual returns is the best yet for such a time span. Soros made good use of the economics and theoretical philosophy courses he took at the London School of Economics. Philosophy gave him a skeptical view of mankind's foibles, while economics made him a keen market timer. Soros made money because he understood government intervention in economies, how it affects economic systems and, specifically, how money supply intervention affects interest rates and securities markets. His early career in arbitrage only added to his ability to move fast in the market.

Jacob Rothschild. In 1984, *Business Week* called him London's new financial whiz, congratulating Rothschild on his rebound from a feud that had exiled him from the Rothschild family's investment bank, N. M. Rothschild and Sons, three years earlier. A maverick, Jacob, who is the great-great-great-great-grandson of Mayer Amschel Rothschild, the German financier, had taken large equity positions in companies for years, through a passive investment fund that eventually became Charthouse J. Rothschild, a holding company for all his interests and the largest banking group in the City, London's financial district. The feat was breathtaking, performed with a quintessential dealmaker's drive in accomplishing that much that fast. His sudden retreat and later mellowness puzzled and disappointed many of his most ardent fans, who felt that, at last, here was a Rothschild in action.

My legendary investors thrive on competition. Roy Neuberger stated categorically, "I am competitive," when he told of a dinner that Eastman Kodak gave to honor him for being their best money manager. There he was, eighty-two years old, competing against the best brains in the country at managing pension funds—and winning. Dreyfus told me he had just returned from Australia where, at seventy-four, he had won the senior doubles tennis championship with Gardnar Mulloy, that he didn't mean to brag, but he was thrilled. John Templeton was evasive when asked who his competition was, saying, "If I knew, would I tell you?" But then he admitted to feeling competitive with other money managers, the Standard and Poor's Index and the averages of other mutual funds. Soros sounded like a childhood playmate when we discussed my writing this book, challenging, "I have a book, too, so perhaps it will be out before yours." Rothschild certainly was competitive against his family legend, and Warren Buffett is the ultimate loner, always trying to outdo by a nanosecond his latest record, even though he knows how difficult that objective is. The daily work of choosing investments is the ultimate competitive experience. You have to like being graded and knowing if you're winning and doing better than your competition.

All my legends are also intuitive investors. Important clues are tantamount for them to codes that spies love to break. These investors are able to take creative leaps requiring both judgment and decision-making, using information that might seem trivial to less seasoned players. The minds of these legends store information and past experiences that, when drawn upon, activate intuitive insights in amazing ways. And these six men love their work passionately, treating it with intensity. But they are different from stereotypical workaholics. They are a new breed altogether, one that I call achievement addicts.

Achievement addicts act differently from the traditional workaholic. They seem relaxed at social gatherings; they don't boast about how they carried two heavy briefcases filled with reports to read at home that night. And they don't make others feel guilty for leading a normal work life. Yet there is not a moment, even when lying on the beach or in a garden chaise longue, that achievement addicts are not forming a plan or trying to work through an idea. They may look as peaceful as a downtime computer, but their thinking is as rich and thick as boiling fudge. They are easy and exciting to be around.

Conventional wisdom advises that a money manager should be seasoned, a broker or investment adviser who has already done his learning with someone else's money. John Train, in his book *The Money Masters,* suggests that a successful investor needs "ten to fifteen years of intensive theoretical and practical training, including a number of years under the greatest investors before you start in for yourself." None of my greats had that kind of background. When John Train himself visited Buffett in his early years, looking for someone to manage some capital, he decided against giving it to Buffett because he was working in a sitting room off his bedroom and would not reveal his holdings. One has to sympathize with this story, but it would have been equally difficult to give over money in the early years to John Templeton, who had merely two months of investing training before he opened his firm, or to Dreyfus, or to Soros with three years of unemploy-

ment behind him and no investment record. We can only
wonder if it would have been easier for Roy Neuberger
and Jacob Rothschild to entice money out of us.

Yet each of these men showed his mettle immediately.
Investing, like horse racing, is one field where you show
early whether you are good or not. Our legends' stars
shone early and only kept getting brighter.

Some of these six investors have defied the laws of averages and become long-term investment winners. The
Green Bay Packers had the greatest run of any football
team, one that lasted for ten years; many professional
investors would happily settle for a ten-year top performance record. One has to wonder, then, what separates
the middle-distancers from the marathoners and gives the
latter the motivation and energy to keep going after having reached their pinnacle. Perhaps, as another student of
such miracles suggested to me, it's their style, more patient
and oriented toward the long term. Such men as Neuberger, Templeton and Buffett are value investors who have
a longer time horizon and are not involved in deals, as
Jacob Rothschild was, or, in Soros's case, in capturing a
big interest rate move in the market. Nor are they technical traders excited by a new product, as was Dreyfus. Yes,
style certainly could make a difference, but appetite is important, too. Certain people in various walks of life simply
have insatiable appetites for just one more good meal, one
more good deal, one more good investment. The memory
of the last success only stimulates the taste for another,
and for the excitement the search entails. This is, I think,
what creates marathon investors who run a race with no
finish line.

ROY NEUBERGER—A LIFETIME LOVE AFFAIR

*"Stay in love with a security until the security gets
overvalued. Then let somebody else fall in love."*

"Always searching to know more is my philosophy in life
and one I follow daily," Roy Neuberger said, when I asked

for his thoughts on his Wall Street experiences over the last half century. Hyperactive and alert, his mind switches from point to point deftly, the way a painter works with watercolors. Neuberger calls this skipping pattern an investor's "stream of consciousness," after his early study of James Joyce. Memory and experience, he feels, are necessary qualities for a good investor, and his own way of sorting information and tapping his memory bank, as though with a feather, adds a powerful dimension to his investment analysis.

In the early 1920s, Neuberger spent three years as a buyer at B. Altman's before going to live abroad, mostly in Paris, between 1924 and March 1929. In Paris, he became infatuated with art, especially the work of living artists who he thought were neglected because of the French preference for already recognized work. If he wanted to buy the works of even these new artists, Neuberger decided he would need a fortune. Where and how to make such a fortune was the problem. He considered real estate, but finally his ambitions led him to Wall Street. He began working at Halle and Stieglitz, after being introduced by a friend of his father's who cleared his transactions there and whom Roy saw only once.

He arrived in the spring of 1929 and progressed from being a runner to working in the department where purchases and sales were written out. There he managed his own inheritance, which had made his stay in Europe possible—approximately $30,000 that yielded $2,000 in income when he needed it during his travels. Only about 10% of his capital had been in stocks; the rest was invested in guaranteed real estate securities offering a high yield, for the time, of 6%. Until then, Roy says, he had been young, idealistic, scornful of money, and had hardly glanced at the market. Luckily, he moved all his funds into equities soon after his arrival in New York (those guaranteed bonds went down the tube in the Thirties). What he learned in the infamous year 1929 in Wall Street formed the basic investment philosophy and style that he follows to this day: to hedge his positions by being both long and short.

**Rule 1:   When you are not sure what is going to
happen in the market, it is wise to protect
yourself by going short in something you
think is overvalued.**

Roy Neuberger's original $30,000, invested in equities,
became $35,000 by that fall. In September, he went on
vacation for two weeks. On his return, those equities were
back to $30,000 again, and moreover, he reports, he was
having "a funny feeling that they were about to go to
nothing." That was when he discovered the possibility of
shorting something that was overvalued, thus protecting
capital. In his first real company analysis, of the Radio
Corporation of America, he decided that since it was the
most expensive stock in the market, 574 a share before it
split 5 for 1, it had been pushed far too high because of its
glamour. His investment on the short side turned out well
in the debacle that followed. With that experience behind
him, staying short became a habit.

I asked Neuberger if he had made more money going
long or short on a stock, and though his 1929 experience
had been an exceptional one, he replied, "The long side."
He had made money in Capital Cities Broadcasting and
American Telephone and Telegraph; in fact, he had been
sorry he had sold Capital Cities and wished he had stayed
in it. Neuberger thinks his technique has been right about
80% of the time, when he thinks a stock is either undervalued or overvalued. The kind of stock he likes to short
is that of a company that has performed perfectly for
years, when reality can no longer keep up with the company's image. He compared this phenomenon to the public perception of Marilyn Monroe. "When a company is
perfect, it is selling overpriced because everybody loves it."
Such companies as Avon, Schlumberger and, currently,
Wal-Mart are examples of the perfect companies he likes
to short, but Roy added that if he had gone long on these
same companies early, the returns would have been much
higher.

The method that he has developed is to study the simpler aspects of a stock closely. (Others would call it a commonsense review of its basic fundamentals.) He first looks at its capitalization (its market price times the number of shares outstanding) to see if it is overvalued in comparison with other companies in its industry. He went short Schlumberger when it topped $25 billion in market capitalization. Today he is short Wal-Mart. At its closing price of 50 a share, with 140 million shares outstanding, its cap is $7 billion, greater than any other retail store except Sears, Roebuck, which has other businesses. After checking capitalization, he looks at the balance sheets to see if the figures are getting better or worse, then closely evaluates the company's competition. In the case of Wal-Mart, he estimates that the inroads of competition in small towns, as well as a falling dollar, will finally affect the steady quarterly earnings increases of a company that has a high price-earnings multiple of 26 and doesn't own the land under its stores. "They've done an immaculate job, but they're in a competitive world." Technical analysis convinces him that the stock's performance pattern is in a familiar decline. "At any rate," Neuberger adds, "I'm going to keep the short position until hell freezes over because it's an unbelievably high valuation at seven billion." He has also studied the insider trading patterns and noted heavy selling in 1985.

Another stock he is looking at is Coca-Cola. He finds that every year, its current assets and liabilities are a little worse and its debt, while not great, is a little bigger. He asks himself, "Where does all the money they make go? Why are they buying five million shares of their own stock?" He may have another overvalued candidate.

Part of Roy Neuberger's investment philosophy is to hedge when he is ahead. In his own words: "I try not to have too much greed or too much fear. I would have great fears now if I were vulnerable to either side of the market."

**Rule 2:   Whatever the rules of the game are, you
must take advantage of the ones that are
legal.**

Every day, Neuberger runs his accounts through a computer—a modern miracle, he thinks, in keeping track of
investments—to find the portfolio positions that are going
long-term. Looking at the dates tells him that, next week,
80% of his bond position will qualify for long-term gains,
and this pleases him because he has made a great deal of
money in bonds since March of 1985. "Even if they're
going up in price from here, I'm going to cash in. I love
to pay long-term gain taxes." (Neuberger will look over
the new tax bill carefully to see how he can profit from the
new rules.)

One of Roy Neuberger's many investment protégés,
Jimmy Rogers, says the most important skill he learned
from him was to distinguish between moves the market
made on the fundamentals and on people's perceptions,
and that is not quite as easy as it seems. "I'd see," said
Jimmy, "companies making terrible announcements and
stocks [would] collapse, and I'd say, 'Let's short more,' but
Roy would have said, 'Buy them.' He knew the news was
disastrous, but he'd make money on it."

Famous for his trading ability and his knack at reading
the tape, Neuberger admits that tapes are no longer valid,
now that individual investors have less influence in the
market. Instead, he relies on the new computer charts and
the daily papers to help him guess where the market will
go.

But it is as a superb trader that Rogers remembers Neuberger best. "He knew every tick for thirty years in the two
to three hundred stocks he followed." Rogers figures Neuberger doesn't use the tape any more because, he can just
sense it.

In looking for near-perfect companies that are overvalued and taking gains when they go long-term, Neuberger
shows that rare skill, the ability to sell at the right time.

Rule 3:   In investing, remember the bottom line.

"You shouldn't worry," says Neuberger, "about a position going against you." He takes his losses if a position goes 10% against him, but breaks that rule 10% to 15% of the time when common sense dictates. Then I asked Neuberger how he normally judged when to sell a stock. Does he say, "I've made enough on this"? "Sometimes," he responded. He had owned and liked Carnation for a long time, because for more than 25 years it had shown constant high earnings. When a deal came along to sell the company at $82 a share, he said he was not going to wait for the $82 if he could get $79; he thought it already was overpriced, despite the fact that it went up another 20 to 30 points in the battle for control that followed. "My own Ben Graham theory," said Neuberger, "is that I try to buy a stock when I think it should be accumulated, and I let somebody else make the last two thirds of the move. And, if something goes from ten dollars to twenty dollars and I think it's worth twenty-five, I'll let somebody else make that five."

Rule 4:   To make a round trip in a stock is a mistake.

Years ago, Neuberger was infatuated with the restaurant chain Schrafft's and thought it had a perfect product that attracted civilized people. Customers could eat in a clean place with a friend at moderate prices, and not get a stomachache. So he was bullish on Schrafft's and rode it from 4 to 8, and at 20, still bullish and holding on, he made a mistake and watched it drop again. That's when he developed his own Ben Graham theory of letting somebody else have the last few dollars.

Roy Neuberger began his own firm in 1940, eleven years after his entry into Wall Street. Neuberger Berman now manages a minimum of $7 billion of assets. Roy himself, at eighty-two years old, manages his family money and a pension account for Eastman Kodak. With great pride, he told me that Kodak was having a dinner for him at the "21" Club to celebrate the fact that the pension account performed better than any of their funds in the last six years. Then he smiled. "I've always been competitive."

Though Neuberger invests for Kodak and for the family accounts, he says, he speculates for himself; he thinks he is better at that. When I asked him to define the difference, he responded, "Investment takes so long, I get bored with it." But whatever he calls it, his field has paid off handsomely.

The assets he has accumulated and his interest in his firm are indeed the fortune he hoped for. But most amazing is the excitement he still exudes about the market; his enthusiasm is intoxicating. He wanted to show me one of his technical tools, the "Bridge Machine," and insisted that we stop by his desk in the trading room. Delightedly, he called up the two-year, six-month and two-month charts for Wal-Mart, his current short, on the screen. Earlier, another friend had urged me to try this machine. Kneeling on the floor beside Roy for a closer look, I had to agree that there is something to Neuberger's philosophy: Learn something new every day.

JACK DREYFUS—THE LION'S LEGACY

"Nobody in my family, neither my mother nor my father, ever thought I'd make a dollar, and neither did I," admitted Jack Dreyfus, in reflecting on the extraordinary coincidences that have occurred in his life. "All these things happened to me," is the way he describes what he considers his good luck. "The Wall Street adventure happened to me. I didn't do it out of ambition; a series of things happened." As Dreyfus sees it, he fumbled around in business until he arrived in Wall Street, where he hit on one of his aptitudes. He had never had any ambitions to go to Wall Street; it was the last thing on his mind in school. When I asked him what academic subjects he was good at, he chuckled, "Recess—I got a straight C average." He explained, "I have a terrible aptitude for mechanics, my sense of direction is backwards and I can forget names faster than you can tell them to me." I suggested math. He replied, "I didn't have any mathematical training, but I do have a sense of probability that had to come from the cradle."

After trying his hand in the insurance, candy and industrial design businesses, Jack Dreyfus went back to playing afternoon bridge, listening to Clyde McCoy playing "Sugar Blues" until 3 A.M. and visiting his psychiatrist. One night at the bridge table, a player who knew Dreyfus was unemployed offered to set up an appointment for him at a branch of Cohen Simondson and Company in the garment district. He got the job, answering phones and keeping the charts of a customer's broker at $25 a week. His father, despairing of his son's working habits, had accompanied Jack to the appointment, and many years later, Dreyfus learned that his father had paid his new boss twenty weeks of his salary in advance.

Not a propitious beginning, but it clicked, and Jack quickly grew interested when he found he had a natural ability for the work. A few years later, he managed to buy a seat on the floor of the New York Stock Exchange with a golfing companion, Jerry Ohrbach, whose family became their chief investors. The Ohrbachs' purchase of Lewisohn and Sons, Dreyfus said, pushed him into the commission business, and then the Dreyfus Fund walked in the door when John Nesbett applied for a position. Nesbett had been the sole proprietor of a struggling mutual fund for several years. Since he collected fees of only $3,000 a year, it had become impractical for him to continue.

These two lucky coincidences were followed by a third, when Dreyfus bought the right stock for the wrong reason. Most of the legends about Dreyfus's investing acumen center on his amazing discovery of the wonder stock Polaroid, in the Fifties. He first was attracted to the company because of the glasses it made for viewing three-dimensional movies. He was excited about them. "Those glasses never did amount to much," he commented, but he bought the stock and then discovered the camera.

Dreyfus used his own wits in assessing the potential market for Polaroid's camera. When it was first produced, it made sepia pictures. This news spread through the financial community and gave Polaroid a reputation that was hard to dispel. But the pictures Dreyfus took were excellent. He photographed old ladies in the park, who were pleased with the results, one of them slipping a quarter in his pocket and saying, "Buy yourself some cigarettes." He kept the quarter, of course. Jack was even more excited about the stock's potential performance as long as no one else realized how good the camera's pictures were. (His enjoyment in people's responses to its photographs brought back memories of my trip to China in 1977; the Chinese in rural communities had never seen instant pictures of themselves and were filled with wonder.)

Besides its potentially big market, Polaroid had a strong patent. Its weak point was product promotion, according to Dreyfus, who paid his own advertising agency, Doyle, Dane and Bernbach, to provide ads for the camera. "A patent is what gives you the advantage," he commented. "With that, you're in control and you can overcharge for your product or be inefficient." His Polaroid stock was around 32 when he bought it; it has split forty times since then. Jack is still in awe of his baby.

"I never saw a stock as clearly as Polaroid. To see something like that, that nobody else has got, and a product that people want, is very rare." Dreyfus's thoughts for other investors incorporate his experience with this exceptional stock.

Rule 1: Look at things freshly.

Many investors could not believe that Polaroid cameras were marketable, because there were no negatives. Dreyfus guesses that having a backward sense of direction here gave him insight. He could see the value of the camera when others were only dismayed by what it lacked. He presented this hypothesis: "Suppose the Polaroid camera had come out first and you brought the Kodak fellow to somebody, saying, 'This is a new camera with a wonderful picture that has negatives.' And you then told them, 'You don't get the picture now but forty-eight hours later, at the drugstore with negatives.' You'd hear the same retorts: 'Are you kidding?' " If Polaroid had been first, it would have been difficult to accept Kodak's system—and that was Jack Dreyfus's way of looking at the new product with fresh eyes.

Rule 2: Treat an investment portfolio as though it were your mother's money.

Jack Dreyfus and Alex Rudnicki, who joined him in managing the Dreyfus Fund, came upon this notion when they were working on the fund and thinking of it as a single account. Let's think of it, they agreed, as our mother's money, not somebody else's mother's money. With somebody else's mother's money, they would have to do things that look right. They would think about her lawyers, her relatives and her accountants. "But if it's your mother's money, you've got your heart in it, and you do the best you can," said Dreyfus. He made a point. With your mother's money, you are more willing to take both risks and losses and thus can be more objective. Yet you are egotistical enough to want to show her how good you are.

Rule 3: Technical analysis helps you to judge the trend of a stock and to determine the appropriate time to buy or sell it.

In the early years the Dreyfus Fund didn't have a large research group, so Dreyfus used the weekly charts to keep up with the major trends. (Polaroid was an exception. Legally, the fund could put only 5% of its money in one stock.) In discussing technical analysis, Dreyfus said, "When you look at a chart, most of the time it doesn't have an opinion. But maybe seven or eight percent of the time, a stock gets into a position where your experience tells you that the probabilities are that it will go up or down. About sixty-five to seventy percent of the time, when you get to that probability point, you act." The use of charts became more important because Dreyfus was too shy to call up treasurers or corporate officers. Rudnicki provided fundamental analysis by studying a company's assets and book values. Dreyfus's technical ability filled the gaps, simply because they didn't know enough about the companies they bought to be willing to keep a stock if it did not act right. (Dreyfus must be one of the few technical analysts who really made money.)

Rule 4:   Keep your mind open and keep thinking.

"You have to keep your mind open," Dreyfus advised in an advertisement for his fund. "You can't go back and say, well, three years ago this condition happened and therefore it's going to happen now. You have to review the changes and the conditions today. . . . It's not safe to apply yesterday's methods and theories, just because they were successful in the past." (Writing advertisements turned out to be something else he excelled at; in an early ad he portrayed Columbus as America's first speculator.)

Rule 5:   Understand probabilities and use them in buying stocks.

In his book, *A Remarkable Medicine Has Been Overlooked,* Dreyfus points out that the stock market appeals to both his sense of probabilities and another aspect of his psyche, the gambling instinct. He was lucky enough, he reports, to have practiced at games of skill, such as bridge and gin rummy, handicapping horse races and, in early days, marbles. Dreyfus distinguishes between two kinds of probabilities: the precise mathematical probability, which can give you the odds on a toss of a coin, and what he calls "the freeform probability." This refers to the sort of guessing we do casually, for instance, when we telephone someone we know well and estimate the ring they will answer on. "Gin rummy deals with exact probabilities; the stock market deals largely with inexact probabilities," he says. Then he explains how to buy stocks.

Jack Dreyfus's Stock-buying Recipe:

- earnings: take a company's current as well as five-year earnings record into consideration;
- then, compute its book value and net quick asset;
- study its competitive position in its industry and the prospect for new products;
- relate its industry to other industries;
- opinion: How does its management perform? What are the prospects for the stock market as a whole?
- technical: How does the stock look on the charts?

Finally, he adds, as Julia Child would, "Put all this where you think your brains are, circulate it through your sense of probabilities, and arrive at your conclusion. Be prepared to take a quick loss: Your conclusion may be wrong even though you've approached it the right way." (I can hear Julia saying, "Start again," as she cracks another batch of eggs in the mixing bowl.)

Rule 6: Never complain about bad luck; it's an excuse for defeat in advance.

"Each hand is a new hand. Each investment, a new one. Each stage of your life, new, wherever you are. If you keep your mind in a negative mode," Jack continues, "you're not doing yourself justice. I learned that in golf. If you miss a putt on the seventh hole and you go the eighth tee feeling badly, you're going to hit a bad drive. You've got to concentrate and say, 'The problem is to hit a good drive.' I think it's unhealthy to bemoan the past. It interferes with the future, and the future is the only thing you can do anything about."

Rule 7: **Your investments should reflect your financial position, as well as what Dreyfus calls the human equation.**

If an investor has a decent income and, let's say, $20,000 in his bank account, if he wants to take $15,000 and gamble with it, he can, because his income is sufficient. On the other hand, Jack believes, if someone with $1 million and no income were offered a ten-or-nothing flip of a coin ($10 million if he won, zero if he lost), he would be foolish to take it. The human equation is the personal decision to invest or to speculate. Once chosen, the path must be followed. To do both, an investor must have two accounts and steer a straight course in each.

In the twelve-year period before he retired in 1965, Dreyfus's fund was the number one performer. After this success, he decided to leave it and, in 1965, passed his mantle to Howard Stein. In his book, Jack explains how he chose Stein: "Whenever I'm stumped as to how to find someone or locate something, I have a simple method. I ask Howard Stein. I don't know how he does it, but he never lets me down." He still comments proudly on the continued success of the Dreyfus Fund, saying: "Hasn't Howard done a great job?"

When Dreyfus offered the management company of the fund for public sale, taking $26 million as his personal share of the $45 million subscription, the question was: Why would a man who thrives on competition want to leave the investment business at all? But Dreyfus, with his amalgam of abilities, still feels that he never was ambitious, that he simply fell into amazing situations. Competitiveness he can't deny. When he took over Nesbett's fund, it had a value of $580,000; one of the investors heard that the fund was no good and immediately withdrew $80,000 from that $580,000. It took the new partners four years to reach $1 million, with the help of Dreyfus's inventive marketing ideas.

Jack's prowess at golf, bridge, the racetrack and especially gin rummy are legendary. He was capable, during his investment heyday thirty years ago, of lying in Battery Park in a three-hundred-dollar suit, shoeless, wriggling his toes, under the eyes of the president of the New York Stock Exchange. Dreyfus once hired a psychiatrist for his firm, to deal with interpersonal problems in the office that Dreyfus didn't want to worry about.

He likes to refer to the writings of Mark Twain, especially a piece called "What is Man?" In it Twain explains that everything we do is motivated by self-interest, even the kind acts that make us feel good. "You also," Dreyfus says, "in reading the piece, get the feeling that everything in life is luck, who your mother and father were, and how all the influences in your life programmed you, so that it's difficult for anyone to really credit you with being smart."

Dreyfus's luck continued, he says, when researchers developed a drug called Dilantin, which controls epileptic seizures. He was able to contribute to its wider use with the money he made in Wall Street. "If you're lucky enough to run into something that could help so many people in the world, it's such an extraordinary privilege, one that happens only once in a billion lifetimes." Dreyfus has thrown his skill, heart and money into a foundation that researches and promotes the extensive use of Dilantin, which his foundation's research shows might be used for a wide variety of conditions. This possibility is gaining recognition around the world. Newcomers to Wall Street sometimes are skeptical of Jack's medical crusade, for a crusade it has been. Yet I recall his conviction about Polaroid, as well as about the Dreyfus Fund itself, and see this same pattern of tactics and tenacity repeated here. Dreyfus has recognized an opportunity, something exciting that others don't yet see; he studies ways to market the product to make it successful, and he won't give up. One of the early Dreyfus maxims was, "Look for outcome (capital growth), not income." Perfectionist and competitor, Jack is following his own maxim.

JOHN TEMPLETON AND WARREN BUFFETT—
THE TWO GENTLEMEN OF
WALL STREET

John Templeton and Warren Buffett are the padishahs, crown princes and tribal leaders combined to the many colleagues who toil in investment offices. Esteem from one's peers is usually considered the highest accolade, and the two gentlemen of Wall Street have been placed not just on pedestals, but on an Olympian plateau, one so broad that it would be impossible for them to fall off. Both men practice their art far from Wall Street, John Templeton in Lyford Cay in Nassau, and Warren Buffett in Omaha, Nebraska. From these outposts, Buffett and Templeton have piled up thirty-year investing records and awesome reputations as successful investors. Their distance only helps them to research the way they like, their retreats acting as base camps from which they can extend their long arms and sharp eyes in search of unusual opportunities.

Buffett currently seems more in fashion, the result of a style that has proved profitable over the last few years. He seeks a specific kind of undervalued company in which he can buy a decent-sized position. Buffett's hits have been extraordinary, including, Geico, the Washington Post and General Foods. His personal investing success has been advertised to the world by his inclusion in the list of the *Forbes* 400, with a personal net worth estimated at over $1 billion.

Templeton, modest by nature, seems more mysterious. His absolute wealth is a secret, yet his investing record is in the public domain, registered with the Securities and Exchange Commission. This record shows that for thirty-one years, his performance has averaged a yearly increase of 15%, which means that, during bull markets, it has been much higher. Since he competes against the Standard and Poor's Index, what Templeton is most proud of is that, during this time, his funds averaged 8% a year better than the index. This investing record is rare and, as in baseball or football, such records are thought about daily, so that the new generation has a goal to beat and a mentor to follow. But it is interesting to estimate Templeton's wealth, however hypothetical the figure. He started his firm with a small amount under management and today controls $6 billion in assets worldwide. He has faithfully put 50% of his personal earnings each year into an investment program. Then, compound these figures at 15%, for a possible guess.

Some investors will get into heated arguments over which of the two greats is the best. Fundamentally, both are value investors who analyze value differently. Templeton prefers to look for a variety of bargains worldwide. When I asked him whether he was a value or a growth investor, he responded, "I'm everything, but I like to think of myself as single-minded and open-minded." A commonality that Buffett and Templeton share is that both were classroom students of Benjamin Graham. Templeton studied with Graham when he taught at New York University in the late Thirties, and Buffett at Columbia University in the early Fifties, so that the two were weaned on Graham's quantitative analytical skills.

It has usually been written that Buffett was Ben Graham's star student, but the competition for such an ephemeral title would have included Templeton and would be equivalent to a battle of the Titans. John Templeton had straight A's through high school, worked his way through his last three years at Yale, capturing Phi Bete in his junior year, and winning a coveted Rhodes scholarship to Oxford. Since both Templeton and Buffett speak publicly, Buffett at Columbia and Templeton at Oxford, where he founded the Templeton College for Management Studies, I have culled from the talks and conversations some investing rules that reflect their individual styles and experiences.

John Templeton

I first saw John Templeton at a lunch for Templeton College at the Racquet Club in New York. He was sitting only two places away from me, and I overheard his conversation. He asked the president of Purolator, "If you were not allowed to buy Purolator shares, what other company's shares in that industry would you buy?" And the reply was, "Federal Express." Searching out such information from secondary sources is one of Templeton's favorite techniques. He always learns more, he believes, when he asks a businessman about others. Businessmen will go right to the heart of the matter and put their fingers squarely on the problems or the advantages of their competitors, their suppliers or their customers. It is only when businessmen discuss their own companies that they filter information.

I met with Templeton again in Nassau and, like other Wall Streeters who had traveled to his base—a trip to Mecca for capitalists—I was enchanted by his charm and his quick mind. He is multifaceted and broad-ranging, and I had to work hard to focus on Templeton the investor, rather than on Templeton the giver of religious prizes, the educator or humanist.

When he was a sophomore at Yale in 1931, taking elementary economics, Templeton was fascinated by the fact that share prices fluctuate so enormously and so widely that they cannot represent the true value of a corporation. The true value, he thought, had to be somewhere in the middle. If, then, a person could determine the true value, he would know which stock looked promising, and when to buy or sell it. At eighteen, he decided to prepare for a future as an investment counselor. As a Rhodes scholar at Oxford, he had intended to continue in this field, but after searching the university from one end to the other, he could find no way to major in investments. There was no lecture on it, there were no courses, there wasn't even a book on the subject. Therefore, he took a degree in law at Oxford. When it came time to find a job, he wrote to twelve investing organizations in America, saying he would like to interview with them when he finished at Oxford. The job he accepted was the lowest-paying, at a company called Fenner and Beane, which later merged into Merrill Lynch. The company had just started its investment operation a few months before, with only two people; that attracted Templeton. He felt that he could learn more if he got in on the ground floor.

Templeton stayed there for only a short time, until he was offered a job in the Texas oil business. In 1940, four years after leaving Oxford, he moved back to New York and opened his own investment counseling company in the RCA Building in Rockefeller Center. Clients were scarce for a young person starting in the field; for two years, he could not pay himself a salary. I asked him just one question about this period: "John, was your performance good right away?" "Yes," he answered. "It was very good."

After his economics courses, three months at Fenner and Beane, then three years in the Texas oil fields, his self-reliance in starting his own firm and the abilities he then displayed seemed incredible. But self-confidence is fueled by successes. A few early incidents helped him develop his natural business talent, confirming his keen analytical judgment and his decisiveness.

At Yale, with $300 surplus from his earnings, he bought stock from his roommate, a broker: the $7 (dividend) preferred stock of Standard Gas and Electric. In the Twenties, there had been many mergers of electric utility companies. With the Depression, most of those utility holding companies failed, including Standard Gas, enabling Templeton to buy a $7 preferred for about $12 a share. Utilities, he reasoned, would continue to have good earnings in the long run. Templeton did get an immediate psychological return on his first choice; it rose immediately, and he ended up by quadrupling his money. Modestly, he remarked, "It did happen that way, but that's not always wise for a young man starting out in investments;

it's much more educational if he has a failure to begin with instead of a success."

Perhaps he is right, perhaps a failure would be more educational, but the rewards of the glow from the psychological effects of quadrupling one's money can instantly boost self-confidence and the eagerness to continue. Templeton was more than able to handle such successes.

When the Germans and Russians invaded Poland, Templeton saw that there was going to be a widespread world war. Since there had been a great worldwide depression, a war meant that demand for goods would pick up: During wartime, everything is in demand. There were over a hundred stocks, then, selling below one dollar a share on the New York and American stock exchanges, so, from Texas, he called Fenner and Beane and gave the order to buy $100 worth of every stock at a dollar a share or less. There were 104 of these stocks and 100 of them turned out to be profitable. The most spectacular investment was the $7 preferred stock of Missouri Pacific Railway. It had been offered to the public at $100 per share, paying a $7 cash dividend. The railroads had had a particularly rough time in the Depression, and this one had gone into bankruptcy. The preferred stock had gone down to 12 cents a share, or ⅛ point. For his $100, therefore, Templeton was able to buy 800 shares of stock that were each supposed to pay $7 in cash dividends. After the war, the stock moved from ⅛ to 5 a share or forty times what he'd paid for it. Templeton said, "I thought how wonderful it was and took my profit, and within two years it went to 107."

After Oxford and before starting at Fenner and Beane, Templeton had gone with a friend on a trip around the world. One of the countries he visited was Japan, where he was impressed with the hard work of the Japanese and the quality of their products—a great contrast with the perceptions of Americans back home, for whom "made in Japan" in the Thirties was an indication of a junk product. He observed also that Japanese accounting understated true earnings. So, with his own money, he began to buy small amounts of shares in Japan, about two years before money could be taken out of that country. What he observed on his barebones grand tour eventually led to a significant commitment to the Japanese market, as Japan's economy exploded after the war. When Templeton bought them, the finest companies' shares sold for three times earnings, and Westerners still believed that Japan only made poor imitations.

Templeton found all these bargains before he opened those Rockefeller Center doors. To him, a good investment is nothing more than finding a bargain; these are superb examples of him at work in his best bargain-hunting period.

One of my favorite questions of other investors concerns their mistakes or some investment they made that might in retrospect seem foolish. For years, the Templeton group kept a record of what happened when they took their clients out of one stock and put that same money into another one. In studying that record a year later, they found out that, a third of the time, it would have been better to have stayed with a stock they had sold. But even that doesn't seem foolish to me. To be right two thirds of the time is to be tops in the investing field.

Some of Templeton's tips:

Rule 1: **Make an investment plan, commit a certain percentage of your income to it each year, and don't spend the capital you've put aside, for that would defeat your investment plan.**

When they married, Templeton and his wife agreed to set aside half of their income each year for a personal investment portfolio. He has always followed that plan, even in the early years when it was difficult, but his propensity towards thrift saving was extremely strong. He actually did what many counselors advise their clients to do, though they don't always suggest 50%. He went into debt only once: when he borrowed $10,000 from his boss to buy the 104 stocks under a dollar. But he soon repaid it from his profits of $40,000.

> ### Rule 2: Enjoy making capital gains and paying taxes on them when you sell securities; for long-term investors, there is only one objective: maximum total real return after taxes.

Templeton finds that many people spend too much time trying to avoid paying taxes. They would do much better if they concentrated on making money with their investments.

I agree. I have been amazed at how difficult it is for some people to sell a security and pay capital gains taxes —a problem, surprisingly, for some of the richest and savviest families. A friend once asked my advice about the trust department that managed her money. She lamented their poor performance record and wanted me to recommend another manager. I reviewed her portfolio and found that 80% of her money was in one stock that she had received when her family company was bought with shares of that corporation. "Oh!" she said in a shocked tone, "I can't sell that. The capital gains would kill me." Still, the bank that managed her money could not perform well unless her one big position was in an uptrend. Another family I have known just rode stocks up and down over the years rather than pay capital gains taxes.

Rule 3: Diversify your investments.

Templeton believes that the best investor is only right two thirds of the time and that it is only prudent to protect yourself, because you will make mistakes. He developed his theory of prudent diversification to minimize risk; he thinks that an investor in stocks should own at least ten companies of 100 shares each. Some of his large mutual funds even have over 100 names.

He followed his diversification theory in applying to

.earch encourages strong convictions, don't delay too
ng before acting.

I think that many investors form a judgment after
ound analysis but then vacillate about taking action. A
successful investor must do both.

Rule 6: Decide which risks are worth taking and which are not.

To secure admission to Yale, Templeton weighed risk
in deciding how to take his entrance exam. As an investor,
the one risk he refuses is to invest in socialized countries,
where capital cannot be taken out, or, for that matter,
even in countries where there are price controls. The climate for capital accumulation is best in an open society.

Rule 7: Let the numbers tell you whether management is good or not.

The numbers will tell how well management is doing. In
interviews, most managements sound enthusiastic; it is
hard to manage a company without being optimistic. Visits
to companies provide a little information, primarily that
most of the managements are composed of intelligent people. But only the numbers reveal what you need to know.
Measure management by quantities, not qualities.

Rule 8: Keep a flexible, open-minded and skeptical attitude as an investor.

This is one of Templeton's two most famous axioms.
The second: Focus on value, rather than on outlook or
trend-in-the-making. To Templeton, everything has a season and he is suspicious of anything that blooms longer
than four years. He also believes that when a particular
industry or type of security becomes popular with investors, that popularity will always prove temporary and will
not return for many years when lost. In a world where
people like to label investing styles, Templeton thinks that

Yale. It was necessary to take ⟨
for Yale, and there were two
could take a comprehensive exan
years, at the end of their third yea⟩
an exam for each course the year th
chose the latter, considering the forn
Something might happen on that one ⟨
day to keep him from doing his best jo⟩
get accepted at Yale. To bet everything on
when he had another choice was not a wort

Rule 4: Look for bargains when you bu⟩ rity.

By this, Templeton means not just any bargain b⟨
that have true value. And he does not have a mag⟩
mula that can help others in their search. Each positi⟨
a company or industry is distinct; for instance, he focu⟩
on earnings per share for grocery chains, and depletion ⟨
minerals for mining companies. He does use a large variety of yardsticks for value: how high the price is in relation
to earnings, to potential earnings, book value or net working capital after subtracting the debts, to sales per share,
to prices of other stocks in a similar industry or a similar
situation and so on. "These yardsticks of value are never
very reliable or very accurate, for that matter," he added,
"but if you know enough about them, you can come out
with an estimate of the value of the company and then you
can price the companies once a month to see which is the
cheapest." Perfection is to divide the total value of the
company by the number of outstanding shares, and find
that the market price is less than that figure. Then it is
attractive.

Rule 5: Learn the art of decision-making.

Research the company, weigh all the factors and make a
judgment. Anxiety accompanies any new path, but if the

no investment approach should be graven in stone, because no selection method will ever be permanent. To stay ahead of the competition, an investor must experiment with methods that no one else, or very few others, are looking at. At any given time, Templeton is trying six or seven or eight different methods.

He remembers one time, thirty years ago, when he was not flexible or skeptical enough. When his group was organizing its funds, one of the underwriters on Wall Street persuaded them to bring out a new fund called Nucleonics Chemistry and Electronic shares; at the time, these new buzzwords excited the public. Templeton says that his firm appointed a board of scientific advisers from all these fields, and at the offering, the fund was very popular. But they stayed with the fund too long. They should have known that new buzzwords are just a fashion, their popularity temporary. Once Templeton's group realized its mistake, the fund was folded into one of its larger mutual funds. But the delay lost money for their shareholders.

Rule 9:   Be positive.

This rule applies to everything in life, according to Templeton. Negative thoughts are psychological poison that may distract investors from important goals. If an investor keeps dwelling on mistakes, it becomes harder and harder to take the next risk. To add to that, Templeton then developed his theory of the extra ounce. He has observed in all fields that outstandingly successful people always do that marginal extra bit; they practice more, they recheck their research, they make just one more telephone call. And their results are dramatic—as they clearly have been, year in, year out, for Templeton.

Warren Buffett

"No doubt about it, he's the best." So Peter Lynch, of Fidelity's Magellan Fund, evaluated Warren Buffett as an investor. Then he added, "What makes him so good is that his investment abilities seem to evolve and grow stronger." An interesting remark about a man who feels he is doing the same things he has always done, picking a few stocks a year that are undervalued, companies he knows well and has confidence in. What has changed is the vehicle he has used for his investments: Originally it was a private part- nership, now it is a listed corporation. His current $2 bil- lion asset pool also dictates changes. It means that, if investments are concentrated, there is a much larger com- mitment in each one.

Such an accolade from another respected investor is in- deed a compliment but not a necessity to Buffett's self- respect. At all costs, he wants to avoid being influenced by other people's opinions or actions, particularly in invest- ment decision-making. In fact, he has structured the money he manages so that, as much as possible, he reports only to himself. If investors know what the manager is doing, chances are, they will worry and start telephoning. Sooner or later, the manager will be influenced. Once, Buffett compared such conversations to a surgeon's hav- ing a running dialogue with a patient during a major op- eration.

After graduating from Columbia Business School, he worked for two years with Ben Graham at Graham-New- man, believing that the best way to learn was to apprentice himself to the smartest person in the field. Then, return- ing to Omaha, Nebraska, he started Buffett Partnership in 1956 with $100,000 he had borrowed from members of his family. In 1969, when he disbanded the partnership, it had grown to $100 million, and he had made $25 million for himself (his take was 25% of the profits after a 6% return on capital to his investors). The return to his inves- tors was approximately thirty times their investment—a $10,000 original commitment was worth $300,000. One of the companies he had taken over in 1965, Berkshire Hath- away in New Bedford, Massachusetts, then became his investment vehicle for the next sixteen years. This diver- sified holding company clocked in yearly compounded gains of 23% (surprisingly close to the returns he netted for his partners in his partnership). Thus we see a thirty-year record of amazing consistency, despite Buffett's warning that concentrating investments as much as he does would lead to some weak years.

In describing Warren Buffett's style, Chris Browne of Tweedy Browne, a firm commonly thought of as son and grandson of Graham-Newman, said that Buffett has "a stamp collector's mind." Browne told me a story about Tom Knapp, who had joined his firm from Graham-Newman in 1958. Tom liked to buy things that nobody else had the sense to buy because these stocks were so inactive. He and Buffett—two like minds—decided to corner the market in four-cent Blue Eagle stamps when they went out of production. They thought that there would be a scarcity, that these stamps might be worth six cents. But the investment never panned out: The stamps weren't in short supply, and they never carried a collector's premium. Chris continued, "What they did do, then, was to pay their postage for the next ten years. And they did have fun. Moreover, they carried that stamp concept over to other things." Still, such an investment fits into Buffett's thinking. When he started his partnership, he promised his clients not riches, but two other objectives: value rather than popularity, and an attempt to keep permanent capital loss to a minimum. His four-cent Blue Eagle stamp adventure met those objectives.

Buffett's students in the marketplace have focused on a few of his disciplines, which can essentially be boiled down to the following "rules." They describe the way I think he invests, and they certainly give good advice for intelligent investors to follow.

Rule 1: Resolve to make only a few investment moves.

At least ninety percent of Buffett's performance in the past ten years came from ten positions that he held in his portfolio. To him, fiddling all day with a portfolio or being overstimulated by looking at a hundred ideas is bad tactics.

Wait instead for a company you can understand and that you know to be a bargain. Buffett thinks that investors should aim for the skyscrapers—companies with comprehensible businesses which seem to be worth more than they are selling for. Try to keep the investments simple. He looks for skyscrapers in companies he can analyze to his satisfaction. He tries to find a discrepancy between price and value, stocks selling at what he calls auction prices. Investors who find only seven such companies in a lifetime will do very well.

Rule 2: Make your own decisions.

Jot down the reasons for buying a stock and don't try to find a crowd that will agree. Later on, you'll find out if your facts and reasoning were correct. The trick is to avoid overstimulation, a frequent occurrence in cities like New York. It is not easy. Buffett has found that going beyond his understanding can lead to big mistakes. He does better, he says, sitting in a room all alone.

Rule 3: Concentrate on return on capital when you look at a company's figures.

Return on capital produces the earnings, and it is harder to manipulate than earnings per share. To grow fast, a company needs a high return on capital; if it is developing rapidly, investors can hold it longer in their portfolios.

Rule 4: Look for bargains.

There are rare times when exceptional businesses are almost given away. When this happens, investors must seize the opportunity. Buffett's favorites are businesses that can improve without needing extra money. Since he often looks at things with a fresh eye, he once realized that there is a group that has virtual franchises on controlling companies' access to consumers—a group that receives royalties on other companies' sales. This royalty group includes the advertisers, broadcasters and newspapers. He found some bargains there that turned into great investments:

The Washington Post. The company was selling for around $100 million in the mid-Seventies when Buffett bought the stock. The business was probably worth $500 million; the television stations alone were worth $200 million at that time. It was a good business, but the stock was down because earnings for the next quarter or so would be disappointing.

Disney. In 1966, the company was selling for $80 million. Buffett said that Disneyland itself would have sold for more than that in a private transaction, but investors were worried that earnings from the movie *Snow White* could not be duplicated the next year.

American Express. Buffett bought 5% of the company following the salad oil scandal, because he was attracted by the profit from the float on their traveler's checks. The company was selling for $150 million. After pricing the liability of the salad oil scandal at $60 million, Buffett decided it was a great opportunity; the market was acting as though the company had lost more than its total market value.

Rule 5:   Look for great businesses to invest in.

The communications industry has been Buffett's favorite. There are 1,700 newspapers in the United States; all but 20 are monopolies. The business is good not because of management, but because it is inherently good. The *Daily Racing Form* is the highest-priced daily newspaper in the United States at $2.00. This publication, owned by Walter Annenberg, has $130 million in sales and, like all monopolies, extraordinary pretax margins. People are hooked on the *Daily Racing Form;* they are relatively insensitive to price. To Buffett, a good business can be run by just about anyone.

Rule 6: Avoid companies with a great many variables.

When it is impossible to analyze all the variables of a stock, Buffett avoids it. This includes companies that may be regulated and smokestack companies.

Rule 7: Try not to be concerned about stock market fluctuations.

Simply be concerned about the business you bought and how well it is doing.

Rule 8: Work out your own ideas.

Buffett generates all of his. He leafs through Value Line every week to keep abreast of things. (You can take someone else's idea. It just means that you have to do enough work on it to make it your own idea.)

Rule 9: Figure the value of a whole company in the market.

Buffett thinks of companies and talks about them in terms of how much he could buy the company for—its market value (shares outstanding times market price), not its earnings or its price-to-earnings multiple.

Rule 10: Concentrate your investments.

Buffett uses Billy Rose's description of the problem of overdiversification: "If you have a harem of forty women, you never get to know any of them very well."

In 1969, when Warren Buffett disbanded his private partnership, he sent a letter to his partners telling them he felt out of step with the market then, and couldn't participate in something he didn't understand. In his 1984 Berkshire Hathaway annual report, eagerly read by ambitious young Wall Streeters, Buffett mentioned the dismal choice in prospective purchases that year and warned his investors that, over the next decade, his company would have to net $3.9 billion merely to maintain 15% annual earnings. He had no strategic plan for this, he went on, but would need big ideas. Small ones just would not do.

Berkshire Hathaway's return was up 48.2% at the end of 1985 (a $613.6 million gain). One stock, General Foods, accounted for the majority of that gain. "Our experience has been that something popped up occasionally," says Buffett in the company annual report.

Our two gentlemen of Wall Street are the long-distance runners, winners of the investment marathon as measured over a thirty-year distance. Buffett could be declared the winner for clocking in a minimum of 23% returns annually. His Buffett Partnership, during the thirteen years from 1957 through 1969, averaged 29.5%, annually earning the limited partners 23.8% (the difference was Buffett's profit). This was followed by Berkshire Hathaway's twenty-year 23% annual return. Templeton accomplished his thirty-one-year record of 15% in the public eye, and in an arena that many say was more difficult. He had to deal with numerous reports to shareholders and clients, daily review by his peers and stockholders and with marketing his services, as well as managing the enterprise itself. Because others in the investment business know the pressures of these responsibilities, their respect for his performance has placed him on that broad pedestal.

In his book *The Money Masters,* John Train referred to Buffett's style as that of the hedgehog, who knows one thing well, whereas the fox knows many things. Whether John Templeton can be called a fox is debatable, but he does invest over a broader range, domestically and worldwide. Templeton's more diversified strategy dictates a broader number of investments, unlike Buffett's concentration in a few securities. Templeton likes to talk to many people about his investments and treasures secondary-source information, although he thinks the figures themselves show if management is doing a good job. Buffett likes companies in a business so foolproof they do not need great management. He does, however, make subjective judgments based on qualitative analysis of a company's franchise and future. Their tutor, Ben Graham, distrusted both subjective ideas and talking to management.

Both disciples have strayed a bit from pure quantitative analysis, although their searches for bargains remain rooted in Graham's discipline. Templeton's style is more flexible, and he does not believe an investing philosophy must be predictable, while Buffett has chosen a narrower viewpoint and likes only a few, special companies; he focuses on the easiest part of the game. Both men think that investors should be patient and take a long-term view, that they should focus on the value and progress of their investment, rather than on the market in general. And both have found that they think better more than a thousand miles from Wall Street, away from the daily pressures and the chain-letter mentality that prevail in the investing community.

GEORGE SOROS—THE HUNGARIAN WUNDERKIND

In April 1981, the *Institutional Investor* featured George Soros on its cover, calling him the world's greatest money manager. This profile had a dramatic effect on others in money management. Billy Salomon, the ex-managing partner of Salomon Brothers, called me, with wonder in his voice, to ask if I knew Soros. Many participants in Wall Street had never heard of him or of his Quantum Fund. And with good reason. It was an offshore fund using money from international investors rather than from Americans who often invested in foreign markets. And

Soros, a passionate student of philosophy, believed in keeping a low profile, which has always seemed strange to Wall Street's status-seekers.

But the article blew George's cover. The investing world now knew of his talent and of his personal success, a fortune estimated at $100 million at that time. The Quantum Fund, eventually renamed the Soros Fund, was structured like the old-fashioned hedge funds, which today seem to be called private partnerships, in which the managing partner earns 20% of the annual profits over some yardstick, usually the Dow or Standard and Poor's average. Soros computed his compensation percentages after subtracting a stable cost-of-money figure of 5%, or what an investor would average on a bank deposit. Thus 20% of capital gains earned each year, after subtracting the 5%, belonged to him and whoever else shared the management of the assets. But he only accumulated his own $100 million because he made large sums of money for the fund's investors. In the fall of 1985, George gave a celebration party for the original investors in his fund, who had put up $12 million. These investors, after fifteen years, Soros said, would have made a hundredfold on their original investments. A $50,000 investment, then, would have grown to $5 million. Awesome best describes this performance, in any other investor's view.

How did he do it? What were his secrets? I asked a broker in England recently, who had been one of those original investors. "I don't know," he responded. "I wish I did, so I could do it, although I think he made more money in big bets in the fixed income area than anything else." Then he added, "And I think we've done even better than a hundredfold on our money." When I asked Soros this same question, he answered with an irreverent remark that I teased him about. He replied, "It's just as well that people treat making money in the market in an irreverent way. No one can tell you how to make money before you do it and, after the fact, most people become too serious. Irreverence makes sense."

Could a savvy analyst of money managers have spotted his talent? It's doubtful. Certainly, no professional pension consultant would have directed a client to Soros, who had no performance record of any kind. When he started the fund, he had worked in England, specializing in what he calls internal arbitrage, trading the parts of security packages, such as bonds with warrants or shares with warrants, when the units are broken up. After this period in England, he became a one-man institutional salesman and analyst, selling European securities for Wertheim and Company in New York. He enjoyed this stage of his career, but it ended with a bang when President Kennedy signed the interest equalization tax bill, and Americans stopped pursuing foreign stocks.

Soros then retired and spent three years at Arnhold S. Bleichroeder, a New York brokerage firm, resting, writing and studying philosophy. He thinks of Bleichroeder as his home base. Though he still managed his own money, he admits that during those three years, between 1963 and 1966, he lost touch with the financial world, and his own investments deteriorated. The turning point came when he realized his thinking had become so abstract that he tried one day to reread what he'd written the day before and couldn't understand it. That was the end of the road, he could go no further. "You have to reach the point where you've done everything and you're worn out resting," he said of his three-year thinking sabbatical.

It would have been difficult to hand over one's mother's money to this abstract philosopher in 1969, but some people did. For in addition to his personality, he had the necessary ingredients for success as an investor.

A Strong Ego Drive.   After three years on the sidelines, Soros wanted to prove himself. When he moved to the buying side from the selling side, he began identifying himself with his performance. "My ego was on the line, now that I was investing," said George. "That's a very good thing to have on the line, for success."

Motivated to Make Money.   Soros had always been motivated to make money because he didn't have any. The financial incentives in the fund partnership were perfect for him. "I really wanted to make it a success, I identified with my investors. We were the same."

Balanced Talent in His Money Management Team. Soros balanced his intuitive stock selection by choosing as his junior partner Jimmy Rogers, a superb fundamental security analyst. In selecting Rogers, he showed that he understood Rogers's abilities well. Soros's selling ability helped in raising the capital. And he used his arbitrage background masterfully in the trading of securities. Adding the talent of a financial analyst to the careful perception of a Sherlock Holmes created a dynamic team.

Sitting in his sunny Long Island garden close to the beach, Soros made some observations on what he'd learned from his own career managing and making money in Wall Street.

Rule 1: The only way you can stay ahead is to look for new rules.

"Yes," George said, "I made rules, and I think probably by now I've broken all the rules, and I've forgotten all the rules as I have made them." Rather than play with a given set of rules, Soros is more interested in how the rules of the game change. He offered a simple example to show a shift in perceptions: the case of conglomerates of the past. Originally, people had watched for earnings growth per share to evaluate these companies. Soros thought they were mistaken "in not recognizing that there is a difference between growth that is somehow internally generated and one that uses the stock to play with and thus devalue the earnings." The rules of the game for evaluating conglomerates were about to change. If you recognized that, and Soros did, it was possible to make a lot of money before the conglomerates collapsed and the old game came to an end.

Rule 2: The first task of any investor is to survive.

"If you're doing poorly, the first move is to retrench, not to do things differently nor to do more some place else." Years ago, for example, the global funds mistakenly doubled their bets to try to recoup, throwing good money at weak ideas as they declined, and ended by losing everything, Soros pointed out. Since he always had his own money invested, he quickly reexamined his position when he felt he was overdoing it. "Don't try to recoup, that's the big mistake," according to Soros. "When you start again, start small." In short, "He who fights and runs away, lives to fight another day."

Rule 3: Test an investing concept or thesis in a small way first.

"You can get an edge on other people when you have an investing concept or thesis, but, as with any scientific thesis, you should start testing it in a small way, adding to it if the hypothesis looks good. Then, if it passes the tests, you'll have a big reward." Soros used this policy often. In the Seventies, he developed two major assumptions: that defense spending in the United States would increase, and that oil prices would go up. At first his positions were small; then, as these theses passed "the tests," he added to them dramatically. "Big plays never were big in the beginning. They became big," says the man famous for big plays.

Rule 4: Other people may know less than you do. You don't need to know everything about a situation to make money.

When George started out, as what he calls the one-eyed analyst of European securities, he was surprised to find that he was the expert, that there were no analysts in America who understood anything about European companies. His first selections were the German banks, because these banks sat on portfolios worth more than the market value of the banks' shares, and in addition, they had banking businesses, thrown in free. While he did not know everything about Germany and its institutions, he nonetheless came up with a valid and simple analysis, without researching other companies.

Rule 5:   People are influenced in the marketplace by events around them.

As a philosophy student, Soros developed a rather complicated theory that he calls his theory of reflexivity. Simplified, it means that a participant in the market tries to base his actions on his understanding of a situation, but, since that view is necessarily distorted and affects events in its turn, the bias acts to reinforce the trend. The more the trend is affected by bias, the farther removed from reality it becomes.

There is a sequence, Soros observed, of self-reinforcing and then self-defeating actions. Analysts who are aware of them can make a lot of money. An example of such a sequence, a paradigm to George, can be seen in real estate investment trusts. Originally, he had written a four-act scenario for this industry, a pattern of boom-bust, in which everything would be great, and then end in disaster several years away. So he played it both ways. A few years after he'd made money on the long side, he reread his original piece and found his case for disaster, in black and white. Even though the stocks were already down, he shorted them—and kept selling short. As a result, his million-dollar investment on the short side made more than a million dollars. I liked Soros's comment: "So, that was rather nice. That was sort of the nicest."

Rule 6:   Timing is much more important when you sell something short.

"In a sense, you're going against the grain," George replied when I asked him why so few people are good at shorting a stock. After all, he continued, a company generally earns money and pays dividends, and traditionally brokers recommend buys, not sales, of securities. But the short side is no longer exclusive, and more people go short when the market facilitates it. But few, I dare say, have made a million on a million-dollar short investment.

Currently, Soros spends a lot of time on his foundation, in many ways the inverse of an investment fund, disinvesting his surplus capital profitably. He believes the same criteria apply to making money as to giving it away. He does not allow people to sell him things, and he does not aim for instant gratification. That is why, in this new endeavor, he intends to maintain the same low profile he kept so long in Wall Street.

Perhaps Soros's evaluation of market activity also applies to him—that boom-bust attitude, what he refers to in his career as a manic-depressive element. The bust side is hard for most of his friends to discern because his irreverence, charm and formidable talent are contagious. When I left him, easy in his relaxed setting, I remembered another day fifteen years ago, at the start of his magic streak, when he looked like a panther ready to strike and behaved the way Olympic swimmers do when warming up before a race, shaking and vibrating, readying themselves for the competition ahead.

A postscript should be added to my bucolic view of Soros in the summer of 1985. When, at the end of that year, his fund's results were in, his performance, at 121%, was four times the market averages and the best single-year return of Soros's career. Under his management, the assets increased from $449 million to more than $1 billion. Hearing of this, some people said, "Well, don't forget that George had that bad period." Soros's so-called bad period came in 1981: The net asset value per share was off 22.9% that year, declining from $1,849 to $1,426. The size of the overall fund went from $381 million to $193 million because of that decline and redemptions. That was Soros's only down year in seventeen years; he tripped twice in the bond market, anticipating the turn too early. His aggressive comeback, when his fund crossed the $1 billion mark, only shows that champions need not strain as obviously as beginners. Soros has established a performance record of 35% compounded over the seventeen-year life of his fund, the best money management record to date. His friends anticipate that next year his net worth will earn him a place on *Forbes*'s megamillionaire list. (Listings start at $150 million.) George Soros's record does beat Buffett's, but Soros still lags behind Buffett's accumulated net worth of over a billion dollars. The question for those of us who know George is, for how long? (The Quantum fund was up 43% in 1986, a happy return for George and his investors. And to the original investors, a 250-time return on their money.)

THE ROTHSCHILD LEGEND—"GREEN FINGERS"

No legend in the historic annals of investing has fired imaginations for as long a period as that of the Rothschilds' financial acumen. Four of the five sons of Mayer Amschel Rothschild left the Frankfurt ghetto, their birthplace, in the nineteenth century, and for the next fifty years rode astride Europe. The five brothers, working as partners, lived the famous chant from *The Three Musketeers:* "All for one and one for all." Before long, the Rothschilds were assumed to have "the Midas touch"; their participation was considered necessary for any financial undertaking to get off the ground. Wild rumors circulated about any investment they might be interested in, the crowd anxiously seeking confirmation, so that they, too, could participate in the venture.

Folklore attributes the bulk of the Rothschild fortune to Nathan's market transactions, to the way he took financial advantage of his advance knowledge of the outcome of the Battle of Waterloo, what currently would be called inside information. Some of these romantic accounts even trace Nathan to the actual battlefield, close to the duke of Wellington. These tales describe his journey through stormy seas across the English Channel to Dover, to arrive in time to stand at his post at the London Stock Exchange. Once there, he was able, supposedly, to place sell orders, thus convincing the City that the news was bad, defeat for England and victory for Napoleon. In the panic that purportedly followed on the exchange, Nathan Rothschild's unknown agents secretly bought up every issue they could find. One pundit estimated that this financial duplicity netted the Rothschild family £135 million. The current head of the English side of the family, Lord Victor Rothschild, categorically denies that Nathan acted so fraudulently, saying that it is slanderous to accuse him of pocketing a fortune by using his knowledge to speculate on the stock exchange. Yet, Lord R., as he is known, admits that Nathan did have this knowledge ahead of time, either by pigeon post or his own couriers. (Fast information has always been considered the key to financial success. The Rothschilds then had a network of couriers all over Europe. Even today, Citibank bought its own zip code to receive mail a day faster.)

Lord R., in his book *Random Variables,* analyzed the plausibility of making the fortune so often discussed in the financial markets around 1815. His research shows it would have been technically impossible, considering the rules of the markets at that time, to make anywhere near the fortune described in the two possible investment vehicles—British government securities consols 3% or an investment trust then named Omnium, which contained only government securities. And it shows that Nathan's profits, assuming they existed, had to have been less than a million pounds. Stories also report that Nathan first informed the prime minister of the news, which seems plausible in view of the Rothschild family's part in financing the war effort, and considering the importance of the Rothschild brothers in their newly adopted countries. The gratitude of governments was always profitable.

The absolute truth remains a mystery. The reason for the Rothschilds' financial success over their rivals seems to

have been their keen ability in short-term financial transactions. Their business evolved from their first acting as
money changers, then as traders; next they handled financial transactions for such clients as the elector of Hesse.
Once the family accumulated capital from these activities,
its members were able to enter the world of debt financing. Anka Muhlstein, a family descendant, in her book on
Baron James (Nathan's brother, who represented the family in France), says that the Rothschilds believed "it was
better to borrow in order to purchase rather than to remain on the sidelines." This strategy then meant borrowing money at the best rate, buying and selling aggressively
and as fast as possible. Muhlstein captures the essence of
the Rothschilds' tactics when she says, "None of these ventures—not even lending—entailed the prolonged commitment of capital." The Rothschilds, for the most part,
avoided betting on the long-term future of anything. Why
tie up money for long periods when so many opportunities presented themselves for quicker profits?

Modern-day Rothschilds, the inheritors of the famous
Rothschild brothers legend, have not been greatly attracted to the worldly pursuit of making money with
money. Baron Guy de Rothschild, in his memoirs *The
Whims of Fortune*, poignantly reveals a lifetime search for
others who had green fingers, so that he could benefit
from their financial abilities.

Yet there is one Rothschild, Jacob, who flashed his
Midas touch over the English landscape, and with his
forceful and dashing style and aggressive maneuvering,
appears to be the true descendant and inheritor of the
nineteenth-century Rothschild financial wizardry. Jacob
has excelled in the same remarkable way as his forebears.
With his transaction-oriented style, he has shown the ability and courage to move aggressively when opportunities
arose.

The vehicle that Jacob Rothschild used so successfully
for his financial transactions was a passive investment trust
that he built from $10 million in the early 1970s to $265
million by 1980. Ironically, a family feud first assigned him

the responsibility for managing the trust. Jacob fought with his cousin Evelyn over the firm's future. Since Evelyn owned 60% of the firm and Jacob owned 20%, Jacob lost all the battles. The family's way to try to remove him from the main activities of the firm was to give him the trust to manage. Their intention was certainly not to give him what turned out to be the catalyst for his success. That smoldering feud, along with his aggressive success with the trust, ended in an eruption. He left his family firm, N. M. Rothschild & Sons, Ltd. (named after Nathan of Waterloo fame), and gained the trust as part of what *Business Week* called his divorce settlement. These family arguments fueled Jacob's natural talents. Just a few years after his departure from N. M. Rothschild & Sons, Ltd., he started a firm—still using RIT (Rothschild Investment Trust), now called Charterhouse J. Rothschild—to purchase an assortment of financial companies. Lionized in the press, portrayed on the cover of *Business Week* as the English financial genius who might rule that country's financial future, Jacob Rothschild was king. Yet, within the year, he was unraveling his purchases at hefty profits. The press, in an about-face, was now debating the decline of Jacob's financial structure, blaming it on his inability to manage a business.

When we discussed the outcome of his maneuvers, Jacob expressed surprise that the press had expected him to manage the empire. That had never been his plan. He had intended to let the best manager, Mark Weinberg of Hambro Life Assurance, PLC., do what he excelled at, once the acquisition was complete. What those critical observers had ignored was Jacob's penchant for investing in the Rothschild style—knowing when to take a profit and keeping to the near term. An acquisition today, after all, is just another buy transaction and always can be traded at the right price. Both sides of financial transactions were fundamental to those big, nineteenth-century profits.

There are lessons for other investors in Jacob's experiences:

Rule 1: **When you invest, stay with the areas you think you know and feel comfortable with.**

Jacob believes that he never was a real investor, since his career in corporate finance started at N. M. Rothschild in London. His background and thinking evolved entirely around mergers and acquisitions; when he thought about buying a firm, it was through mergers and acquisitions, and when he thought about buying a position for the Rothschild Investment Trust, he chose what we call today a prearbitrage stock, one that can be taken over. His thinking started with ways to restructure a company. He asked himself, "What could the company do to become more profitable?" or, "What's wrong with the business?" In fact, all his subsequent ideas came from this questioning.

His first choice, a 20% stake in Sotheby's, had takeover possibilities because the company had a proprietary niche, only one competitor, Christie's, in a big market for luxury items and it had a small capitalization. Sotheby's, then capitalized at £4 million, was eventually bought for £80 million. Another company, Watney's, was a candidate because it seemed to be weakly managed, but with good prospects. Jacob started a hubbub, at the time, by instigating a takeover offer. His group had gone to visit one of England's larger companies, Grand Metropolitan, and suggested that they make an offer for the company, stimulating the bid. This was a natural process for someone whose roots were in corporate finance, but was considered then to be slightly aggressive by the investment community.

Rothschild Investment Trust appreciated from under $10 million in 1970 to $265 million in 1980, and even further when it issued shares to merge with Charterhouse. Today, as a result of increasing its percentage of capital, it has an asset base of about $550 million. The trust had been inactive when Jacob had taken it over, but using an investment style that he felt comfortable with, he was able to work wonders making money with money, regardless of his own estimate of his purity as a real investor.

Rule 2:   If an investing plan that looked good starts to unwind and no longer seems attractive, listen to the evidence and change your direction.

Rothschild thinks that very few people understand his about-face in building a financial empire. Originally, his group thought that the financial services sector in England was ripe for change, ripe for deregulation because England was lagging too far behind the Americans and Japanese. This analysis motivated the group to put its hat in the ring, by merging with Charterhouse. Rothschild says he thought they had been right about their strategic plan and that, in the future, only the strongest financial services, with good proprietary lines of business and excellent management, would survive. The combination of Charterhouse J. Rothschild, as it was called, was not strong enough and therefore they took the initiative and merged with Hambro Life. This combination would have introduced extremely good management (what Jacob considers probably the best in England and in this field) and could also have provided a strong proprietary line of business in retail financial services.

The acquisition with Hambro didn't come off. The market started to weaken, and analysts then questioned the price-earnings ratios applied to financial conglomerates. Charterhouse was having problems, as was its American business, which was going through a weaker profit cycle in 1984. Everyone was hesitant about moving ahead, considering the markets and business conditions at that time. What the group already had in place was analyzed, and Jacob said, "We didn't think we were strong enough to be successful for our shareholders. When you come to such a decision, you have to take it to its logical conclusion in an orderly way, and in a way which is not unprofitable for our shareholders. So we decided to retreat from Moscow." Jacob still believes that retreat was the right decision, yet he regrets that the financial company never came to pass. And not because he had pretensions about running a business, which the press seems to intimate; he honestly does not know if he could manage such a business, but he does know he did not want to, then. What he did want was to build, through acquisitions, a well-managed, strong financial services company, but it was necessary to back off when the plan became unstuck. In smaller things, however, Jacob says he is not very good at changing his mind. When only he is involved, he tends to try and try again.

Rule 3: Seize opportunities and use whatever investment arena you can be successful in.

It is not surprising that the nineteenth-century Rothschilds became masters in dealing with money, when we realize that, in the Germany of their day, all other professions were closed to Jews. The changing and lending of money was not an esteemed occupation for European society. Still, the family used the one option available, and they became successful by taking risks and moving aggressively when opportunities arose.

Jacob himself took the option open to him—the trust—and did the same with it. The trust was not a treasure when it was given to him.

In looking toward the future, Rothschild says that he does not have imperialistic ambitions; his goal today is patiently to increase the total return for his 40,000 shareholders, using the style he is comfortable with, trying to spot companies with takeover potential way ahead of time, in the manner that Warren Buffett has honed so brilliantly. Jacob admits that he no longer is intense and aggressive, as he was ten years ago when he had more energy and fewer distractions, and that, if anything, he is more mellow, having already gone through his achievement-addict period. The selection method, one part of his winning formula, will remain the same; he will just have lengthened his time frame.

A persuasive myth always seems real. The legend of Nathan Rothschild, knowing that Waterloo had been won, coolly leaning against his post at the stock exchange selling consuls, while amassing them secretly, has become a part of English history. Researchers will debate whether it's a false or scandalous story for years to come, as they go through the dusty family archives. The actual truth does not matter and fortunately is not provable. So the myth of the Rothschilds' Midas touch lives on in the minds of investors everywhere. The media believed for a moment that one heir to this legend, Jacob, could revive the success achieved by the five brothers almost two centuries ago. It is easy, then, to understand the disappointment when he pulled back and spoiled the dream. Jacob proved to have the legendary talent but not the hunger driving him to concentrate so intensely on business, once he had succeeded in making his mark on the financial community.

THE EPILOGUE

Are there common threads in the careers of these six major money managers? Four of them were hungry for capital, success or fortune: Roy Neuberger, George Soros, John Templeton and Warren Buffett. One, Jacob Rothschild, no doubt wanted success, but carrying the family legend on his shoulders made him hungry for financial recognition. Once that was satisfied, it lost its importance. Jack Dreyfus seems to have dropped into Wall Street, but once there, like someone sent into a football game, he played continually, catching every ball thrown and running for a million touchdowns, until one day he asked himself, "What am I doing here?"

4

THE TRENDSETTERS
Two Investing Romantics—
Peter Lynch
and Jimmy Rogers

ROMANTIC INVESTORS ARE LIKE BURMESE RU-
bies, that scarce gemstone filled with fire and mystery.
Idealistic and unspoiled, romantic investors are strangers
to cynicism, ordinarily a natural by-product of years spent
dissecting facts and figures, misperceptions, outright lies
and a million mistakes. Such cynicism is accepted in Wall
Street as a normal state of maturity, just as a patina of
age is deemed advantageous, even when it covers with a
dustlike crumb an original eighteenth-century French gilt
mirror.

Every now and then, a romantic figure comes along,
eager to conquer nations and hearts in the battle for investment success. These figures, like all romantics, have
mystery and charm, yet are vulnerable and intense. A romantic hero must be someone whose success has been recognized, such as Mikhail Baryshnikov in ballet or Jeremy
Irons in the theater. Once in their presence, we feel as
though we have entered a magnetic field. We want to look
at them, listen to them, smile at them. And they keep their
power over others, as long as the secret of their strength

is never revealed. Romantics remain romantics as long as they maintain the illusion.

The modern investment world has two such romantics: Peter Lynch and Jimmy Rogers. They both retain their mystiques, despite publicity about their investment thinking and track records.

JIMMY ROGERS

Jimmy Rogers was easier to pursue, living only a taxi ride away, in his six-floor Victorian mansion on Riverside Drive in New York City, a purchase he had made with some investing winnings. He had invited me for lunch and suggested that we spend our time on his roof, so we could enjoy that lovely early spring day out of doors. The size of the roof, the panoramic view of the Hudson River and, across it, New Jersey, were spectacular. I made sure to sit facing the wall, giving him the better view, lest my mind wander from the purpose at hand.

Born in the backwoods of Alabama, Rogers is today, at forty-four, filled with a sense of good fortune at having found his way into the investing business, and at the money he was able to earn.

In his senior year at Yale, he was a confused young man, trying to choose between law, business and medical school. One day, he went to New York for a variety of job interviews. In one of them, he hit it off with a man who had grown up in New York's Little Italy and had gone to Harvard. Rogers took a summer job in his brokerage firm, Dominick and Dominick. At Yale, Jimmy had studied philosophy and history. He knew nothing about Wall Street except that it was located in New York and that something unpleasant had happened there in 1929.

"I went down to Wall Street and fell in love, and it was wonderful." When I asked what had made him fall in love, he answered, "I remember it very well . . . not the moment so much, but the summer. They were paying you just to play this game of what the future was going to bring, what was going to happen in the world, which I love to do, anyway, since I was always figuring out revolutions in Chile or whatever. So I saw, then, that if you could figure out what was going to happen in the world, you could make a whole lot of money."

After that summer, Rogers went to Oxford for a year on scholarship, and there decided that his future would be on Wall Street, not in law or medical or business school. After an army stint, he joined Bache and Company in the summer of 1968, right at the top of the market.

"I shouldn't be in business on Wall Street any more with my entry before the worst bear market in thirty years, but somehow or other, I survived."

Following Bache, Rogers worked at three jobs in five years: at R. Gilder and Company, then for Roy Neuberger, until someone introduced him to George Soros, whom Jimmy joined at Arnhold S. Bleichroeder. Rogers got along well with Soros and made a lot of money quickly. Eventually, they became one of the most successful investing pairs ever. But in 1973, Congress changed the law, making the team's money management methods illegal, so they left Bleichroeder. Brokerage firms could no longer have subsidiaries managing money for a percentage of the profit.

"Thank God somebody changed that law. We wouldn't have done it otherwise," reflected Rogers, on what turned into his golden opportunity, after three job changes in five years. Of the $33 million in European money that Soros and Rogers had been managing, $12 million came into their offshore partnership originally. Most of the rest followed a few years later, when the investors took a look at their performance record. In 1979, after making a great deal of money for their clients and for himself, Rogers retired from his partnership with Soros.

"I'd made more money than I needed and I'd always dreamed of having more than one career, although I'm still not sure what the other careers would be. Besides, I think that in the investing business there is a law of diminishing returns. When you've had the kind of success we had, you get bigger and bigger, and then there are more and more people around, and not that many people are that good at investing and can think the way you do, and I have enough trouble getting along with myself, let alone with all those other people."

Rogers is a security analyst's analyst. His two greatest strengths as an investor are his passion for doing the analytical work himself, and the way he conceives of investing, starting with a central theme that flows into connecting investments over a period of time, all derivatives of his core theme. Rogers's rules for other investors include observations on these two strengths, as well as other advice.

Rule 1: Do your own work. Don't be afraid of being a loner.

"I learned early in my career that if you read the annual reports, you've done more than 90% of the people on Wall Street. If you read the notes to the annual report, you've done more than 95% of the people on Wall Street, and if you actually sit down and do a spread sheet, you've done more than 98% of the people on Wall Street." Rogers then told me about what it was like when he started in 1968, when stocks would sometimes double in a week. He shared an office with another analyst, and one day he was sitting in his office doing a financial spread sheet (which is like a doctor analyzing an array of X-rays and scans done on a patient—in this case, on a corporation). A broker came rushing in to see the other man, and he said to Jimmy, "What are you doing?" Jimmy told him and the broker said, "Nobody does *that* any more," devastating Jimmy with his scorn.

The Rogers spread sheets have become famous. At the beginning, they were fairly simple. Jimmy first figured out profit margins and return on equity, and formed in his mind a historical overview of the company. Then, in the years that followed, he'd add on something else. A company in one year would take a receivables write-off, and Rogers would say to himself, "Hey, schmuck, why don't you figure out about receivables?" and so he would add them to his spread sheets. Then he added inventories, then equity ratios or lease commitments or pension arrears. Jimmy still is a devotee of spread sheets. He prefers the old-fashioned paper-and-pencil approach to today's quick computer run.

"If you do it yourself, it will mean more to you. Yes, it's boring and seems like drudge work, but it still sinks in that way." He has learned by doing hundreds, maybe thousands, of them.

In researching an investment idea, Rogers says that he doesn't talk to anybody on Wall Street. No broker or analyst calls him. He calls the company, the competitors, the suppliers, and the customers, as well as trade associations and the publishers of trade magazines.

"Somewhere there's a guy who has the information you want," he said. "If you read the stuff and talk to guys out there in the real world, one thing will click, and that's all you need to know."

Any investor can read an annual report and, after he is seasoned at it, its footnotes. Doing a spread sheet may be asking too much, but the three basic points that Jimmy started with can be mastered. Ask, or compute for yourself, whether the profit margins and return on equity are improving or declining. Try to research the company's history: Under what conditions did it do well? When did it do badly? Talk to people who know the business. Investment research can be more fun and certainly more profitable than reading a spy story.

Rule 2:   Good investors need a historical perspective.

"The best investment training," says Rogers, "came from what I studied in college: philosophy and history. People usually look at me like I'm a madman when I say that," he added. "Philosophy, because it taught me how to think, and history, because it taught me that the world is always changing, and things will not always be the way they are today."

This belief made Rogers take his spread sheets as far back as possible to understand a company. "How else would anyone know that U.S. Steel was a growth stock in 1959?" he asked me. "The farther back you go, the better you can understand the cycles."

John Brook's classic, *Once in Golconda,* influenced Rogers by showing him the historical pattern of bull and bear markets.

"You've got to remember that the same kind of madness happens in a bull market every time, and the same kind of madness happens in bear markets." Looking through Ben Graham's book and flipping through the charts and stock prices for thirty-five years added to Rogers's investment perspective.

Rule 3: Think conceptually about the world.

His most profitable investment area has turned out to be the aging population. An annual report of Beverly Enterprises came across his desk in 1978 or 1979. The stock was selling at $2, but, with surprise, he noticed that the earnings had gone up every year for five years. Something is going on here, he thought. And then he got out all the annual reports of the nursing home industry, and found the stocks were all cheap and the companies doing reasonably well. Getting out his spread sheets, then, he found that in the late Sixties, these companies had sold for huge prices. One company, Four Seasons, went bankrupt, and all the stocks had a dramatic collapse. Some of the wonderful things that were supposed to have happened were starting to come true, but nobody cared on Wall Street. So he went out and visited all the nursing home companies.

"It's typical," Jimmy said. "You spend hours and hours doing research into something, and you'll run into one thing, one statement or one guy who says it all. It's all you need to know. Of course, you never would have found the one sentence if you hadn't spent all those days dragging around." The chairman of Beverly said, "We are ninety percent full and starting to have a waiting list in some nursing homes. Where we are full, we'll drop the government-paid patients, if we have the demand, and take the private patients." When Rogers asked him why demand was increasing, the chairman told him that since the nursing homes couldn't raise money from Wall Street, the number of beds was not growing, but there seemed to be more and more people out there who needed one. Rogers tracked down government birth charts back to 1890, and there it was, in the number of people born in 1890. The population was getting older. There would be increasing demand. Yet the chairman had told him that supply could not go up because they couldn't raise any money. So it is that simple, he thought. The Rogers-Soros funds bought every nursing home company in the business at that time, and eventually bought companies that grew out of this phenomenon, companies that would care for people in their homes when they couldn't get into nursing homes. The next step will be public hospice companies, he added, in five or ten years. "They're going to be growth stocks, and I'm going to buy them." Hospices have no house rules. You can bring anyone in, even your dog, at any hour. Basically, it's a way to die happily in peace and dignity.

Other investment concepts that Rogers believes have a future are prisons and nuclear plants. Right now, it costs $30,000 a year for New York State to keep someone in jail for a year. It would cost less at Harvard.

"Remember," he added, "that forty years ago hospitals in this country were run by charities and municipalities. Eventually prisons will be run by private companies. All the utility companies that have been having problems, like Long Island Lighting [Lilco], will survive. Even New York State, which may close down the nuclear plant at Shoreham, is suggesting 'a limited write-off' for the company, two billion at the most. A lot of money is going to be made in nuclear companies. When someone comes up with a way to take care of all that nuclear waste lying around, as well as to transport it, riches will be made. No such company exists today."

Jimmy's concepts sound interesting: public companies that are in the hospice, prison management and nuclear waste businesses. I will watch for them to arrive in the marketplace.

Rule 4:   Don't buy stocks at high multiples.

"I don't buy them because, by the time they reach a high multiple, it's probably about time for it to come to an end. Wall Street and politicians are the last to catch on to anything," said Jimmy. He doesn't sell a stock just because it happens to have a high multiple. He either waits for a fundamental change or for an indication that something is about to go wrong.

Rule 5:   Be selective in your investing and look for one good idea.

"The most important trick for getting rich on Wall Street is not to lose money. There are many guys," he said, "who do well for two years and then get creamed. Wait until you have a winner and are sure. In the meantime, keep your money in treasury bills. Professional money managers feel that they have to do something all the time and are the worst at following this advice.

"Even if you only have one play every ten years, you're going to do a lot better than most people."

Rule 6:   Every investment should be considered a commodity that will be affected by supply and demand changes. It's just a question of when.

Everything has its own supply and demand cycle, which may be a twenty-, thirty-, or fifty-year cycle, and everything is basically a commodity in the end. American Standard was a great growth stock when people went from outdoor to indoor plumbing, but it isn't considered one today. Avon, a cosmetics firm, boomed after the war when the country became more affluent. By the late Sixties, Avon had a multiple of 50, and the market was saturated with many competing cosmetics brands.

"Everybody, even in the backwoods of Alabama, was using cosmetics," Jimmy noted. There had to be a change, and along came the hippie movement with its natural look, followed eventually by the women's movement and the surge of women into the work force.

"When you're in any stock, what you really want to do is understand the supply and demand factors, and remember that it's going to change. It's just a question of when. Such changes are caused by changes in society and economics, and there are always reasons for them."

Many investors would have done well to remember this rule in late 1979 and lock in some of their hefty profits.

Rule 7: Every investor should lose some money, because it teaches you about yourself.

Jimmy Rogers thinks he has made two serious mistakes.

In the late Sixties or early Seventies, he shorted the three listed machine tool stocks by buying puts. Four months later, he had tripled his money. Then he said to himself, "I'm so smart, I'm going to be the next Bernard Baruch. I'm going to be rich and triple my money every four months, while others are in a frenzy over their losses."

He sold the puts, waited for the industry to rally a bit, then shorted the stocks themselves to avoid the premium in the puts. Two months later, he had lost everything. Fortunately, it was not a lot, but it was devastating to him.

What happened? He felt that he hadn't understood the market. Two or three years later, these stocks collapsed. His fundamental analysis had been perfect, but there is more than that to the market, he found.

"I learned it ain't quite as easy as it seems, just knowing and being right." It taught him to pay more attention to the market. It taught him that people's perceptions are different from the fundamental outlook of a company.

Things often don't happen tomorrow, they may take a while to sink in. "I used to think that if I'd figured something out, then everybody else had to. Well, I now know that I may be early." This mistake made Rogers try to learn more about timing.

Another time, Jimmy figured out that the market penetration had peaked for Masco, the company that made the single-handled faucet. There was a lot of competition, and he saw that the company had started to diversify. At the same time, he was buying the stocks of citizens-band radio companies, eventually making money on that trend. Masco bought a little company that Rogers did not pay much attention to, a scanner company whose product allowed people to listen to police, fire and ambulance calls. It had no two-way signal, as the CB radio had. People just listened to the conversations. Rogers did not realize that people might like to do that. As he worded it, the same hotshot who figured out CB radios didn't figure out that people would like this scanner. The stock went through the roof, and he had gone short. He'd been right on the peak in the fundamentals of Masco's single-handled faucet, but the company had been smart enough to diversify and acquire the one product that would send its earnings through the roof.

"I lost a lot of money, and it was so stupid because I was so sure of my facts about the market peaking for Masco that I didn't look at all the parts of it. And, you know, I've seen it so many times, where people get carried away with a concept that something's going to be great." His advice is to challenge everything, to look at all the other company divisions and to know it all.

Although we talked for two and a half hours, my interview with Jimmy Rogers seemed short. We were waiting for the elevator, adjacent to his rooftop Jacuzzi, which is on a platform to ensure an even better view.

"What now?" I asked. I mentioned the course in money management he had been teaching for the past two years at Columbia University. "It's the same course that Ben

Graham taught," he said. I also know that Jimmy spent his time managing his own money.

Like a good romantic, he gave me a Mona Lisa smile. "I'm looking for adventure now," Rogers said. While descending, we wondered what a today adventure might offer. What could equal, for this forty-four-year-old from the Alabama backwoods, the adventures he had already found in the ephemeral world of investing.

PETER LYNCH

The other "Burmese ruby" investor, Peter Lynch, was away from his desk at Fidelity Management in Boston when I was ushered into his office. Looking around the room, I felt immediately at home. The desk was covered with annual reports marked up and left open, a cascade of pink slips with telephone messages to be answered, plus assorted other corporate documents and data. Stacked up to one side, as well as littered below his desk, were twenty-eight clean yellow pads, ready to be grabbed and used at the appropriate time. Paper was everywhere. At the windows, there was a long table with approximately three-hundred pounds of brokerage reports to be read, scanned, filed or jettisoned, a week's supply for one of Wall Street's institutional money managers. Lynch later estimated that fifteen inches of reports arrived daily. Just to be sure that he would see internal meeting notices or special telephone messages, a thoughtful staff member had pinned them to the two chairs facing his desk. When Lynch came in and we started to talk, it was apparent that his appearance and personality were in direct contrast to this paper chaos.

In his classic book on money management, *The Money Game*, published in 1967, Adam Smith said, "Fidelity has been the Green Bay Packers of the fun[d] league for some time now. They don't win every year, but are the team to beat." That was twenty years ago, when they had assets of $3.5 billion. Today they have over $35 billion under management, and their long-term investment results are a source of pride for the founder, Edward C. Johnson II. These days, Peter Lynch is the man to beat in the professional money management field. The mutual fund he manages at Fidelity, the Magellan Fund, has been number one, measured over five- and ten-year periods against the 380 mutual funds monitored by Lipper Analytical Services. Over a ten-year period, Magellan's total return, market appreciation plus reinvested capital gains and dividends, was 1,702%. This compares with a 292% return for the Standard and Poor's 500-stock index over the same period. Lynch's fund was not the best every year, but the compounding of steady good results piled up.

Lynch said that he was always interested in the stock market, even as a child, when he worked as a golf caddy at a club outside Boston. The golfers often discussed investing. There, he said, "people get to know you very well because you start working at eleven and now you're twenty-one, out of college, and once they see you're going to business school, they start to inquire." Fidelity had fifty applicants for three positions, but only Lynch had caddied for the company's president.

The first investment Peter made was buying $600 worth of Flying Tiger, which he had discovered in 1961, while in high school. He considers himself lucky because the Vietnam war bailed him out. The stock went from $7 to $70. He hadn't known about the impending war. He had simply thought that the air freight industry was going to become a big thing.

After a summer apprenticeship in 1966 at Fidelity, a graduate year at Wharton, and two years in the army, he returned to Fidelity in 1969. Soon after, he was given Gerry Tsai's office, one of Fidelity's most famous former stars (for a rookie professional investor, the equivalent of being assigned Mickey Mantle's or Joe Namath's locker).

One of his first assignments was to research some industries: metals, textiles, apparel and carpets. He remembers that he had to find the outlook for molybdenum and couldn't even say it. He had taken chemistry at school and thought the word was pronounced "moly bidium." But whatever it was, he had to find out within two weeks whether Fidelity should have more of it or less of it.

"This," he said, "is the traditional way at Fidelity. You learn by yourself." Eventually, Lynch became director of research, a role that he shed gladly in early 1977 to assume responsibility for the Magellan Fund.

Rule 1: Concentrate on the profitability of a company, not on economic projections.

"The problem I have with looking at the economy is that I can't judge whether economists are looking at today or what's going to possibly happen next year. I try to be in on what's happening to a company, and when I talk to companies I'm interested in, it's whether business is getting better or getting worse. I want to know if the competition in steel is intensifying or fiber prices are collapsing." Looking for red lights, yellow lights or green lights is what is important to him. And Lynch stays 100% invested at all times in his $9 billion fund, even when he is bearish on the current market outlook.

Rule 2: Sell stocks when whatever you are looking for has not happened.

Lynch had made quite a commitment to steel stocks in 1984, but though the economy was going up, things were not getting better in the steel industry. In fact, they were getting worse. The operating rate had gone up, but prices had not firmed, and earnings were still poor. By 1985 Lynch still had not seen improvement, and it was getting late in the cycle for steels. "The final killer," Peter said, "was that the dollar strengthened," so he cut his steel position dramatically. If, as steels went down, he had doubled up, adding to his position, he would have had 12% of his portfolio in a group that fell 50%, hardly an enviable position.

"When whatever you're looking for hasn't happened," Lynch says, "sell. Otherwise it's a hope and a prayer that something will happen. If you thought that a company could turn around one of its problems or introduce a new product or get rid of that one, and it doesn't happen, sell!"

Rule 3:   Buy as many stocks as you really like.

"If you find ten stocks you like, you should buy all ten." Lynch said he reasons that shortening the list to four could produce the four losers. But if you buy all the stocks you like, when a few go up and do exactly as expected, you can sell them. If the fundamentals of the companies are still valid, you can buy more of the ones that haven't moved.

For a *Vogue* investment article, I picked four stocks that I thought would do well and ended up owning three of them. The fourth went up 80% immediately.

Rule 4:   Small companies usually have big moves, and big companies have small moves.

There is a direct relationship between a company's size and its potential return to you, Lynch said. A company like Dow Chemical is not going to go up sixfold. "Yet, at the same time," he said, "you can't make rules in estimating potential returns from an investment." He has bought stocks that he expected to make 30% to 35% on and made tenfold, and bought stocks he thought he would make tenfold on and lost 80%.

Rule 5:   Try to avoid buying exciting companies without earnings.

In reviewing where he had made the most mistakes, Lynch put most of them into one category: "The companies that were the most exciting."

They were the companies that had the greatest possibilities but were not making money. "If a couple of things went their way in a few years, they would be enormous stocks." Peter counted at least twenty developing companies in which he lost money, and he could not remember once breaking even. Whenever he bought them, he had expected a ten- to fifteenfold return. After these experiences, Lynch means to follow this rule but still finds it a hard one to keep. "I try as much as I can, but these stories are so powerful."

Possibilities like these can be intoxicating, and I, like Peter, bought my share of them. Sometimes I have made money in them, mostly through luck. I moved out of the others right before they tanked.

Rule 6:   There are two ways to make top money in the market: Invest in a small growth company or in a turnaround.

Successes in the investment business come from buying a small profitable company, owning it for a long time, and letting it become a medium-size one that is even more profitable. "It's not magic," said Lynch. "If a hundred people had seen that company, ninety-eight of them would have bought it. They just weren't looking at companies of that sort." He believes, too, that good money can be made in a company that has been doing poorly for the last few years and that will suddenly improve.

Rule 7:   You are not going to do well as an investor unless you learn to accept mistakes and deal with uncertainty.

This is one of the harder lessons for investors to learn. Often people do well in high school, college and graduate school. Then they go into the money management business and, even after years, can't get used to feeling a little stupid half the time. In investing, the picture is never black and white. Instead, there are usually three or four negatives and three or four positives in a company's outlook, and a lot of uncertainty. Lynch asked, "What if you can't deal with that? In school, when you do pure research, you circle around from one angle until, six months later, you say 'Aha, I've got the answer!' Well, in the investment world, by the time you say 'Aha!,' the stocks have either doubled or been cut in half."

Rule 8: Buy only a small amount of stock you're interested in until you know a lot about it.

This will ensure your closer look at the company. Lynch's expression for this rule is, "I'll go up to my ankles in anything. But, when I start getting up to my knees or my waist, I want to really understand the business."

Rule 9: You have to understand the business of a company you have invested in, or you will not know whether to buy more if it goes down.

If you understand what you own and what it does, for instance, Dunkin' Donuts, then if nothing is wrong with the company and the price of the stock goes down, you can buy more. But if you own a software company or one in random access memory or digital data, you don't know whether to buy more or to sell it. How can you tell how good your company is? "You have to know what the right things are to worry about and what you expect to happen."

Rule 10: Don't bottom-fish.

This is a mistake we all make. A stock has fallen a lot, and it is bought for that reason alone. Imagine if you bought Polaroid at 65 after it had dropped from 130, and you watched it go to 16. It is one thing to find a real reason. But too often a bottom-fisher strains for that reason, to crank out an explanation.

Rule 11: Be careful whom you take a tip from.

When you get a tip, you have to look at the source. Does the tip come from the president of an electronics company, telling you that the semiconductor industry has got-

ten dramatically better in the last two months? Or is it a
tip from the president of a semiconductor company, telling you to buy the biotechnology firm Genentech, or
Union Oil? What does he know about these fields? You
generally buy on a tip because you think the person giving
it is informed. But you've got to find out what the story is
on this tip, what the fundamentals are. Otherwise, what
do you do if the stock goes down? The tipper is usually
not available and won't want to hear from you if the tip
doesn't work out.

You can use tips about an industry that the tipper knows
well. Of course, you would love to have known about a
wonder drug like Tagamet and bought Smithkline Beck-
man, or known someone in the retail world who could see
Zayre turning around. Observations such as these are sensible tips.

"People do a lot of research," Peter said, "when they buy
a dishwasher, a stereo or a VCR. They read *Consumer Reports* and talk to other consumers. They do all that work
before buying something that costs $500 to $2,000. Yet
they'll put $10,000 on a stock without having the foggiest
idea why. Here's a good comparison: In college, when
you're dating, and someone says they know this really nice
girl, you ask, 'Have you got a picture?' You don't want to
rely only on the person. And that's what I want to do. I
don't want to rely only on Joe Doakes. I want to know
what the story is on every investment I'm dealing with."

One year, I analyzed my own mistakes and found that
they all were violations of this rule. The tips did not come
from someone who really knew, and I myself hadn't done
enough fundamental work on the ideas.

Peter Lynch, the star investor, has this in common with
Jimmy Rogers: He is still amazed that he is paid to do what
he loves. He comes into his office every Saturday to work
his way through those piles of investment reports. Each
year, he calculated, he visits 300 to 400 companies, some
years more than 500; he'll often make a cold call just to
hear what is going on in that industry. Lynch seems to

thrive on the responsibility of his 800-stock portfolio, as well as on the esteem and envy that come from being number one, the man to beat in the professional investment derby.

These romantic investors stand apart from many of their colleagues in another way. They refuse to fit themselves into one investment dogma, rebuffing nonplayer consultants who like to dissect money managers as if they were botany specimens. Both Rogers and Lynch have had the luxury of managing funds. Thus they can afford to focus on making money, instead of pleasing consultants so the consultants will recommend them to their pension-fund clients. If we tried to give a name to their styles, we could call Rogers the supply and demand investor and Lynch a hedged mélange investor, for the way he uses growth, value, cyclical and special situation stocks to balance his portfolios. However we describe the way they work, we must recognize their talent and be caught in the force field of their success.

5

THE CLASS OF 1985

The Changing World of Wall Street— Profiles of Four Highly Successful Investors

INVESTORS' STYLE COMES FROM TWO COMPO-
nents: where and from whom they acquired their training
and experience, and when they practiced their art in the
marketplace. Some of the newcomers who are doing well
today and attracting notice for their ability to manage
money have adapted a value orientation to their selection
of stocks. This group, the Class of 1985, has been weaned
in the roller coaster years of the 1970s, when in one decade they saw the extremes of optimistic and pessimistic
valuations of securities. And, because of that experience,
they have successfully adopted a conservative, long-term
outlook in their investment decisions. "The fewer decisions, the fewer chances for mistakes," is their credo. They
study each situation and deliberate for a long time before
they make a purchase, estimating how much money they
could lose as well as how much they could make. The Class
of 1985 represents today's neo-ascendancy in America, as
well as showing how the Eighties have influenced the se-

curities market. Its members have a different brand of optimism from that of the speculative Sixties.

America embraced the start of the Eighties in a semioptimistic mood. Tired of the binges of excessive adventurism in the Sixties and the economic debacle that followed in the Seventies, the country chose an optimistic leader, Ronald Reagan, over Jimmy Carter in the 1980 Presidential contest. The new decade began with an upbeat tone, punctuated by bass chords. A sweet-and-sour combination, a delicate balance among ever-increasing budget deficits, a strategic defense buildup and surprising statistics on new jobs and personal financial well-being that became the envy of the Western world. This yin-yang economy shaped the character of the stock market, the most volatile barometer of perceptions and change. More than twenty years after what the author John Brooks called The Go-Go Years, Wall Street in 1986 was thriving. Yes, dramatic changes and subtle shifts had occurred, but these only assured the participants that they were operating in the casino they knew and loved so well. The most notable difference in that twenty-year span was the institutionalization of the marketplace; everything else recedes in importance.

The Institutionalization of the Marketplace

Individual investors in 1960 accounted for 69% of Wall Street's daily volume. Today, the institutions have taken over, accounting for approximately 90% of daily trades. In 1960, an individual investor was a significant player; his transaction costs were *pari passu* (Wall Street's wonderful term for the same or equal) with all other investors; today, on the other hand, an individual can pay ten times the commission that an institution does. (It can range from 50 cents to 90 cents a share, versus 5 cents to 8 cents a share.) Daily volume has changed even more. In 1960, 5 million shares were traded daily, but more than 140 million are traded currently, a twentyfold increase. Institutions, the dominant investors, for the most part pay no taxes and therefore can move freely in and out of the market. In addition, they have cheaper commissions and first access to information. Yet, despite the declining role of individual investors, all that has really occurred is a marked increase in volatility and a decrease in the ability of many professional money managers to show better-than-average results. In short, the individual may still be ahead, since he can command attention from an adviser or broker who has learned to value steady customers as well as those higher commissions.

Investors' Attitudinal Swings

The saga of changing investor attitudes, swinging dramatically from positive to negative, can be seen in reviewing price-earnings (p-e) multiples. These always reflect levels of optimism in the market. Value Line computes an industrial composite of over 900 companies, which account for about 80% of the income earned by all nonfinancial companies in the United States; their multiples tell the tale.

Multiples

1972	19.2×
1979	6.7×
1986	14.2×

average annual p-e ratios

The growth market broke in 1972 and Value Line's multiple of 19.2 is an average figure that year. I remember a discussion at Dreyfus in which two of us argued that Levitz Furniture's multiple of 60 was reasonable.

Different Stock Selection Focus

During the Sixties, investors looked for growth stocks, then considered wonder stocks, companies so good you would never have to sell them. These plums were called one-decision stocks. The favorites offered innovative breakthroughs in technology and medicine: Syntex, Polaroid and Xerox. Unfortunately, as shown by Glenn Greenberg of the Class of 1985, people who believed such growth was invincible went down with their Titanic portfolios; these high-multiple stocks fell the fastest in the market decline of 1973–74. Today the value seekers have taken over; "value" has become the Eighties investment fulcrum. Corporate restructuring, either forced (like Goodyear's) or voluntary (like Gulf and Western's), is the watchword in the marketplace as long as it will benefit shareholders.

Yesterday's Cinderellas, waiting for an offer from a corporate fairy godmother, are today's wonder stocks. After the briefest flirtation, the company is at the ball, dancing with Prince Charming.

The Evolution of Security Analysis

Security analysis developed into a distinct career only in the 1960s. Fred Alger, a seasoned money manager, remembers telling his uncle that what he really wanted to do after graduating from college in 1956 was be a financial statistician, as analysts then were called. His uncle was not pleased with Fred's choice because it was at that time considered the most unprofitable of all possible jobs. The only textbook on the subject was Graham and Dodd's *Security Analysis,* which newcomers found only by chance or through their own curiosity.

As a discipline and career, security analysis has come a long way. Slide rules are no longer used (a blessing for those of us who have graduated to reading glasses). Now calculators are as familiar a tool to security analysts as slide rules once were. Another significant change from those early days when Alger was first intrigued by the research process is in the amount of data available to any market analyst. Alger had become fascinated with financial research, as though it were a great detective story. Whoever could decipher all the clues would make money. But today the mystery has become far more difficult to unravel, even when the analyst has an individual computer and instant access to data. There is much more information to sift. Therefore, any serious investor must spend considerable time in assimilating all the information available before he can find those clues and select the ones that are relevant to the analysis.

A Changing Cast of Stars

The investment world has always admired its stars, its members who appear glamorous and larger than life. In the 1960s those stars were Gerry Tsai and Jack Dreyfus. Ross Perot emerged as the hero of the corporate culture; his frustrated attempts to bring our boys out of Vietnam were finally satisfied when, years later, he organized and personally led a raid to bring out his own personnel who were stranded in Iran. There is an even larger cult of admiration in the 1980s for the investing acumen of Warren Buffett. Ivan Boesky, accepted in the star category, was treated with some skepticism by his peers and the press, although they envied his success. (That envy turned to anger and disgust in November 1986 when Ivan Boesky agreed to pay $100 million to the federal government for insider abuses. His crime was compounded by the revelation that for three months Boesky had been "wired" in order to entrap his friends and thus lower whatever prison sentence might follow. The ultimate arrogance and crime to many was the discovery that Boesky was allowed to sell $400 million worth of securities out of his partnership before the public announcement of the scandal. Thus he was allowed to profit from inside knowledge of his own demise.)

Lee Iacocca is the equivalent of Ross Perot as the 1980s corporate hero. As flamboyant as Perot, Iacocca led a turnaround at Chrysler, a company that had been written off by many. Then, to describe the details of his accomplishment, he produced an all-time best-selling book telling just how he did it. He earmarked the book's profits for charity and then helped raise millions for the repair of the

Statue of Liberty. Certainly, Iacocca is a splendid match for Perot's earlier altruism and social involvement.

The Broker's Tango

Success as a Wall Street broker brings significant financial rewards. Many have been lured to the Street by visions of the wealth that will be generated from commissions. A broker today has been trained to be an account executive, a financial consultant with many products to sell. Twenty-five years ago, we expected a broker to have some hot stocks for us, and that's all. Now, we still expect good stock picks from him, but it's a diminishing part of his repertory.

As the institutions in the late Sixties increased their participation in the market, firms were organized to service this new client breed with special research and to provide them with their own institutional salesmen. Donaldson, Lufkin and Jenrette was formed to focus on this new, thriving business. I remember a visit to the firm in early 1969, when I was shown what they called the war room, geared to plan institutions' investment strategies and decorated so dramatically that the material presented seemed custom-made for each client.

In 1967 George Goodman, using the pseudonym of Adam Smith, wrote the first book that wittily mocked the antics of this institutional sport on Wall Street, *The Money Game*. In this book he introduced a character called Scarsdale Fats, modeled on one of the new institutional brokers, who courted the money managers—also known as the kids, or sometimes, deprecatingly, the gunslingers. Scarsdale Fats, in his pursuit of commission dollars, was shown entertaining a gang of clients over a pastrami-sandwich lunch, while quizzing them on their fastest hot stock and insulting them with his quips. Since managing money has always been a lonely job, these kids enjoyed meeting their peers and Scarsdale Fats's teasing and generous hospitality.

Those lunches have continued over the years, although

the sandwich fare has been replaced by a more formal menu at an uptown club. And Scarsdale himself has mellowed. He recently admitted that he no longer could travel, since the airlines had made the men's rooms smaller. Still, for the past twenty years, this tough-sounding veteran has given shelter in his office to an army of displaced Wall Streeters who became victims of the financial evolution. Scarsdale has been a friend for all seasons to those kids who shared his table back in the go-go Sixties.

The Eighties version of the institutional broker has just been discovered by the press and the investment community at large. A mystery man suddenly surfaced in three leading publications, after an extravagant trip down the Nile that he hosted with the wife of one of America's richest men for a few of their special friends. Now the Nile may seem a long way to travel from Scarsdale Fats's pastrami lunch gabfests, but that distance and style reflects the internationalization of our times. Some people referred to this Eighties broker simply as the Greek. Others called him the Greek typhoon, because he created a whirlwind when he appeared, but I prefer to think of him as the Greek godfather. Unlike the traditional godfather, the Greek godfather selects his own godchildren, in a fashion that appears random to many. It is not.

There is a reason for every favor he bestows, for every person he asks to dinner. Everything he does is part of a Machiavellian puzzle that he alone understands. It seems, though, that his candidates usually fall into one of two categories. The first is a practical one, current or possible clients, or those who are well connected, who will help to cultivate even more important clients. The second category of godchildren is a catchall, one you might call festoonery. This category is simply for amusement, and it includes writers, deposed royalty and personalities in the public eye.

The guest list for the moveable feast of parties that the G. G. offers evolves continually, but a few faithful retainers are invited to court as long as they please him. In these settings, the Greek godfather easily wins over his prey, proving his theory that no one in the world has ever had enough attention. Doing business and generating commissions are the consummation of his relationships; that is why he offers his affection, along with the continuous entertainment that his godchildren have come to expect.

On reading about this model of the Eighties, a keen observer of Wall Street remarked, "It's refreshing to know a broker like this still exists." Will the G. G. go the distance? Only time and the markets will tell. In the meantime, he gives full value—whatever the client wants, whether it's a nanny for the children, a merger partner or a permanent mortgage for a large real estate project—just by waving his magic wand.

Greed as Motivator

An off-Broadway musical that ran for years in New York City (and was eventually made into a movie), called *The Little Shop of Horrors,* revolved around a plant that had to be fed human beings to thrive. The plant grew and grew into a fat, grotesque version of its original self while it kept demanding more. The audience found this gluttonous display highly amusing. Wall Street, in its hunger for more and more profits, has indulged in the same excesses. At the end of the speculative period of the 1960s, when the bull market reached its peak at over 1000 in December of 1968, the "fail" level had risen to more than $4 billion. Fails are a good way to measure the paper mess and disorganization in the back offices of Wall Street; they occur when a stock certificate is not delivered by the broker who sold a stock to the broker who bought the stock by the settlement date, five days after the trade took place. In early January of 1968, fails had gone over $1 billion, the level then considered acceptable. All attempts to correct the problem by closing trading an hour and a half early on the New York Stock Exchange did not help, and the early closing stopped. The fails continued to climb during the rest of 1968, until they reached that $4 billion figure. But Wall Street, hungry for more, could not stop;

it kept writing orders. The market only halted this growing nightmare of chaos in the back office in early 1969, by
starting to decline, rather than by choice.

The same gluttonous forces are at work in the 1980s.
The principle of "more" is still alive but is expressed differently. E. F. Hutton pleaded guilty to multiple felonies
in a check-kiting scheme in the early Eighties. Griffin B.
Bell, the former attorney general brought in by Hutton to
analyze what went wrong and who was responsible, chas-
tised Hutton's middle management for failing to exercise
control, thus allowing this scheme to proliferate. (This
same critique could have been made against all brokerage
firms in 1968.) A firm's demand for more profits, when
personal compensation is based on a percentage of either
the person's or his department's contribution to that firm,
must present a conflict of interest to any middle manager,
easily leading to some form of aggressive looseness.

In the 1980s version of brokerage greed, someone, of
course, was being taken advantage of, but this time it was
not a naive, individual customer but the banks doing business with Hutton. It seemed fitting that, as the markets
became institutionalized, the institutions themselves became the victims of Wall Street greed.

But there are still individual culprits, such as J. David
Dominelli, who prey on the innocent, people who promise
the road to riches, if others will only invest along with
them. Still, the 1980s con men seem somehow to lack the
flair and color of an Eddie Gilbert or a Bernie Cornfeld
from the 1960s. These two were F. Scott Fitzgerald–size
characters, with a hidden social agenda that gave their
behavior poignancy when their foibles were exposed.

Greed is still thriving. The tale of how Lehman Brothers
fell apart and then was sold to Shearson is witness to how
individual greed destroyed one of Wall Street's most formidable and prestigious partnerships. The startling disclo-
sures in 1986 of insider trading, from the Dennis Levine
case to Ivan Boesky's fall, may become, as the saga continues to unfold, the greediest escapade ever in the financial
community. This "new crowd," unlike the greedy fictional

man-eating plant, arouses neither sympathy nor amusement, only repugnance.

The Private Casino

Financial pundits have called Wall Street the casino, a place where anyone can go to gamble or speculate. The requirements for opening a brokerage account are minimal; unlike college students, no one has an identity card; not even a driver's license is requested. That is the way it always was, and it still is. What has changed, though, is that the stock market has become two-tiered. The casino has the familiar gaming tables, but it has added an assortment of new, popular games—options, commodities and so forth—so people won't say they are bored. But it has also installed a new, private and exclusive room where a certain group plays poker. The game is difficult to understand outside the golden rope separating this room from the rest of the casino. The poker players are members of corporations, raiders, arbitrageurs and the institutions who use a company's stock for chips, once it has received a bid from another company or group. As in all poker games, the players are not equal, but the general public is excluded from their table.

This is the investing world that the Class of 1985 inherited. Unflappable, this group ignores the crowd and market volatility, and tries to focus on what it does best. They go home early on days like September 11, 1986, the day the Dow plunged 86.61 points, to avoid worrying about the volatility of program trading. And they try not to envy the class of 1986, which has won its laurels in the takeover game. Our class members are all value investors, although each one defines value in his own individualistic way. Warren Buffett, their hero, said in a talk at Columbia University that the portfolios of different value investors would include totally different names. As in all things, value is in the eye of the beholder.

THE DELAWARE DYNAMO—TED ASHFORD

Ted Ashford watches over family, foundation and pension funds as the president of Ashford Capital Management in Greenville, a suburb of Wilmington, Delaware. He is known for his recommendations as a consultant for the State of Delaware pension funds, because of the way he has guided the state in its overall goals and its selection of outside money managers. Quiet and unassuming, Ted rarely gives interviews. He states flatly that he must be the worst marketer in the history of money management. His strengths, he says, are in setting goals and disciplines for himself, goals that he meets and disciplines that channel his investment decision-making. Early in his career as an investor, Ashford decided that he should try to be as good as he could be at what he took on, so he set himself three objectives: (1) to find an investment approach that he could live with; (2) to beat the thirteen-year performance record of Warren Buffett's private partnership, which terminated in 1969, and (3) to prove that a large state public fund could be managed with flexibility and imagination.

What pleases Ted most is that he has been able to meet the goals he originally set. He found the right investing approach, one in which he purchases small companies, not owned by the institutions, that have something unique about them, companies he can live with for long periods of time.

In 1970, Ashford chose a small foundation as the competitive vehicle to test himself against his hero, Buffett, with his thirteen-year record. Ted estimated Buffett's return to be 30% compounded, before subtracting interest costs, which would lower the net return to about 23%. Ashford's fund started with $30,000; thirteen years later, in 1983, it was worth $844,073. It went up an incredible 3,149% (after regular annual payments, some additions and adjusting for cash flow) against a 71% return on the Dow Jones average over the same period of time. (The $30,000 original market value of this portfolio is a representative sum with which to start an investment account.)

Ted Ashford surpassed Buffett's record with the advantage of a smaller portfolio than Buffett's, but Ashford also had the disadvantage of two down years in 1973 and 1974; Buffett never had a down year. Ashford was also proud that his turnover rate (the percentage of a portfolio sold during a year) was a low 15%, reflecting good original stock selection, right after Buffett's comment in 1969 that there were very few good ideas. Quips Ashford, "He sure was right for the first few years. The irony is that the largest holding in my portfolio today is Berkshire Hathaway, Warren Buffett's company."

Ted Ashford's investing career started at college in the early Sixties. He had intended to become a nuclear physicist, but while at Harvard, he started a company, a pro-totype of today's financial services conglomerates—managing money, selling insurance—that combined numerous financial transactions. One of his first clients was an investment club of the Harvard Business School. One of the club members came to him with the idea of buying the Dow Jones average. A new idea at the time, but what has today become indexing. "We executed the order form," Ted reminisces, "but the transaction costs were incredible." He was attracted early in his career to smaller companies and more adventuresome ideas, such as Disney and Xerox, companies that did something unusual (and, remember, Disney and Xerox were small, back in the early Sixties).

Early in his career Ashford began the practice each evening of taking home ten annual reports to read. He says that is how he taught himself accounting. Later, he learned about the variety of ways to make money: arbitrage and private placements, convertibles or even foreign securities. Some people chose to invest in large-capitalization stocks; some in asset plays. Ted's niche became small situations, often illiquid companies, with something special about them. These companies usually have little debt and therefore can provide their own financing. Ashford believes that if they have positive cash flow they can control their destiny. "You know, also," he says, "if their internal growth rate is twenty percent, you can reasonably expect the long-term return from the company to be about twenty percent. You could have a welcome surprise, if they have good management, because they may find a way to improve that return."

Ashford's investing precepts, in summary, are:

- set goals that fit your abilities and temperament;

- search for facts, not opinions;

- look for a business you understand;

- sell when you see a problem management has created;

- review all your investment decisions afterwards because you always learn the most from your mistakes.

Rule 1: Learn early to avoid losing money.

Ashford learned this lesson from studying Warren Buffett's record.

Rule 2: Get the facts, make a decision and act.

Of the three, acting is the most difficult for an investor to do.

Rule 3: Go to the source for information.

At one point Ashford went back to the daily papers during the Civil War to get some information. "If you don't get to the source, it's like that game we all played when we were kids, 'telephone.' You'd whisper something all around and never recognize at the end what had first been said."

Rule 4: Invest in businesses simple enough to understand, businesses that you can put your hands around.

"What you're looking for in analyzing a company is information, not data, and it's getting less likely that you'll get information from a large company.

"I used to cover IBM and learned my lesson. I was given an hour, an hour and a half, with management. I worked for weeks, putting all the data together, before going to my interview. My interview concluded within thirty seconds of the time allotted. The corporate treasurer was poker-faced on every single question that would have given me any insight that wasn't available to anybody else. And finally, he smiled, ten seconds left to go, and he sort of threw me a ball. And so I had one modicum of incremental information that no one else had—totally useless, but I had it—and I had this great yen to go charging right out, and—But where was I going to go? Nowhere. And behind me came the next three hundred fifty to four hundred analysts covering IBM."

I had an experience similar to Ted's. I once visited a company in Philadelphia. Instead of one person, five came to the meeting and not one of the five gave me a straight answer about anything. I had no incremental information —except for my own reading of the annual report. I recall thinking that they really did not want any independent judgments about this company; for some reason, they felt defensive about it. Since then, I have taken multiple attendance as a warning: Quite possibly, something is wrong. And something was, in Philadelphia.

Rule 5:   Look for monopolies.

Ashford wished he had concentrated more on broadcasting and newspaper companies, which most people consider the ultimate monopolies.

Rule 6:   Don't hold on to other people's stocks.

Investors who don't feel comfortable with a stock and do not know why it is going up or down cannot know whether or not they should sell it. Ted Ashford inherited some stocks in a portfolio that he took over in 1970. From that, he learned how hard it is to sell a stock. It is harder yet in a group environment. This experience taught him that he had better buy a company that he was prepared to live with for a long time and happily never sell, to be able to follow it even through its down cycles. The decline in price does not bother him, provided that management and the fundamentals of the company are still intact. And he found the guts to do it, once he decided that this was the way he was going to invest.

Rule 7: Find companies that you can live with a long time.

Ashford said that without this philosophy, he wouldn't have been fully invested in 1975, when the small company mutual fund he was managing was up 88%. In the fall of 1974, he had attended a board meeting in which he had to defend his investments. Everyone around the table was saying that the world was going out of business. He showed them the balance sheets of the companies in his portfolio and how his selections were in much better financial condition than the big companies were, and that the p-e's were so low that this was clearly a time to buy stocks. "Once they saw the facts, the board became supportive and protected me from turning defensive at the wrong time."

Rule 8: Avoid buying the big companies that have made multiple acquisitions.

Some companies, it seems, never know what to do with their cash. Ted cited CBS, with its high positive cash flow, showing how they bought everything from the New York Yankees to a publishing company, at 50 times earnings. Xerox did the same. But Ashford usually sells a big company, if he suddenly finds that he owns it because it has acquired one of his investments. When Federated Investors was taken over by Aetna, he said to himself, "Who wants to own one of the biggest property and casualty companies? There's no way I can understand it." When I asked Ted if he ever broke this rule, he stopped to think and then told me about Hunt Manufacturing, one of his big winners. "I agonized over that because it was apparent that they were going to make acquisitions." But he was won over by George Bartel and the fact that he planned the purchases sensibly, cleaning up his balance sheet along the way. "All Hunt's acquisitions have been small," Ted added, "and they are still a relatively small company."

Rule 9 : Study all your buy and sell decisions.

You should appraise all your decisions afterwards. Ted says that he goes into board meetings today and explains actions of three years ago. He reviews all the transactions but underlines the mistakes, not the winners.

Rule 10: Don't get machine-gunned into buying something you don't know enough about.

In reviewing his mistakes, Ted found that if he had waited until he'd had genuine convictions, he could have avoided many of them.

Rule 11: Be willing to open yourself up to ideas even if your first impressions are negative.

Ted told me some stories about how he would find himself scratching his head, after he had bombarded a company with questions, and thinking to himself, "This is an interesting company," when originally he'd thought it deplorable. One of his favorite examples concerned Agency-Rent-A-Car, a company that went public in July 1983 at the top of the small company market and, since then, has more than doubled in price. At first Ted thought that renting cars had to be the worst possible business to be in.

"I couldn't imagine how anyone could sell it to the public."
Then he learned what the company does: It rents cars to
insurance companies to replace their customers' stolen or
wrecked cars. Ted analyzed the business and discovered a
gold mine that earned 30% on its equity.

THE ROTHSCHILD TOUCH—APRIL WALSTAD

April Walstad is a refreshing surprise. Deceptively frag-
ile, she combines a southern charm, acquired in Atlanta,
Georgia, in her magnolia blossom years, with the midwest-
ern common sense of her birthplace, Joplin, Missouri. Yet
managing some of the Rothschild family money in America awes even her. The chief executive officer of Rothschild, Inc. once said, after reviewing the competitive
investment returns of all the money managers in the asset
management division, "How does she do it? She's just a
slip of a girl. I mean, she doesn't look that formidable." In
1983 and 1984, two years when 75% of professional
money managers failed to do better than the Standard and
Poor's 500, April's returns were solidly outstanding, outstripping her peers'. In 1985 she quietly streaked ahead
of them.

While other more seasoned investors were floundering
around, what was Walstad's strategy? How did she clock
in those returns and win the respect, however reluctant,
of her colleagues? (Money managers in the same office are
highly competitive, often behaving like rival sopranos in
the same opera company.)

In analyzing her investing principles and style, April
said that she did best as an investor when she understood
why she owned what she owned, when she had bought the
company at a reasonable price and had done enough work
to give her a strong conviction about the purchase. Without that conviction, it would be impossible to be patient if
the stock stayed dormant or to have the resilience to stay
invested if a temporary reversal occurred. "If you're not
sure of the idea, it's too easy to get nervous and sell your
position." All her mistakes, she said, came from not un-

derstanding the company, not doing enough homework, not being patient enough. And the mistake that troubles her most is finding herself out of her realm, owning stock with a high price-earnings multiple.

April focuses her investing research on good businesses selling at reasonable prices. The qualities she seeks are:

- a high return on equity and a high return on assets;
- low debt;
- consistent earnings growth;
- low-to-reasonable price-earnings multiple (when it goes over 12, she gets dizzy);
- insiders who own positions in the stock.

Reasonable prices usually come about when companies that fit her profile have temporary problems. Perceptions about the real value of the company can become confused when one division is losing money. "But," she said, "if you separate the individual parts, you can see that they are worth more than their current market value." Walstad searches the "new-lows list" in the morning papers to see if she can find some of these tarnished gems to start her cleanup analysis.

I asked her what assurance she had that a corporation would do something about its trouble? Sometimes, companies go on for years with these problem areas. Walstad replied, "I don't know, except that, given its past history, that division has had pretty good, consistent earnings. You figure that everyone, once in a while, stumbles. You never know for sure, but you can bet, if the other parts are pretty good, that a company's management will put all their attention to doing something about their losing division."

Some of the companies that fit her profile and that she did well on were Rollins Corp., Tyco and Time, Inc. Of the companies that she was attracted to and owns, only two have high price-earnings multiples: Rollins Corp. (before it split into three parts) and IMS International. These two she allowed, feeling that they represented special situations, IMS because of its specific niche, the health database market, and Rollins because its assets were undervalued in the marketplace. After a succession of unfortunate acquisitions, IMS had begun a program of divestiture, April noticed. Its core business, the health database, was a gemstone and, she said, "a good, if not great, business." People would recognize it, once the acquired debris was removed.

Rollins, on the other hand, was an asset play. The market price was unrealistic, once the parts were evaluated on their own. Again, a major problem, its oil division, disguised the real worth of the main business.

So most of Walstad's successful stock choices have resulted from a search for value, when a company's market price has been affected by a problem that disguises the value of its main business. Her mistakes, according to April, were caused by going afield from what she's comfortable with. She made such a mistake with Adac, a small company in medical technology, when she was assigned to monitor the health field. Adac was touted for its advance products in nuclear medicine radiation therapy, as well as in digital radiography, and it appeared to have growth potential in these new fields. The multiple had been high. Investors expected success in this company's future. The first shares she bought at 21, but street rumors began reporting price cutting in Adac's type of products. The stock dropped to 17 a share, so she bought more. Then investors worried about hospitals' ability to purchase Adac's expensive machines in light of new guidelines for Medicare reimbursement. The stock crept lower to 12 a share, where Walstad sold it. (It eventually sold down to 4.)

"It wasn't my kind of merchandise," April said. "And, with a price-earnings ratio over 20 on my original purchase, I was taking too much risk—and I found out soon enough that I had. Adac was a small position but a big lesson." She continued, "When you buy something with a high price-earnings ratio, you lose your flexibility. There's no margin for error. What you want to do as a money manager is to lose less, because it's difficult to make up your losses in a portfolio. The truth is, you don't start over. A loss is a loss, and your clients can't afford it if you shoot for the moon and miss."

Most money managers are always on the lookout for a good idea, so they respond immediately to the suggestions of friends and brokers and buy their ideas. Walstad, reflecting specifically on life in New York said, "People here are rife with ideas, but it's too difficult to do something new or clever every moment."

Now, when she is presented with a new idea, she asks herself whether it meets her good business criteria: a low p-e multiple, low debt and a high return on equity. If not, she ignores it. That is, unless the idea is presented as a tarnished value, and she agrees to lower her screen.

April developed her style from her own investing experience and from studying the experiences of investors she has admired (Graham, Buffett and Templeton). She feels fortunate, too, that she has had the chance to develop her talent without needing approval from a rubber-stamp organization. Looking at me quizzically, she asked, "How did you know that I'd be good when I first came to New York and you hired me?"

"That was easy," I told her. "If you follow any field closely, it doesn't take very long to spot potential talent. Theatergoers can immediately spot a new actor or actress with presence; when a Doug Flutie passes a football, football fans know that he's special. Then the question becomes, 'Is this person motivated enough to work hard and take advantage of the opportunities that come his way?' "

April has that natural talent. She also had the determination to prove herself to be good, and not to disappoint anyone, particularly her clients, who was depending on her.

April's Investing Rules

1. Have a long-term horizon.
2. Be realistic; too many people are already searching for another IBM or Xerox.

3.   Don't believe anyone; keep questioning, reviewing and monitoring.

4.   Remember, you don't buy the market. You look at it. People tend to inspect the market too closely when all they are buying are a few ideas.

5.   Try not to waste time debating economic theories. It is more important to focus on individual companies.

6.   Don't forget to compare frequently the after-tax returns of cash, bonds and stocks to determine their relative attractiveness.

7.   When you buy a stock, set a target price at which you would like to sell it.

8.   Look for good companies that have temporary problems and therefore are reasonably priced.

9.   Don't worry too much about p-e's, just avoid the overly high ones; worry about what a company is worth. What would other people pay for it in its entirety?

10.   You can buy someone else's idea. But you first have to find out why it is attractive, and be convinced yourself of its attractiveness.

IN PURSUIT OF A CATALYST—MARIO GABELLI

The name of Mario Gabelli became more familiar than others of the Class of 1985 because of his participation in Barron's year-end panel. Only eight years after starting his brokerage firm, Gabelli accumulated $600 million in assets to manage for other people, and an enviable seven-year 27% compound return. Gamco, his firm's money management arm, was not a planned expansion. One day, when he was visiting a Toronto firm, the chief executive said to him, "Mario, you made me money with ideas before. I want you to manage some of my money." When Mario told him that he didn't do that, the chief executive opened his desk drawer, wrote out a check and said, "You're now in the money management business. Charge a fee."

Picking stocks has always been Gabelli's forte. Before starting Gabelli and Company, he was a security analyst with Loeb, Rhoades & Co. His original responsibilities were to analyze cyclical companies, auto stocks and farm equipment, and later, the conglomerate and growth companies in health-care and business services as well. As Roger Murray's student at Columbia University School of Business, Gabelli had studied Graham and Dodd. And in the real world, as a security analyst, he learned the variables that move stocks. Then, selling his ideas to institutional money managers taught him how to see portfolio strategy through their eyes.

He started early. In fact, he began investing for himself in the market at the age of fourteen. And, in Mario's words, "That's when I became a player." What attracted him to Loeb Rhoades and kept him there was that they encouraged their analysts to manage some money. During his years there, he was fortunate enough to manage some of the Loebs' family money.

Later on, he joined William D. Witter and Company, where he tried to encourage a focus on small companies that were dominant in their area of activity, like Binnie and Smith, which had 90% of the crayon market. Witter pointed out the small size of the overall crayon market, doubting that there would be buyers for such insignificant stocks. So Gabelli began to identify possible buyers: substantial individuals who were buying businesses, institutions with special funds and foreigners. This was the market he focused on after Witter was merged into Drexel Burnham Lambert and he started his own business.

During this period, Gabelli honed his analytical ability, developing a selection process in his stock choices that focused on the internal dynamics of a company. He would begin by projecting cash flow for the next five years. But the cash flow analysis led him to questions about depreciation, the status of pension funding and other accounting issues, making it necessary to see each flow before all the expenses: taxes, interest, corporate expense and depreciation. Finding it close to impossible to put a multiple on these cash flows, his next question became, "What could we sell the company for?"

Gabelli was looking for "the private market value of a company," as he put it. What would somebody pay to own this business, and why? I wondered how anyone could determine a company's worth to an informed industrialist. Mario thought it could be done. "If I had in the room ten guys who knew the movie business, I'd say, 'Winner-take-all on Warner's. What would you pay?' Or, 'Winner-take-all on Twentieth Century-Fox.' And why?" Once he has estimated the private market value, and the difference between it and the company's current market value, and if he finds this difference significant enough that there could be a 50% appreciation if this spread is closed, Mario starts looking harder at it. (If, for example, he could buy Twentieth Century-Fox for 30 a share in the market and it was worth 50 a share in a private transaction, then this company would meet his investment criterion, his "hurdle rate" of 50%.)

He chose this hurdle by stepping back and saying, "I am in the business of earning a rate of return. I am not competing against the Standard and Poor's average. Mario Gabelli wants to make money for himself and the same standards should apply to clients." So he aimed for a real return after taxes and inflation of 10%, which he decided was a sufficient rate considering how the A. W. Jones crowd (an aggressive group of money managers) performed, as well as Warren Buffett and other investors in the Fifties and Sixties. It became apparent to Gabelli that few people had done better than a real rate of return of 10%. He decided he would be happy with that figure himself. Aiming for investments with a possible 50% appreciation, Mario found, gave him a cushion in shooting for 10%.

Mario's Analysis. At his start-up time in 1977, the long-term capital gains tax was somewhere in the vicinity of 35% to 40%, much higher than it is today. If he could make 50% on an investment and then pay capital gains taxes, he would keep 35%, leaving him enough to cover inflation, which was then at 8%. A bond investment then could have earned him 15%, but with the marginal tax rate of 70% on passive income, it might only earn 4% after tax. Inflation at 8% meant he would be actually losing 4%.

An investment commitment should be made, Gabelli said, when a "catalyst" is spotted, and he defined this as "a visible element that helps to identify the dynamics in place," which will close the spread between—in our example—the $30 value in the public market and the $50 it might bring in the private market. Possible catalysts for identifying change might be:

Takeovers in an Industry. A trend sometimes develops, as seen recently in oil and broadcasting stocks, in which offers are made one after another for companies in a specific industry.

Internal Dynamics in a Company. In one of Gabelli's early successes, American Manufacturing, a senior manager and owner in his early seventies, Gurdon Dwattles, announced that he was going to sell off holdings in Eltra and liquidate his company. Once Gabelli calculated the values, he bought the stock and it turned out to be a spectacular investment. Another internal catalyst was the death of Charlie Bluhdorn of Gulf and Western. "The company would do nothing," Gabelli figured, "but continue to do what they were doing as long as Charlie was there, but once he died things would change." Yet another success for Mario was Cowles Communications, when Mike Cowles and Marvin Whatmore said, "We want out." By buying the stock, Mario said, he got a television station in Orlando, free.

A Capitalization Shrink Without the Threat of Greenmail. Company A buys back its own stock. "We start," says Mario, "by asking ourselves why?" It is not as impressive if there is a greenmailer in the picture (someone who has accumulated a large percentage of stock in the company and would like to have this position bought out at a price above the market). "We like it when we feel that they're buying a stock for a dollar that they know is worth two dollars. Then we start looking at the company more and more." Mario uses as examples Iroquois Brands and Metromedia as well as Chris-Craft, attractive investments because of their capitalization shrinks.

"The search for the catalyst before an investment is made is the real thing that differentiates us from other value-oriented investors," Mario says. When I asked if he ever broke this rule, he said that he did and named an exception, Earl Scheib, Inc. "Mr. Scheib owns forty-odd percent of the company. He's seventy-five and in great health, God bless him, I hope he lives forever. The value spread was so significant between the public and estimated private market that if a catalyst comes along, we want to be in a position to take advantage of it, so we now own twelve percent of Earl Scheib."

Gabelli's Investing Formula

1. Search for and follow "niche" companies, with some kind of franchise, if possible.
2. Evaluate their cash flow. This he does by estimating the multiples of other companies in the business or what they would pay for this operating income, and why. If the company is in different businesses, he takes each apart.
3. Determine from the cash-flow estimates what the value would be to an informed industrialist.
4. Study the prospective investment as a snapshot and then in a two-year framework. What variable could influence the value two years hence, positively or negatively?
5. How does the potential increase in this investment match up against your goals? Gabelli matches them against his "hurdle rate."

6. What catalysts could develop in the future that you should be looking for?

Some of Gabelli's steps may seem too difficult, but you can easily look for companies with franchises, such as bottling companies or newspapers. And you can watch for areas where there seems to be a flurry of takeover activity at much higher prices. You can start to look for possible catalysts by asking, "What could happen in the future that would allow the company to realize a higher value?"

One of Gamco's largest investment positions, Rollins Communications, is a good example of the kind of company Gabelli's team searches for. In the late Sixties, they started following Rollins Inc., then a company predominately in broadcasting and business services. In the late Seventies, it entered the energy service business, becoming a big stock because of this expansion. But Gabelli did not buy it in any size until December 1983, when the chairman and CEO, Wayne Rollins, announced that he was going to split the company into three pieces.

Mario's team asked themselves the question, "Why would one of the wealthiest guys in America, on the *Forbes* 400 list, do that? What's he thinking about?" In March 1984, as part of the spin-off process, Rollins issued a prospectus so that the company, stripped of its other parts, could really be analyzed. "The company had no debt, the businesses in broadcasting were all cash generators," Mario says, "so we picked up the phone and called media rep agents and friends of ours in the industry and asked, 'What would you pay me for a television station in Potsdam, New York, or in Pensacola, Florida, and why?' The television side we evaluated by looking at industry trends, growth in the market, competition and new signals that could come into the market. Then we called everyone we knew who could aid this analysis. Afterward, we did the same to their radio and cable businesses, looking for everything that was right and wrong about them. When we added up the pieces, we came up with a value of thirty dollars a share, so we started recommending the stock."

The first trade on the New York Stock Exchange was at 11½. Rollins closed the first day at 13½. Figuring they were getting more than a 50% discount, they bought most of the stock that traded. Gabelli, in recalling their reasoning, said that the catalyst was vague because no one knew what Wayne Rollins ultimately had in mind. What they did know was that a seventy-four-year-old guy who owned more than 40% of the company was splitting it into pieces and that he wasn't going to sit down and say, "Well now, let's see, I got three pieces of paper, and they're worth more!" "He knew they were worth more. He had some objective in mind." The stock appreciated to 26 after the day it opened at 11½, and Gabelli still finds it attractive, estimating its private market value at $45 a share by 1988.

Rollins Communications is a good example of a "Gabelli special," but Mario has a dream investment. He describes it this way: "We're not awfully good at self-discipline, so we like our self-discipline made for us. We want the companies we own to go private and no longer be public. But if someone asked me what's a great play, what's the greatest music you could hear, my dream is a hostile tender offer [a demand for control by a corporate raider] for our biggest position." One, the stock will go to a premium and, two, Gabelli will avoid a sell decision as he and his clients enjoy their profit from the merger.

CHATEAU CHAMBORD 1985— GLENN GREENBERG

Glenn Greenberg, as he recalls, was always good at memorizing numbers and symbols. As a small boy, he spent many hours at his father's office in front of an old ticker tape, memorizing ticker symbols and having contests as to who could name more symbols as they came across. All investment people have such an affinity with numbers, he thinks. When he was first introduced to Warren Buffett, Glenn told him that meeting him made Greenberg understand for the first time how so many people felt when they came to his father, to introduce themselves and worship him. Buffett asked Glenn who his father was, and when Glenn replied, "Hank Greenberg," Buffett said, "1938, fifty-eight home runs." All of it was there in his head and it just came out, Glenn reported.

Later on, after Yale and Columbia Business School, he remembered those distant days with their excitement and anguish and, not surprisingly, how the only courses at business school that captured his imagination had to do with investments. "There was an element of something being won or lost as a result of your efforts," he said. "If you're good at it, you're going to move forward and get more responsibility, more pay. In many other businesses they measure people's performances subjectively. In advertising, you can work on a campaign for months and have it pass your boss and his boss and then get to the client who says, 'I don't like it,' and that's the end of three months' work."

There are two best routes for investment training. Either go to a bank like Morgan Guaranty and spend a few years there, going through their training program, or go to work as an apprentice to the most interesting and successful investor around. Glenn Greenberg did both. He started his career at Morgan, working his way through the labyrinth of that large organization. Later, he worked for Arthur Ross of Central National Corporation, a man Greenberg feels is one of the great investors of the last fourteen years, although very few outside of the New York investment world have heard of him.

What Glenn learned about investing at these two different schools gave him the security to start his own firm, Chieftain Capital. In the first year of its existence, he and his partner researched five hundred ideas and invested in only twelve. They are looking for those same dream franchises that others in the Class of 1985 like, but Glenn and his partner insist that their companies have low multiples.

At Morgan in 1973, Greenberg was working for the firm that had by far the most money under management and the most commissions to give out. He got a great education from all the street-side analysts who wanted some of those commissions. But working there also "taught him the ability of crowds to influence and to make really horrible mistakes under that influence, and then to justify them later." That environment makes it difficult to see change coming: A bank is too far from hands-on analysis, which requires going out and seeing changes taking place in the world. Group-think and the inability to see change, Greenberg thinks, accounted for Morgan's remaining in growth stocks long after the party was over. "Being there taught me something about never buying stocks at high multiples," he said. "They got carried away with a brilliant idea and let it get to excessive levels," so that in 1973 and 1974 they were hurt badly in performance and reputation.

At Central National, for five years, Greenberg found Arthur Ross's style inherently appealing: buying value stocks in understandable businesses, avoiding stories of any kind and looking for intrinsic value in a franchise—always low-multiple franchises. Ross often preferred to look for what he called "a Château Chambord," a reference to the château in France that has been added to and built over by many different people over the generations. He searches for companies that have the ability to start out in one attractive field, but when business opportunities present themselves, to take advantage of the chance for the company to grow and become something bigger and grander, in the same way that Château Chambord evolved.

Some of the highlights of what Glenn learned during his two investment apprenticeships:

Rule 1: Respect the market, and adjust your intellectual beliefs according to what the markets are saying.

The market will do what it wants to do and defies most people's projections and predictions, so don't fight it. And if the market is really acting badly, lighten up. Find things to sell. Do not accept conventional wisdom or you will be blinded the way the Morgan Guaranty Trust was with growth stocks, or even the way the secretary of energy, James Schlesinger, was about oil prices. Glenn recalled that, at a Bob Brimberg dinner, Schlesinger predicted $100-a-barrel oil in the next few years. The price at the time was about $35, and the perception in the market was that oil stocks had already crested. "He had access to all the geopolitical information you could possibly have, but he wasn't paying attention to the market." I asked Glenn how this happened so often. He replied, "These people are very, very bright, but when you are covered with so many distinguished degrees, you get caught up in the intellectual exercise of the issues, and many, many sub-issues, and sub-sub-issues and second derivatives of the sub-sub-sub-issues."

Rule 2: Go out and talk with businessmen, low- and middle-level corporate managers.

The only way to know what is happening is to make friends and develop a network of business people who can be called and asked, "What the heck is going on in your business? How are you reacting?" Then think about their reactions. Greenberg told of a chief financial officer, in town from Indianapolis, who came to see him one day, after hearing Henry Kaufman of Salomon Brothers at a seminar. When Glenn heard that two hundred treasurers had been there, all concerned about Henry's prediction that rates would be moving up with no abatement in economic strength or borrowing, Glenn thought, "That obviously can't happen, if they're all concerned. How are they going to react when they go home? They will do everything possible to cut inventories, capital spending, to husband cash. These issues are very big and difficult to predict. I certainly don't want to deprecate Henry Kaufman, either. He's a brilliant man."

Rule 3: Try to identify a major trend, because you always want to have time on your side by being right early.

Anyone who identified the period when supply and demand changed for the oil companies did very well. De-

mand for oil exceeded supply in the mid-Seventies, so oil
had to be repriced. The concurrent trend was that inflation was increasing, and an investment in asset-rich companies did well. This was also true in wheat and corn, but
not in just a food processing business. All that changed
when the inflation spiral broke and oil prices headed
downward. Spotting the change allowed investors to make
money in consumer stocks and avoid losses by taking profits in the oil and asset stocks they owned.

**Rule 4:   Dishonesty is a real problem; if you feel
uncomfortable, sell a stock.**

The worst investing disaster Greenberg ever had was in
1976 at Morgan Bank, when he started to be recognized
for his stock-picking ability. "I got interested in an electrical contractor with a great five-year record with a booming
business in the Middle East." He bought shares in the
company and encouraged many friends to buy it. But he
couldn't visit such a small business then, and had to rely
on public information; a phone call was his only weapon.
The stock went up for a while, and then it began to act
badly, and he heard questions about whether the company
was getting paid, and then about its finances. "The company," said Glenn, "failed to disclose the fact that they
were making enormous work changes on buildings they
were doing the electrical work for, before negotiating the
price on the work changes with the government." Eventually the government refused to pay, and the company
went bankrupt. They never said anything about these
problems in a press release, or an annual or quarterly
statement. "And," Greenberg went on, "I lost money, and
the people who owned stock with me lost money." Then
he talked about how he could have checked with other
contractors in the Middle East about work procedures to
pick up some warning signals.

I asked Glenn if this experience had damaged his reputation, and he agreed that it had, adding that it has not
happened since. When he feels uncomfortable in a stock,

he sells it. Feeling uncomfortable is a difficult concept to articulate, but he describes it best by saying simply, "Sometimes you get an uneasy feeling." Recently, he visited a land-developing company and found the head of it friendly and enthusiastic about his business. Yet, says Greenberg, he wore an unbuttoned button-down shirt, and he was wearing big gold rings and gold chains. "It's hard to estimate the land's value, because it depends on how he develops the asset, and it didn't help that I felt uncomfortable with him." Later on, Glenn said that it wasn't just the unbuttoned collar; this man had a checkered past. The shirt was a reminder that he didn't have to own this stock, though it might go up.

Greenberg always finds it hard to learn the truth. "More often than not, with bigger companies, they always want to put their rouge on and present their best face to the world." He has stayed suspicious of people's motives. "A company fearful of being taken over is going to tell you great things about their prospects for this or that, in order to keep their stock at the highest level. And I am always suspicious when a corporate manager whom I've never met before takes me aside, puts his arm around me and tells me things he shouldn't tell anybody. It's not because I've come out from New York, or because I'm such a great guy."

Rule 5:   Try to take advantage of what you know and have learned when you invest.

"When you're young and have less money, you're impatient," Greenberg said. "Later on, you learn more patience and you have more money." The first industry he was assigned to at Morgan was media stocks, because new analysts always get the unseasoned equities, and many of them had gone public in the Sixties. They were considered small stocks for a bank the size of Morgan; even if an analyst recommended the New York Times. CBS or ABC, the bank couldn't hurt itself very much. Glenn recommended the group, spotting their advantage as mo-

nopolies and, in the case of broadcasting, their regulated
competition and unregulated pricing. He felt brilliant selecting them, but after nine months he was rotated to another industry group and sold his own media stocks to buy
into the new, more exciting group. He never went back to
them.

It is emotionally difficult to buy stocks back at a higher
price, but the fundamentals of the media stocks and their
perfect franchises should have been a natural investment
for Greenberg. Perhaps their higher-than-average multiples kept him away. The lesson is to reanalyze freshly what
you know well.

Rule 6: Buy low-multiple companies with fran-
chises.

Greenberg has done well investing in two companies
that fit his formula perfectly. Nova is a classic example, a
Danish company with two attractive businesses in sales
where it had half the world market, and also a business in
industrial enzymes where, with only two competitors, it
was clearly the leader. "Nova was selling at the time at
seven times earnings and it had grown twenty percent a
year and had all the financial criteria you could possibly
look for." Here was a high-grade company in the technology area with great research and development, fantastic
margins and a good balance sheet. All that for 7 times
earnings. After buying almost 10% of the company, Glenn
started to wonder about it. Was he missing something important? Perhaps Denmark was going to change its taxes
or nationalize the company. The truth was that government bonds in Denmark paid around 18% interest and
you also got a special tax break on the interest from those
bonds, and that was the reason why no one in Denmark
was interested in Danish stocks and why Nova sold so
cheaply.

The other choice that met Glenn's formula, a company
with a low multiple and a franchise, was the Dreyfus Corporation. He looked at it in January 1984, after it had

already made a big move, but recognized it as a cash machine that generated generous earnings that were going into a great war chest. The nature of the business was to collect fees, and although Dreyfus could not raise prices, there seemed unlimited possibilities with new, inventive funds. Dreyfus, with three million names in its files of people who knew and trusted the Dreyfus name, was a great business franchise. At the time, like Nova, it was selling at about 7 times expected earnings with only one down year, no debt and a slew of cash on the balance sheet. What amused me, having worked there, and what made Glenn Greenberg even more positive about owning Dreyfus, was that the staff was small. The only negative he had ever heard about the company was that people there never got paid and always left. But he laughed, saying, "It doesn't matter, it's a unique business."

What Greenberg never mentioned was that Dreyfus was the perfect Château Chambord for Arthur Ross, his mentor. A company that had grown organically as successive generations took advantage of new opportunities and allowed the firm to become bigger and grander.

THE CLASS OF 1985—CONCLUSION

Three of these four rising stars have started their own firms. Mario Gabelli is better known in the investment community, yet Ted Ashford has managed money and his firm longer. Glenn Greenberg and April Walstad, a few years younger, are still acquiring investing patina. The vital questions for the future are, will the investing records they have established continue? Will they be able to stay focused and strong in a profession famous for burnout? Martin Mayer's book, *New Breed on Wall Street,* was published in 1969. He defined the new breed as "the young men that make the money go" (he will have to redefine the new breed to include women in his next book). Insiders called those people the Class of 1968, as a reminder that, only a few years later, some of the new breed had disappeared completely from the Street.

One of the young men chronicled then who did survive through the twenty years is Fred Alger. He is the proto-typical "earnings momentum" investor (a new term describing someone attracted to stocks with accelerating growth). He chose this style naturally, since he grew up as an investor in the late Fifties, starting his own firm in 1964. These were the years of dramatic changes in money management. In the mid-Fifties, active management of money had just been born. "The buy-and-hold philosophy followed by our fathers," Fred said, "was discarded in the belief that there was a better way to make money." Investors tried to identify the currently favored industries, then move in and out of the favorites, rather than just own fine companies for the long term. (Some investors ignored this fashion and applied the old ways to the new wonder companies.)

Alger's investment philosophy has remained constant; he tries to find those favored companies or industries. In his search for them, he has observed that nine out of ten of his choices have something in common. They are either inventive companies selling a hot product or service with a high unit volume (a technical way to say "more sales") or they fall into the category of companies or industries going through a major life-cycle change. What these two categories have in common is that they are rapidly changing for the better and, consequently, can show rapid earnings growth. "The area where all the big money is made is where there is surprisingly good earnings growth; the rapidity and surprise attracts speculation," Alger said, recommending that investors look in one of these categories:

Rule 1: Look for an industry or company going through a life-cycle change.

We are all familiar with the oil industry because we all lived through that crisis. Alger points out that there had been no growth in units of oil sold in the twenty years previous to the industry's life-cycle change. Yet, following the breakup of the Bretton Woods agreement, and the subsequent doubling of virtually all commodity prices, as well as the halving of the value of the dollar in relation to other major currencies, a life-cycle change for the oil industry began. It only accelerated with the subsequent quadrupling of OPEC's oil price in the late Seventies. The price of oil moved up something like fifteen times in the next decade, taking earnings with it.

In the early Sixties, another big life-cycle change occurred when jet aircraft were introduced in the airline industry. Before that, airline traffic was growing modestly. "Nothing to write home about," according to Alger. Then jet aircraft turned the airplane into a hot new consumer product and revolutionized travel. The use of planes vastly exceeded management's projections and earnings were considerably higher. As a result, the stocks were important in the mid-Sixties.

In the Eighties, there are only a few life-cycle changes caused by restructuring, such as in the automobile industry. Alger observed that, in spite of being an older industry that appeared to have overwhelming competition from the Japanese, the car industry had a certain franchise with dealerships. It was also able to reduce its break-even point dramatically. As a consequence, earnings have been considerably higher, despite the fact that auto sales have stayed flat throughout the period.

Rule 2: Look for a vital company selling a product or a service with a high unit–growth rate.

Alger thinks that here the individual can be on a par with a professional investor, if he is alert to change, to things that are going on around him. If an individual likes a new product and it is important for the company, not merely one of Procter and Gamble's new products, then, chances are, it will be a good unit-volume investment.

A recent example Alger cited was Federal Express. The company originally had a wild notion that they could actually charge $25 to send a letter from New York to Phil-

adelphia. Many people laughed. Yet, in practice, people
living in Los Angeles think the fastest way to send a letter across town is to put it into a Federal Express envelope.
Federal Express had a new, exciting product, its only
product, and people wanted to use it.

Fred cited other incidents in the past that an alert investor might have spotted. There was great excitement in the
cosmetics industry, especially at Revlon, when that company sponsored the *$64,000 Question* television program.
Polaroid brought out its instant camera in the Fifties. Fast-
food chains changed eating habits across America.

The presumption in any search for an inventive company is that it can bring good unit-volume growth down
to earnings. One new industry that Fred is now watching
is biotechnology—companies like Genentech, a leader in
the industry, or Hybritech, the company that has used
monoclonal antibodies to attack liver cancer, or Damon
Biotech, which can produce large quantities of high-yielding monoclonal antibodies. Biotechnology is an industry
with possibilities that, if developed, could fit into his model
(that is, if the companies are not all bought by large drug
companies in the meantime).

Rule 3: Try to sell without recrimination, without worry, without looking back.

Alger has found that the only way for him to follow this
rule is to have done enough new research. Attractive new
ideas make it easier to sell the old stock, based on the
theory that though a few companies are not acting right,
it's impossible to figure out what's wrong. Sometimes the
market refuses to value investments at the high level analysis shows is correct.

Alger, like every other investor in the world, has difficulty selling. He has to come to grips with it because his
investing style requires selling; great earnings growers do
slow down, and the play is limited. An individual has a
luxury that a major professional money manager often
doesn't have: He can sell and hold his money liquid until

a new idea comes along, as Jimmy Rogers so intelligently recommended.

Rule 4: Try to identify the behavior of a stock you own by keeping your own "psych line."

Any investor has to be familiar with the pattern of behavior of his stock. Its price is affected four times a year, when quarterly earnings are reported. In between, everything is speculation as to what those quarterly results will be, so the stock reflects a lot of tugs and pulls during each quarter. Alger recommends keeping a "psych line" of your attitude toward each stock you own. Whenever you hear any news about the company, write down your reaction, along with the stock price. He says this is the best way to face up to what is happening in the marketplace. All too often, investors fall into an avoidance trap, saying, "Oh well, let's wait and see what happens next." Instead, ask yourself, when you read an announcement or item about a company you own, "With this news, do I feel better or worse about my investment?"

There are other investors besides Alger who have achieved superb results, but would not be classified as members of the Class of 1985. Although value seekers are fashionable, remember that making money is classic.

Alger told me the story of his favorite client, who thanked him by sending him a gift, a beautiful pair of soft leather loafers that fit perfectly. Twelve years earlier, the client, who works at a club Alger visits periodically, gave him $50,000 to invest, saying, "I don't care what you do with it; you can lose it, but I don't want anyone to know about it." So they nod to each other when they are introduced at the club now, even after a long, successful business relationship. That $50,000, twelve years later, after taxes, is worth $1 million, and Fred's favorite client is probably richer than 98% of the club members.

6

THE FINANCIAL EXOTICS

Understanding Some of the
Sophisticated New Investment
Approaches

AS AN INVESTOR, YOU MAY NEVER WANT TO
stray far from what you're familiar with—stocks, bonds
and money market funds—but you might, if you understood more about some of the sophisticated new investment approaches and the investors who make significant
returns using them. I have found these to be the most
seductive and hope you will at least flirt with these financial exotics:

- options
- foreign investing
- arbitrage
- junk bonds
- ventures

OPTIONS

The dream of any investor is to have purchased call options on a stock, either before a takeover bid for the company or before the stock has made a significant move. The leverage on such an investment is so spectacular that it is worth learning the intricacies of the option market, just in case one day you want to take a whirl. Remember, though, that the seduction of possible returns has been the siren that has destroyed many an investor. In fact, I worked at Rothschild with a band of former E. F. Hutton employees who had been active in their options department; they had become so addicted while there that they had formed an Options Anonymous group to keep from playing just another one for their own account.

In my interview with Jimmy Rogers, I had asked him if he knew anyone who had made money buying options. He could think of no one. Then he said, "I never buy options, I only short options. Ninety percent of all the money options expire worthless. You pay the premiums and only have a limited time horizon, and whatever the reason, I know I ain't smart enough to be in that ten percent, whereas ninety percent of the people who sell options make money. It's the most wonderful thing."

Irving Zweifler, vice president of Shearson Asset Management, concurs with Rogers's assessment of the odds in option buying, yet Zweifler understands why investors are attracted by the promise and the excitement of the game. Irving is an options guru, writing covered calls for many of Shearson's institutional clients, on the side of the option business Rogers called "a wonderful thing." Zweifler started his career as an electronics engineer and, because of his training and his background in mathematics, was always an active investor. The idea of using options as an adjunct to investing interested him, so he read extensively (the best book by far, Zweifler said, is *Options as a Strategic Investment* by Lawrence G. McMillan) and dealt with a broker who taught him about the subject. Zweifler liked the leverage in options. And he emphasized that to make money in options, investors must have the right attitude toward the underlying stock. When Zweifler started out, there were no options that dealt with the whole market; whether or not you made money depended on your ability to pick stocks that did what you thought they would do. He offered some rules that can help investors interested in options.

Option Language

A friend once reminded me to read the instructions when I was trying to operate a machine. In trying to understand options, it is necessary to review the definitions of the terms continually until you are familiar with them.

An Option—a financial contract for a specific period of time that gives the holder a right to buy or sell the underlying security at a particular price (they are not like stocks and bonds, which give you an interest in a company).

A Call Option—gives the buyer the right to buy a security.

A Put Option—gives the buyer the right to sell a security.

An Option Writer—(or seller) sells stock if a call is exercised or buys it if a put is exercised.

Options Sell—out of the money, at the money or in the money. If you buy an April 20 call on Boeing and the market price is 25, five points above the strike price of your call (20), it is called "in the money." If the market price goes down to 20, the option is at the money, and if it slips to 18 it is out of the money, below the striking price of 20.

Premium—this is the price that the buyer of an option pays and the writer of an option receives for the rights conveyed by the option. The premium represents what the odds are that the option will be profitable before it expires.

A Covered Option—one where if you sell a call you own the underlying stock. In a naked call you don't own the underlying stock.

The Strike Price—the price at which you can exercise your option.

Rule 1: Remember, if you buy options it is always possible to lose all your money.

The deck is really stacked against you, just as it is if you go to Atlantic City or Las Vegas. If you play at it long enough, you will lose. The market often doesn't move for a period of time, and the premium disappears as time passes. If you buy 100 shares of IBM, you have something. It might go down from 130 to 110, but if you believe the shares have value, you've got an infinite amount of time to wait for their recovery, and even to make a profit. But if you buy a call on IBM and in the next few months it goes down, you could lose all of your investment. And that's the one significant difference between buying a stock and buying options—in the latter you can lose all your money.

Rule 2: Decide in advance what your reasons are for buying an option, because that will help you to determine how far out to go.

If you buy an option because you believe that Upjohn has a terrific product and that over the next two or three years, the stock will go up, then the ideal thing, says Irving Zweifler, is to buy a call as far out as you can, and the furthest is nine months. On the other hand, he feels that if you are following the market technically, and you think a particular stock is ready to break out, then you should buy an option that only lasts for two or three months, because the premium is less.

Rule 3: Consider the attractiveness of buying an in the money call.

You always have the choice of buying an option that is out of the money at the strike price or in the money. To show why he likes in the money calls, Irving pressed out on his machine the row of options on IBM, then selling at 132¼.

calls	IBM	$ price	premium	
Aug	115	17½	0	in the money
Oct	135	3	5¾	out of the money
	130	5¾	3½	in the money
	125	9¼	2	in the money

He would delete the August option because it was expiring in two weeks and hence had no premium; the timing would have to be perfect. So he might then go to October, which gives him two and a half months. The first choice, October 135, would cost him $3 for the 135 call. IBM was then selling at 132¼, below its strike price of 135. So that difference of 2¾ he adds to his purchase price of 3 to arrive at the premium. The October 130 costs 5¾, but since it's in the money by 2¼ points, he subtracts that amount from 5¾ to arrive at a premium of 3½. If he then looks at the October 125, selling for 9¼ and subtracts 7¼, the difference between the strike price of 125 and the selling price of 132¼. He finds that his premium on this option is 2 points. And if Zweifler were going to choose one to buy, this is the one he would take with the expiration date just two months away, and for the October 125 he has paid the smallest premium. Zweifler believes you have to weigh the trade-offs. By choosing the October

125s, he has more money at risk, $925, versus $300 if he bought the October 135s, but he prefers to reduce the premium. One option contract to buy 100 shares of IBM costs $925 if you buy the October 125s at 9¼ (9¼ cost per share × 100). Whereas it will cost you $300 to buy an option on 100 shares of IBM if you buy the October 135s at 3 ($3 cost per share × 100 shares). The trade-off balances premium against risk. Zweifler thinks the premium is what hurts; the smaller it is, the better. Zweifler weighs his odds of winning as well as how much he is willing to lose.

Most option investors, unlike Zweifler, pick the option with less money at risk, in which they get maximum leverage and the greatest percentage return on their investment, if they are right. They would pick the October 135s. (The 125s would be called "deep in the money" by 7¼ points, whereas the 130s would be referred to as "in the money.")

Rule 4: Options do not move point for point with a stock.

As a stock moves up, an option becomes deeper and deeper in the money, and when that happens the premium goes down. If, let's say, the stock of IBM moved up 5 points, the premium on an option could be reduced by 1½ points, so the option itself might go up 3½ points.

Rule 5: There are financial advantages to buying options.

I had asked Zweifler about commissions on options, saying that I had heard they were exorbitant. He pointed out that in reality, option commissions are much less than those for stock, because of their relationship to the dollars involved. "Let's say," he said, "if you buy 1,000 shares of IBM without a discount, you'll pay $980. So to buy and sell those 1,000 shares, your cost will be $1,960 in commissions. Now, if you bought an option in IBM around the strike price right now with a short expiration, two or three weeks, at $3 and you bought ten of those options [the equivalent of 1,000 shares], the commission would be $135, or $270 for the buy and sale. The cost greatly reduces the premium you pay for the option and I don't think most people are aware of this." So for a round trip in an option, you're paying approximately a 9% commission, versus 1.5% on the stock, but the absolute dollars are much less.

Irving also believes that people never add their lost interest to the cost of a stock. An investor who buys a thousand shares of IBM is investing $132,000. If he bought even a 13¾ option, he would be investing $13,750 for ten options (the equivalent of 1,000 shares). The difference is $119,000, ten times more. If that money earned 7%, it would cost $8,000 a year, or about $700 a month, in lost interest to invest in the stock, rather than options. Therefore, if you would like to own IBM for two and a half months, it would be cheaper to buy the 120 call.

Rule 6: **If you are not a speculator, consider writing options (selling them instead of buying them).**

Selling covered calls on a stock that you own is not for the speculator because the yields are small, but it is on the conservative side of the fence, where 90% of the people doing it make money. The best time to follow this strategy is when the market is not doing much. If the market goes down, it will reduce your loss, but if the market goes up a lot, you will give up much of your profits.

The yields on pension funds can be increased 4% to 6% by selling covered calls over the course of a year.

Rule 7: **You must make an investment decision before you sell a covered call.**

Zweifler had bought Pfizer at 47½ in an up market, he said, and it had gone to 53. When he bought it, he had picked his selling price; as the stock approached that figure, he sold a September 55 call for 1¼ (he always sells out of the money calls, to leave himself room for appreciation). The net result was that if Pfizer went over 55, the stock would be called away, but since he received 1¼ points for selling the call, he would have effectively gotten 56¼ for it, the price at which he had been willing to sell.

In selling covered calls, Zweifler usually goes out between two and four months. A shorter period yields too low a price, he explained, since the time factor determines the premium. The longer period, nine months, allows too many things to happen. Thus he has found the best compromise between premium and flexibility in this middle range, and he uses it as a discipline.

But, Irving warns, the option investor must not only make a decision on a specific stock, but also on the market itself. If he believes the market is going to go bananas on the upside, he should never sell covered calls, and if he thinks it will go down 20%, he shouldn't sell covered calls, either; he should sell stocks and raise cash. But if the market may go up or down a little bit in the next few months, and the investor has some stocks he is willing to own at their present price but would sell at a higher price, it makes sense to sell out of the money calls.

Rule 8: **If you think you can judge whether the market is going to go up or down, then you can buy a call or a put on the Standard and Poor's index.**

Average investors have found the new index options attractive. Often, they think they can judge whether the market will go up or down, but they find it difficult to choose an individual stock. Most professional investors, on the other hand, have found market timing totally impossible. Index options are liquid, and investors can get in and out quickly. The most popular is the OEX 100, which covers 100 stocks on the New York Stock Exchange; these options go out for four consecutive months, August, September, October and November, whereas options on stocks usually expire at three-month intervals. I asked Zweifler which option he would buy that day if he thought the market was going to turn. He explained that the August option would expire in two weeks, so it would probably be the most popular. Option players usually look at the short term, he said. They trade the option closest to the strike price because they want to invest as little money as possible.

The OEX 100 was at $186.95 as he scanned his machine:

calls	volume	price	notes
Aug 185	50,406	2⅝	in the money and closest to the strike price
Aug 180	1,000	7	deep in the money
Aug 190	27		out of the money

Options players like the call closest to the strike price because it represents the best compromise between minimum investment and minimum time premium. On the August 185, they have to invest $265 for one option, whereas, on the 180, they have to invest close to $700. I asked Irving how much the OEX 100 would move, and he said that typically, for every 8 points the Dow moves up, this option will move up a point, if the market is behaving normally. A 24-point move in the Dow could thus double your money in the August 185 call, moving it 3 points, and that's a lot of leverage. Of course it works both ways; if the market goes down, you lose your money.

Afterward I asked Zweifler about the possible return on an investment in the OEX 100 the day after the Group of Five changed their policy and agreed to intervene to hold the dollar down. This was a bullish move for the American economy, and the Dow moved up strongly in the next three months.

The OEX 100 for December 175 could be bought at 6⅜ on September 23, 1985. The market price of $176.70 put this option close to the strike price. On December 13 it sold at 28½; an investor would have made more than four times his money.

The OEX 100 for December 190 could have been bought the same day at $^{11}/_{16}$, a far out of the money call; you would have had to be a sage to know what was going to happen. This option sold at 15½ on December 13, a twenty-fold increase on the investment.

The first option would have cost $637 per contract, as against $70 for the second one. The leverage is enormous.

Rule 9:   If an option goes against you, as soon as you lose half your money, sell it and salvage the remainder.

This is a rule many traders follow, although it is easy to be too optimistic. Irving says that the thinking goes this way: "It's going down, but it's still going to go up. I still have twelve days, I've got eleven days, I've got ten days. And they stay with it and they watch it all disappear." A seasoned investor, however, knows that it is smarter to take a lot of small losses and play for one big hit. When Zweifler sees an option going against him and that he has lost a third or a half, he gets out, and then he regroups his forces and decides what comes next, often doing nothing until a good idea comes along.

Rule 10:   The worst thing you can do if you play options is to make money the first time.

"It's like drugs," Zweifler said. "You get hooked and sooner or later they get you and they get you all the way." The player gets overconfident and convinced that he is smart, but the fact is, he is smart sometimes and not so smart other times. And those who don't lose too much, joke about it, but those who lose more than they can afford to don't talk about it at all.

Investors often think they have devised a profitable options scheme that can't lose. Irving told me about a friend who had retired and decided he would supplement the family income with his investments. He worked out an options strategy that he thought made sense, selling out of the money puts. As long as the stock market did nothing, those puts expired worthless and he kept making money. Since he thought he couldn't lose, he kept adding to his commitment, making it greater, believing that he had found the perfect system. In early 1982, the market dropped sharply. Those out of the money puts suddenly were deep in the money, and Irving's friend lost all of his large investment. Even though he got burned badly, after a year he tried another system, and lost again.

Now there are people who make money in options, there are some smart investors and nimble traders, but the statistics on probabilities speak for themselves. Even though I knew and avoided options for years, I played this winter, though I was aware that I was buying a deteriorating asset. I tend to be early in picking stocks, an inclination that works against an options trader, since the clock can't be stopped as expiration approaches. In fact, timing is always important in investing, but more so in buying options and in shorting stocks. Good timing, unfortunately, takes practice and you have to be willing to be a player or you'll never develop it. So now that I have developed some option scar tissue from my foray and am one of the fortunates who did not make money the first time, I intend to wait until an idea I'm more sure of comes along. The dream remains for anyone who understands the leverage and the possible return.

The one investor I have known who cashed in on buying options was John Slade, a senior partner at Bear Stearns. In 1983 he made $9 million in what *Institutional Investor* called "one of the biggest stock market killings of 1983." Slade, a few years earlier, had made $4 million in Boeing options. As an inveterate options player, Slade believes it is the only way to make real money (but he has been ac-

tive in Wall Street for forty-eight years and carefully put
$3 million of his Boeing options profits into an interest-
bearing account at the firm, to avoid losing it). In July of
1982 he moved again, buying $1 million worth of April
1983 options for his own account, because he believed the
market was ready to go up. Then, as it soared, he began
exercising those options. Slade said that he'd never made
that much in the market before and that he only buys
options on the number one company in any field. At the
time, I remember him also saying that IBM was a company
that he knew very well and had studied closely for a long
period of time.

So, while knowing that John Slade's killing is a rare one,
and that the probabilities are slight, his success, and the
possibility of making the right move at the right time,
keeps the options dream kindled for me, as well as for
other investors.

FOREIGN INVESTING

Why seek out investments in foreign markets, when
doing so makes it more difficult to find prospects and
follow the companies' progress, and adds the complication
of guessing the rates of currencies? Greenwich Research
Associates estimates that of the trillion-plus dollars in pension assets in America, under 3%, or $35 billion, is in-
vested globally, and the firm considers those account
managers to be sophisticated. The figures for individual
investors would have to be less than the pensions' 1% participation. But the world is becoming much more interde-
pendent. At the end of 1985, when the dollar's value was
off approximately 25% from the beginning of the year in
relation to the Japanese currency (the strongest one),
many investors want to know how to diversify outside
America. This is even more important when one knows
that seven of the ten best-performing mutual funds of
1985 were international funds with annual results ranging
between 60% and 70% for the year.

Michael Lipper of Lipper Analytical Services pointed

out that, "Every American has a dollar risk. He's at risk because, assuming he drives an American brand-name car, parts and some of the materials come from overseas and the price is importantly dictated by imports. If he is watching a new television set, either the parts or whole set are produced overseas, and certainly so if he listens to a radio." Lipper then described Alabama's experience: The state worked hard to attract new industry and when they started to lose it, they estimated that 40% of it was vulnerable to foreign competition. Americans can invest in the international economy by buying an American brand name with major foreign earnings, such as IBM or Merck, or an advertising company like Interpublic, or they can invest in foreign securities. Lipper said there are three attractions to investing directly in such securities: first, diversification, made necessary because the economies and markets in the world are not in lock step; second, the ability to buy certain securities that are not available in the United States; and, third, better value, adjusted for currency and market conditions in overseas industries. Lipper used the example of Peter Lynch's purchase of auto companies on the international markets.

There seems to be good reason to consider such investments, but my question was, "Can you make money at it?" Lipper hedged, saying, "It all depends on your timing and if you're willing to wait it out." He believes that people should have an important part of their money overseas, whether in long bonds, in equities or in short-term debt instruments. Lipper, the guru of investment results who publishes the industry bible, agrees with John Templeton and George Soros that everyone should have a global view.

One of the more savvy and literate managers of international money is Gilbert de Botton. At the age of forty-nine, he achieved his aim of forming an investment firm, retaining 60% ownership, that is active in global asset management. In fact, that is what he named the new London-based company. GAM's philosophy is to use funds in separate portfolios that are handled with individual requirements. Global Asset Management has thirty-three funds to choose from, including GAM International, GAM Pacific and GAM Arbitrage.

His peers consider de Botton one of the two best. He has entered a familiar arena; earlier he had developed the Rothschild bank in Zurich, which he had started for the family in 1968, into a $2 billion concern. Before that, de Botton trained and trained at a variety of firms—Bear Stearns, Goldman Sachs, Hambro's, Warburg's and Kitcat and Aitkin. He laughed heartily about his overtraining as a portfolio manager and told me his favorite story. After working at Hambro's, he went to Warburg's, where, when he complained that he had not learned enough, they responded, "We'll teach you things."

"And they taught me nothing," he said. One day, he grew annoyed because the group of younger associates he was working with was too interested in debutante parties and having a good time to be taken seriously at Warburg's. Gilbert said he wanted to leave and was ushered into the great Sigmund Warburg's office. Warburg said to him, with disdain, "My dear de Botton, you cannot leave because you are a volunteer, and volunteers have no right to leave." That formidable meeting kept him there for a few more months before he moved on. Some of de Botton's thoughts on investing are good ones for all investors, as well as for global aficionados.

Rule 1:   The investor has to decide first of all what it is he wants from his capital.

De Botton thinks investors are simply confused when they say to a money manager, "I have capital to invest, and I want performance." A good manager must ask: "Is this really your surplus capital that you're putting to work with the view to one day enjoying it, or do you think you can get rich this way, rather than by working? If so," says de Botton, "you're in for surprises because when you drive a truck as if it were a Ferrari, you're going to crack up against a great wall. On the other hand, there's no reason why, if you've got a truck, you've got to keep it stalled. It's a question of getting the right proportions."

Rule 2: **Individual clients usually get better investment performance because they don't drive from the backseat as much as institutional clients do.**

An institution tends to abuse a portfolio manager if its investments have had a weak period in the market; yet when the management hired that portfolio manager, they said that they were looking for a stable investing approach, and that the manager would not be judged quarter by quarter. They then grill the manager on his attitude toward investing, while questioning his near-term performance. American clients who did just that at pension fund meetings persuaded de Botton to manage a different kind of money. He said, "It really opened my eyes to the fact that I didn't want to be involved in this rat race of going with a Samsonite attaché case up to Rochester or Buffalo to explain to people who were predestined not to understand."

Those experiences led him to want to produce the best investment vehicle in the world, believing that, like the Gucci loafer, people would flock to buy it. So he organized a no-load, international fund approved by the Securities and Exchange Commission for sale in the United States, to offer clients a one-stop investment in the world economy. A fund, to him, is one of the best ways to perform well for your clients, while avoiding the backseat drivers.

Rule 3: **International investing means professional management.**

Buying foreign stocks without using a knowledgeable broker or investment adviser can cause free-floating anxiety. Many first-time participants fail to realize how many factors are involved. Gilbert describes it as "three-dimensional chaos," requiring a knowledge of economic groupings, countries and currencies. Events in 1984 show the dramatic effect currencies can have on net performance. An investor who innocently bought South African gold stocks when they were up soon saw his investment drop 55%. Similar scenes were played in Hong Kong, when the colony came to terms with its real owner, and in Spanish securities when the socialists came to power. Professionals have to study these markets closely in order to move at the right time.

In early 1985, the dollar was poised for the major currency reversal that followed. The top-performing markets were Austria, where stocks were up by 172%, Germany, 132% and Italy, 128%, all outstripping even a strong U.S. market. International mutual funds gained an average of 39.5% in 1985, in comparison with the average American general equity mutual fund, up 27.2% (Gilbert's GAM International was up 59.2%, one of the best-performing funds in 1985).

Since long-term results are what count, let's look at international investments over different durations of time:

	Average International Equity Fund	Standard and Poor's Index
1 yr	39.5%	31.7%
5 yrs	70.9%	85.5%
10 yrs	204.0%	375.3%

SOURCE: Lipper Analytical (Note: currency changes factored in).

From the mid-Seventies to the early Eighties, it would have been better to have been invested in the United States if you were an average performer. Investors in international funds made better profits in the Sixties and early Seventies, and then spectacular profits in 1985 and 1986.

Rule 4: Superlative portfolio managers act like champions.

A money manager, de Botton said, has to have both intelligence and endurance to support the strains of the business, but the quality that distinguishes a superlative person from an ordinary good one, beyond analytical ability and all the other requirements, is the desire to be a champion. "When you see the way a George Soros or Malcolm Forbes suffers, in spite of all the millions they've got in the bank in their personal accounts," de Botton said, "how humiliated, defeated, nagged and niggled they feel when they haven't got it right, and then everything they marshal to get it right again—then you sense you're dealing with true champions. I've seen those two under pressure, just to name two, and I've also seen the hustlers under pressure. The hustler will go for a drink, or knock off and play golf. They give you thirty-six excuses and go on a spending spree, while champions clench their teeth and go at a problem."

De Botton organized his firm so that he could take advantage of such champions, incorporating their ideas and abilities into his talent bank. One of the more controversial people in the postwar money management business was Bernie Cornfeld, who, despite the misery he apparently caused, was acquitted of the charges against him, but only after spending eleven months in a Swiss jail. But Gilbert used his idea of "a fund of funds" in his own organization. He observed the success of Leverage Capital Holdings (a portfolio made up exclusively of separate offshore entities advised by independent U.S. managers) and adapted this kind of specialized fund so that his asset management company could earn a 1% fee.

"Some of the world's best players are like independent opera singers," de Botton said, "who won't sign a contract even if you give them Covent Garden. But on the other hand, they will come and play for a season." So, along with internal managers, he includes some champions in the mix he concocts for his clients. In their first year of operation, five in his fund group are among the top twenty in Lipper's performance ratings, two managed in-house and three outside by associates. Gilbert expected his new funds to be overlooked at first. Though he said "the start has been gratifying," he now faces the pitfalls of linking a record of good performance.

Rule 5: Other people's opinions are only useful when they are right.

Not a day goes by, for a money manager, without the pressure of other people saying, "Why are you doing that?" The richest rewards come from getting a big move right, and managers don't get it right, adds Gilbert de Botton, "by chatting with colleagues or competitors or clients." Even listening to some of the more respected market pundits is foolish, to him. They remind him of Biblical prophets who sing to the courts while waving their sticks. A manager gets it right, de Botton said, by going into a dark room and poring over the entire situation, and then testing it on his peers. "When they tell you they don't think so, you ask them to say why. In the end you find the people you can identify with."

Rule 6: The best investment ideas come from an adviser without a conflict of interest.

One of the most significant things that Ace Greenberg taught de Botton at Bear Stearns was, Gilbert said, that "a broker is not to be confused with somebody who recommends stocks. A broker is someone who brokers a transaction; he has a buyer and a seller whom he puts together, and that is an honorable function for which he gets a fee." (A real estate agent will understand this situation.) This, de Botton believes, usually makes it difficult to get good investment ideas from brokers, and explains why he prefers to act as an investment adviser and charge a fee. A broker makes his living from selling you an idea, not giving you an idea that will make money. An adviser's job is to make you money.

Rule 7: Despite their reputation, "Swiss gnomes" do not give the best investment advice or do the best job.

Gilbert laughed about the general adulation of Swiss money managers, known as the gnomes, and recalled the old joke: "Do you know how to have a million dollars in a Swiss bank?" Answer: "Start with two million." Essentially, Swiss accounts are nest eggs, not performance-oriented money. Swiss firms are not competitive hothouses; even Scottish widows want more action. Swiss bankers do excel at charging fees, and very few people ever count up what an account there costs them.

Investors who want to purchase a foreign stock should seek out a broker familiar with those markets. Indeed, some firms have long histories in foreign markets. My own broker, a stranger to international companies, turned me away from the stock of Jaguar when I heard of the company's turnaround, because he did not want to do unfamiliar research. I have found that an investor needs extra tail wind to buy stocks in companies far from our shores.

John Templeton advises investors to seek out specialists in foreign markets by calling a brokerage firm and asking for its foreign department. Templeton's favorites are:

- Merrill Lynch—all-around best
- Vickers da Costa—a foreign broker with a New York office
- Cazenoves—London-based, has superb ideas and in-depth research
- Credit Suisse—broad coverage in Europe
- Daiwa—Japan
- Pierson Heldring—Amsterdam
- Potter—Australia

John Templeton, Gilbert de Botton and George Soros all offer global funds, which include American stocks, and seven other outstanding international funds were among the top-performing funds in 1985.

ARBITRAGE

Arbitrageurs are different from other investors. They don't think like traders nor do they think like portfolio managers. They are a breed apart because, when they play, they are taking a disciplined and controlled risk that very few people understand. Irwin Schloss described the difference to me by saying, "Our objectives are different. We don't deal in promises or the future, but in the real world, always knowing that it's what you take away in the end that counts." Carl Icahn, in his frustrated attempt to take control of TWA, told Cable News Network, "If ever I'm dying, send me an arbitrageur's heart. I know it will be unused." This remark caused amusement among the active "arbs," since Icahn started his career in convertible arbitrage.

Some tales of arbitrageurs' stiletto coldness are classic. A corporate executive has said that when his company learned of Ivan Boesky's participation as a major investor, management innocently called him to meet for discussions. The company gave him what it hoped was an exciting presentation of its future prospects, saying, "We're excited to have you as one of our investors and hope you'll stay with us for a while." Boesky asked what "a while" meant. The executives responded, "Six months to a year." He supposedly remarked, laughing, "Six months to a year? The only thing I've stayed with as long as that is my wife."

No one paid attention to arbitrageurs for years. Now, however, they are quoted daily, and such tales as Boesky's are frequent. In fact, they have replaced politicians as savants.

Arbitrageurs are the new stars primarily because of the increasing number of hostile and friendly takeovers and leveraged buyouts that are detailed daily in our morning newspapers. In 1984 and 1985, the value of mergers completed in each of those years totaled $125 billion, two times the annual amount in the previous three years, and four times the merger activity in 1974 and 1980. Goldman Sachs estimates that 70% of the market's rise since the beginning of 1984 was a result of this merger wave.

The term "arbitrage" covers a multitude of financial

transactions. But risk arbitrage involves taking a position in a security after the announcement of a deal, usually a friendly or unfriendly takeover offer, although it can be a leveraged buyout proposal. The stock is generally bought on the announcement, as soon as it opens for trading, and sold at the proposed offering price, making a profit on the difference between the two. An arbitrageur protects himself, when possible, by hedging his long position and shorting the stock of the acquirer by buying put or selling call options. He also calculates his return based on both the time he has to hold the security and "the cost of carry," the term for his borrowing costs (he's allowed to borrow 50% of the money involved). Each arbitrageur makes this mathematical calculation his own way, depending on how he values time, although, to the naive, the formulas may look like hieroglyphics. Investors can learn from some of the disciplines that these arbitrageurs practice, even if they cannot duplicate their every move.

One of the deans of the profession is Alan (Ace) Greenberg, chairman of Bear Stearns, who was once described by a competitor, with admiration: "There's no one colder or tougher in the securities business when it comes to selling. He moves fast . . . like a great white shark. Now you see him, now you don't."

Ace Greenberg: The Pro's Pro

In his office near Bear Stearns's no-nonsense trading room, Ace focused on my questions, but then his mind whirled and wandered. I wanted to say, "Earth to Ace," mimicking my children when they thought I was in a different world. That evidence of restlessness may come from too many years spent in a trading room where, comfortable at his station, he would respond to one of the many buttons as they lit up on his telephone. But others might insist that Greenberg's laconic style simply reflects the nature of the true arbitrageur.

Greenberg frowned when I asked him how he felt about being thought of as "the trader's trader." "I don't think traders make any money. They spot a stock moving on the tape, like the way it acts and buy it. I think to try and make a living that way is hopeless. Others try to make money by running in advance of an order that they know exists, so they can have the merchandise to sell to the buyer the next day. I wouldn't call the latter trading. I'd call that something else," he said disdainfully. Then Ace added that such traders, like technicians, appear knowledgeable, but it is hard to find any who make money.

"Does Bear Stearns, as a firm, buy blocks of stock or bonds or government instruments?" I asked.

"Yes, at the right price," he said, "but I don't call that trading. I call that buying stuff when you have to and trying to survive in business."

Greenberg prefers to be thought of as an arbitrageur, with sound reason, since that's the role with which he started his career in Wall Street. The volume in 1949–50 was around a million shares a day (today it averages over 100 million shares a day), and in those days, arbitrage was the only active area that offered tempting amounts of money. Everything else seemed slow to him. There were major arbitrage opportunities in the breakup of the big utilities, and in the one or two railroads that had not been reorganized. Greenberg started as a clerk at Bear Stearns, putting pins in a map to show where oil wells were being drilled. His first promotion brought him to a clerkship in the busy arbitrage department. He had no real apprenticeship; he learned by making mistakes, and there were a lot of them. "Everybody," he said, "makes mistakes of all kinds. You just try not to make them twice."

Now, thirty-five years later, he pilots Bear Stearns, a brokerage firm that many consider a moneymaking machine, yet Greenberg still identifies himself as an arbitrageur, part of a field, he says, that has undergone dramatic changes in recent years. "There are many more players than there were, because of the publicity that Ivan Boesky created in order to raise money, which I don't blame him for, and he was successful in raising money. But the deals have gotten bigger and bigger. It's been a very bad business the last nine months [from late 1984 to early 1985] . . . more deals have been busted percentagewise than any time I can remember. And, obviously, in a risk-arbitrage business, if the deal busts, you lose ten to fifteen points. . . . You've got to be right about three quarters of the time, or more. Yet it's been a good business, year in and year out."

In reviewing what he had learned from his mistakes, Ace remarked, "I personally think the greatest rule in the world is to limit your loss. I stick to that rule and there's no if-and-or-but about it. If I have a security and it starts going down, I sell it when it goes ten to fifteen percent below where I bought it. Everybody here at Bear Stearns knows the rules. I don't want to hear any reasons. I don't want to hear, 'But I talked to the president.' I don't want to hear, 'It's down because of technical reasons,' or 'There's a seller who doesn't know what he's doing.' I don't want to hear it. But sometimes people hesitate and I say this is not a democracy. People here lose their vote when they're wrong. That's it, you're no longer involved. You can outvote on other things, but not this; you're too emotionally involved. This rule of mine, I believe, has saved more lives than anything I can think of."

Precisely this rule of Greenberg's is what started his reputation as a tough and cold seller of securities. It's why competitors think of him as the trader's trader. He agreed. "At Bear Stearns," Ace said, "we have a meeting every Monday afternoon of all the people that run money, and we ask everyone attending, 'Do you have a loss'? Pretty soon, they don't bring in that many losses. They know I'm going to say, 'I'll see you tomorrow morning and we'll sell it together.'

"No one is ever going to change my mind on this rule. Do I sell something that goes down and then goes back up? Sure I do, but I've also sold things that went broke. If it goes up, we can keep it forever . . . or at least until it goes long term. And, stop and think, if the most you lose is ten to fifteen percent and you can make one hundred, two hundred, three hundred percent, you have to be right one out of five times. And, if they go up, we usually buy more."

Then I asked Ace if he thought other investors could follow this advice. "No," he responded. "Not a chance. They do just the opposite. As soon as it goes up, they can't stand it. There's a profit, so they take it. When it goes down, they start thinking of buying more, saying to themselves, 'I've got a loss and I don't want to lose money and I'm not even yet.'" Ace smiled, repeating, "No, not a chance. I could tell everybody this in the world; it wouldn't alter the mechanics of the market one bit, because they can't do it. People here can't do it from nine to five and they've seen it work for years."

In parting, I asked whether he thought there was any correlation between people who play bridge well and who invest well (Ace, along with Jack Dreyfus and Milton Petrie, often plays in a high-stakes bridge game late in the afternoon at the Whist Club). "It's possible for a good bridge player to be a good businessman. Logic, obviously, is important to bridge, the ability to see things through, but they are characteristics that are good for any businessman. Not all good bridge players are money-makers or even good businessmen." Ace's analysis was good, but I felt let down. I had hoped, knowing how successful these three high-stakes players had been at investing, that there was some secret connection.

Irwin Schloss: The Disciplined Engineer

Irwin Schloss wears three hats in the investing community. Some people connect him solely with Gulf and Western, where he has been a member of the board, an éminence grise and chairman of the audit committee under both Charlie Bluhdorn and Marty Davis. Others know him as the chief operating officer of Marcus Schloss, considered by many to be the number one specialist firm on the New York Stock Exchange, while still others know him for his arbitrage activities. Arbitrage for him, as for Ace Greenberg, is his real background; it is where Schloss

started his career in Wall Street. He learned the ropes—
as did Ivan Boesky—at one of the great arbitrage schools,
Gus Levy's Goldman Sachs. Most in Schloss's separate
worlds are unaware of his background: West Point and
engineering, perfect training for the discipline and analytical abilities that are an arbitrageur's tools of the trade. An
engineer not only is skilled in mathematics but also learns
to work with things rather than with people. That background is far less emotional than a doctor's, a lawyer's or
an accountant's. Their businesses bring them into contact
with people, and their feelings, all the time. An engineer
is trained to be thorough, to dig for details, and these
attributes contributed to Schloss's investment acumen.

Schloss believes arbitrageurs think differently from
other investors in two ways:

1. They have a short time frame—not as short as a
trader's but not as long as an investor's. An arbitrageur
factors in the length of time his money is at risk and calculates his annualized return accordingly.

2. They have no allies or loyalties. If a friend who runs
a company, or another Wall Streeter, asks an arbitrageur
to side with him in a deal, he will be refused. The whole
idea is to limit risk once a position is taken in a company.
Taking sides with a friend increases risk.

Some of Schloss's thoughts on arbitrage and the rules
he follows are:

Rule 1:   An arbitrageur has to be multitalented.

To be successful, he needs entrepreneurial thinking, a
trading background, securities research knowledge, a familiarity with interest-rate forecasting, and a liking for
strategic planning, since the chesslike moves of a takeover
proposal can get complicated. He does not believe that
investors outside the arcane world he deals with can successfully analyze the play of a stock once a bid is made.

If an investor happens to own the stock already, he is lucky.

Rule 2: Discipline is the key to the arbitrage business.

When I asked Schloss what successful rules he followed, he answered, simply, "That's easy: discipline." He pointed out that every arbitrageur forms his individual disciplines. Those he follows are:

- To decide at the beginning of the year how much capital to commit to deals, and not to waver from this figure.
- Always to sell when a deal busts.
- Never to load all his assets on one position, which saved him when Occidental backed off from its offer for Gulf, causing the stock to drop.
- To stay away from deals involving greenmail.

Rule 3: Arbitrage is a field that keeps changing.

The practitioner never feels totally confident that he has learned it all. In the past there were the reorganizations of the utilities and railroads, then classic stock mergers. Deals today are much riskier. Today's level of sophistication is totally different from that of the past.

Rule 4: "If the deal doesn't go, we sell the security. We never look for a second reason to own a security. If it's bought for a deal and it doesn't go, we sell it."

When I asked Irwin how long it takes to find out, he said, "We wait for board approval, the definitive agreements and the setting up of financing. If at any time these procedures miss, then we sell it, we don't say, 'Oh, the assets are great.' " A case in point was Scott and Fetzer. The deal was going, then it was off, four times. The first time it was off, Irwin was out. This rule sounds simple: When a deal does not go through, sell; when it does go through, cash in.

Rule 5: **Smart arbitrageurs cannot recount their greatest investing mistakes, any more than they can tell you about their greatest glories.**

The reasons are those disciplines. "My risks," Schloss said, "are always spread broadly across the board, so I'm not in jeopardy. You know that everything is not going to go through and everything's not roses. When Cities Services broke up on the eleventh hour and fifty-nine minutes, we were hurt but not in jeopardy."

Rule 6: **An arbitrageur does not feel excited about any deal. They are strictly business, not emotional questions.**

As a mental exercise, Irwin will, from time to time, buy stock in a company on the fundamentals, but that has nothing to do with risk arbitrage. He has even set aside a pool of money that he calls the "executive sandbox," for his team to work with between arbitrage ideas. Yet Schloss is cynical about the profit possibilities of such a pool; he is happy if it breaks even. Like Greenberg, Schloss feels strongly that traders do not make money. He said emphatically, "That, coming from Ace Greenberg and me, really says something. We've been active in trading rooms for so many years and have profited handsomely from our work."

There are great profits in arbitrage, and some years are better than others. But since 1946, Schloss has never had a losing year. He seldom bothers with an idea that won't net him an annualized return of 20%. "Everyone has his own rules, but this is one that hasn't changed for us."

Rule 7:   The size of positions has to be manageable.

In a broken deal, getting out can be especially difficult for the biggest player in the marketplace. Irwin does not buy enough stock to be required to file a 13D (the form an investor has to file with the Securities and Exchange Commission when he buys 5% of the outstanding stock in a company), saying, "I never like to play in a ballgame where the impossible has a probability of being there."

Rule 8:   The time span until a deal closes affects the return.

"ABC has been owned for months," he said. "We calculated the return when we bought it. We don't reverse our positions. If we originally agreed that there was twenty percent in the deal, we don't change if it goes to a twenty-two to twenty-five percent return, or down to a fifteen to eighteen percent return. If we decide to do the deal, we agree intellectually to stay until it is consummated." He used the example of MGM/UA Entertainment to describe his point. To get financing, the company tried to deal with Viacom, but could not. Drexel Burnham promised in a newspaper story that it would provide the financing with or without Viacom. The stock moved down to 22⅝, then back to 24. Schloss neither bought nor sold MGM/UA stock during this period. "If the deal breaks," he said, "I'm sure we'd get less than 22⅝, and if it goes through, more than 26. Busting and looking like busting is not our game. We wait until it happens."

Portfolio managers, unlike arbitrageurs, often don't wait until a deal is consummated to sell. Roy Neuberger discussed how he sold Carnation early, locking in his profits, and, in the fight for Union Carbide, John Templeton was quoted as saying that he had sold his 3.4 million shares of Union Carbide at 72, even though the offer was for 82 a share. His profit, he said, "was $40 a share—$136 million—and that was high enough." It is a totally different mentality.

Rule 9:   Rely on standard sources of information.

"Most of our information, like the Viacom news, we get right off the newspaper," Schloss said. "Ninety-five percent of the information used comes off the Reuters, Dow or stock tickers, all published information." Everyone believes that arbitrageurs must have inside sources, but Irwin said that the rewards of using inside information are not worth the trouble, particularly with widespread use of the computer: The Securities and Exchange Commission and the exchange are immediately informed of increased activity in stocks. "Now listen," I said, "stocks do go up a few days before a deal for a company is announced, so someone does know something. Look at the recent action in RCA before the offer was published." Irwin said that he has very seldom owned a stock before a deal is proposed. Even in his fundamental choices, he has rarely grabbed the brass ring. Occasionally, he will do a "buy right," in which he buys the stock and sells the corresponding options. A company's stock may seem a good value when the options sell at a big premium. This may be an indicator that someone has a special interest, great enough to pay the high premium. "If it is," Irwin added, "we're very happy with the rate of return, and, if nothing happens, we've made the premium on the option."

In 1985, investing in the takeover game brought the biggest excitement and rewards. I asked, "Where should an individual go if he wants to put some money in an arbitrage pool? Those minimum twenty percent returns and your positive returns over forty years seemed attractive to me." Schloss cautioned again that it was not a business for individuals, even rich ones, who do not have the right mentality. An arbitrageur cannot rely on one deal, he has to have the right state of mind to play them all. Schloss himself has never worked as an agent on behalf of someone else. He has always worked for his firm, never dealing with a private customer, so his philosophy has stayed the same. The problem with clients, Schloss said, is that, sooner or later, they will say, "I don't want to own that company, it's a dog," or "I'll do more of this one and less of that one." And arbitrageurs can't afford to make emotional value judgments. Instead, they must calculate the size of the capitalization, the quality of the company, the length of time they must be invested and any risk factors. Well-known managers of arbitrage pools are only interested in handling large sums of money.

Whether or not one invests in such a pool, one can use Schloss's basic investing outline for its sound, common-sense approach:

1. Decide at the beginning of the year what your investing commitment will be.

2. Sell if the stock you bought for a specific reason is no longer viable. Do not look for a second reason to own it.

3. Never invest so much in one situation that a loss could hurt you.

4. Avoid companies with which you do not want to be associated.

5. Aim for a minimum return for each stock you purchase.

Ivan Boesky: The Elusive Flyer

Wall Street agreed on only two things about Ivan Boesky, the glamour boy of arbitrage: He totally changed the arbitrage game by raising the ante and he made a great deal of money. Everything else was up for debate. Because Boesky accepted large sums of money to manage for others, his fingerprints showed up in the market. He was able to buy enough stock to boost the market price above the price of a tender offer, thus making the offering group nervous enough to think they had better sharpen up their pencils and pay a bit more. They thought that perhaps Boesky knew something that they didn't, that someone else was in the wings with an offer that would top theirs, or that the intrinsic value of the company they bid for was much higher than they thought.

Before the Boesky era, everybody played arbitrage by the old rules. First, somebody made a bid for a company. Then the arbitrageurs figured out how long the consideration of the bid would take, what the chances were that the bidder would get financing, how long it would take to prepare the technical and proxy material and to get the approval of the Securities and Exchange Commission and the company. Would the bidder try to buy the company or to merge with it? What would it cost the arbitrageur to finance a position for the necessary number of days? But in today's aggressive world, the rules are changing. Financing pressures make it difficult to find the cash needed for such large purchases, and lock-up provisions that benefit one pursuer also make a competitive offer difficult. Companies will do anything to fight off an unfriendly offer, even subject themselves to "scorched earth" treatment. The company remains basically intact and management stays entrenched, but such a policy hurts the company and shareholder values because assets are sold off and debt increased. The risks, as well as the rewards, have become greater.

Ivan Boesky was the aggressor who changed the arbitrage environment. His public relations consultant made at least ten appointments for me to meet Boesky at the Harvard Club (though he did not go to Harvard). Each time, as the day approached, I received a telephone call from Gunther, saying that Boesky had to travel out of town. Are there clues to the man in his own book on arbitrage, *Merger Mania?* It is technically excellent, but the reviewers, as well as the readers, were disappointed. It lacks palaver—insights into the participants, and some sense of the day-to-day excitement that others expect to find in the life of a financial swinger.

In March 1986, the *New York Times* reported that Boesky was building a war chest of $1 billion for his stock market forays. This fund, five times the size of his then-present one, would be gigantic compared with other arbitrageurs'

$20 million to $100 million. Boesky's possible leverage would have presented the same menace to corporations as modern bombs do to civilization. If successful, he would have earned 40% of the profits on his positions, while assuming only 10% of the losses. (Remember, however, Ben Graham's profit-sharing deal, which also looked great in the 1920s.)

The time bomb, it seems, was set even as his war chest was announced. For one year (the same year I kept trying to arrange an interview) Ivan Boesky, based on information received from Dennis Levine, bought prearbitrage positions in companies Levine knew would soon be "put in play" by a merger bid. In the outrage that followed Ivan Boesky's record settlement of insider trading charges, the arbitrage community felt it was attacked unfairly for Boesky's escapades.

Risk arbitrage has been around for years and will continue to be practiced in the old-fashioned way. Once a deal is announced, the "arbs" will take a position betting on its eventual consummation. As both Alan Greenberg and Irwin Schloss said, it's a good business year in and year out. Arbitrageurs will rise again in the post-Boesky era, but perhaps their light will be dimmer once the eye of the scandal passes.

JUNK BONDS AND OTHER INELEGANT INVESTMENTS

The perception has taken hold that junk bonds are destroyers of the American financial system. A modern witch hunt is already under way with the Federal Reserve's suggested imposition of margin rules on the use of such bonds for hostile takeovers. Not everyone in the government feels the way the Federal Reserve does, but no matter, the Fed will proceed on its own. Investing pundits, such as Barton Biggs and Jimmy Rogers, are warning the world of impending disaster. Biggs, in his October 15, 1985, *Morgan Stanley Investment Perspectives*, recommended that:

U.S. government obligations should be owned virtually exclusively, as merger and acquisition activity has made the sanctity of corporate debt ratings ephemeral. Junk bonds and seven-day paper of all types should be avoided as though they had the financial version of AIDS, which is what they will have when the next recession begins to claim some victims!

Now that's a warning. No one ever said there were no risks in buying lower-quality bonds, but if the buyer is careful, he may get an improving rating, as well as extraordinary yields. As Tally Embry, who toils successfully in the junk bond field, said, "We prefer to call it high yield–high opportunity investing."

Then Embry showed me his power-of-compounding chart, revealing only a small difference in twenty-year to thirty-year returns between a U.S. government bond yielding 9.7% and an A-rated bond yielding 10.2%. There is, however, a great difference between either of these returns and that of a lower-rated bond yielding 14.6%. The total return of a million dollars compounded in the different debt instruments makes buying inelegant bonds highly attractive; the higher rate yields 50% more on the investment each year. Investment at the higher interest rate brings $8 million more in twenty years and $41 million more in thirty years.

Such a difference in returns makes it worth the effort to learn about the vagaries of junk bond investing, especially since interest rates have fallen so dramatically that many investors feel cheated in higher-rated bonds.

Tally Embry, today president of Magten Asset Management, started his investing career by managing equities, not bonds, at Fiduciary Trust. When he started his own firm, he decided that equities were too risky. After all, he could be right on the company, but the market might go down, or the multiple might decline or any number of pitfalls that had nothing to do with him might make him lose control of his clients' money. How can anyone tell what Procter and Gamble is going to sell at in the next

THE POWER OF COMPOUNDING

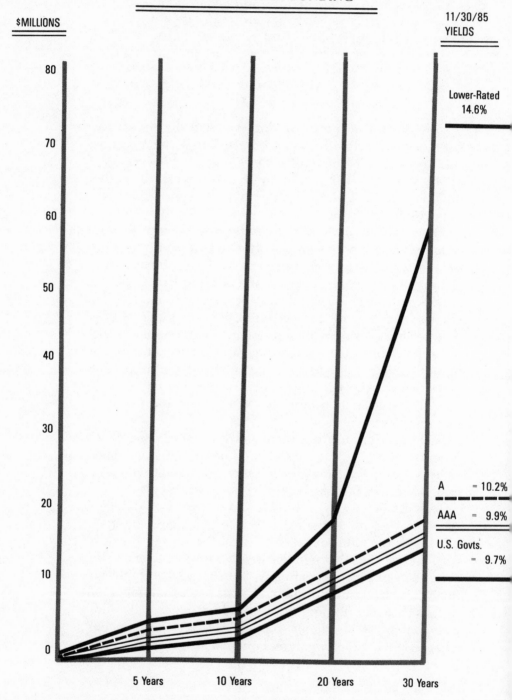

$MILLIONS

11/30/85
YIELDS

80

70

Lower-Rated
14.6%

60

50

40

30

20

A   = 10.2%

AAA   = 9.9%

U.S. Govts.
     = 9.7%

10

0

5 Years   10 Years   20 Years   30 Years

quarter or year? he thought. You don't know where the economy or interest rates are going to be, not to mention what Procter and Gamble's competition is going to be. He strayed away from equities slowly, by first buying REITs (Real Estate Investment Trusts) that yielded 12% when treasury bonds yielded 9%, based on his knowledge of private real estate transactions. Then he found himself attracted to a Bear Stearns report on the Penn Central Railroad, as it emerged from bankruptcy and went through its final reorganization. He suddenly realized that when he worked at Fiduciary Trust, he would never have been able to purchase those bonds. If it is a good-quality investment, a bond has to pay interest every six months. And if bonds do not do that, if in fact they are risky enough to appreciate by themselves, a serious manager gets rid of them or jeopardizes his fiduciary reputation. But Embry observed that there were people who to some degree would risk their money to make money, and clients like these attracted him.

As he looked at Penn Central, he found a rich corporation whose first mortgage bonds were well valued in the market. Tally also read the court documents of Penn Central's bankruptcy. What he saw was not a Wall Street analyst's view of the world five years from now, but sworn testimony about the railroad's assets and liabilities, as well as an estimate of its future outlook. Accountants were highly visible; creditors had their investment bankers available to disprove management's claims. The Bear Stearns report said that though Penn Central's bonds sold at 65, they would probably be worth 100 in eighteen months, and so Embry bought his first junk bond. They sold at around 130 a year later.

There are some misconceptions about buying junk bonds that prevent many investors from recognizing the opportunity to achieve an equitylike return, without taking the risks of equities.

Hostile Takeovers

Using junk bonds is a new way to finance hostile take-overs. There have always been bonds in the investment markets that have offered high yields, but these were bonds that had declined in value after being issued at investment grade, "fallen angels." In 1977, Drexel Burnham Lambert Inc., underwrote newly issued high-yield bonds of companies rated below investment grade, giving many companies access to capital, by using a twist on the old formula. They created and marketed original-issue low-grade bonds with a high yield. Frederick H. Joseph, chief executive of Drexel Burnham, estimated that only 675 American companies had been rated investment grade, though there were 20,000 firms with assets of over $25 million. Of the $122 billion used to finance mergers and acquisitions in 1984, less than 2% came from high-yield bonds. Most of the money came from corporate cash flow or bank borrowings.

Greater Risk

Higher-yielding bonds are riskier by definition. A lower-grade bond always yields more than a high-grade bond. In one study of all bonds issued between 1900 and 1943, triple A bonds yielded 5.1%, while those rated less than triple B yielded 8.6%, a 350-basis-point difference. That spread has been pretty much the same since 1900, though today's differential is higher at 490 basis points (a moveable feast depending on the market's attitude toward junk bonds). The default rate over recent years, as measured by Drexel Burnham, is half of 1%, while Professor Edward Altman of New York University's Graduate School of Business Administration finds the default rate on high-yielding bonds, graded double B or lower by the rating agencies, has been 1.6% a year, compared with 0.08% for all corporate bonds. Since companies often buy back some interest and principal in a default, he estimates that the total loss on such bonds was just over 1%. Since he calculates differently from Drexel, it would be reasonable to figure a default rate of ½% to 1% on such bonds. (LTV filed for bankruptcy in July 1986, so this percentage should rise since the company had $2 billion in outstanding junk bonds.)

Usually one or two industries account for 80% of the defaults. In the Depression, most were railroads and electric utility holding companies, while in the 1970s, the biggest defaults came from REITs. Oil and gas companies should be the leaders in the 1980s. In every case, such defaults occurred in the hottest, most attractive areas, where profits were assumed to have no limit and prices to go up forever.

What is risky to one person is not risky to another. And Tally Embry has found that investors do not like to take defined risks, often preferring those they are not aware of. They will buy a stock like Data General, which went quickly from 70 down to 55, never perceiving that it is as risky an investment as a Muse Air equipment trust certificate that will pay a 19½% annual return. An investor will buy into a biotechnology company that has no prospects for meaningful profits in the next five years and feel that it is not an unusually speculative place to put money. That same investor, says Embry, can then say that owning senior or senior subordinated debt of Metromedia, with its ownership of attractive broadcasting properties, is highly speculative because its bond is riskier than one issued by AT&T. Such analysis, he feels, makes no financial sense. Recently, Embry added, Barton Biggs of Morgan Stanley recommended the Singapore market, after it had dropped 40%. "Now," he said, "if you had bought stock three months ago in Singapore and lost 40% on your money, that would be as bad as you would have done if you had somehow chosen to buy all the bonds that had defaulted since 1960. You would on average have lost 40% of your money if you'd bought them at par."

Undecipherable Bond Grades

There are many more gradations of bonds today than in the past. There used to be government bonds and good corporate bonds and, after those came bonds of companies that got into difficulties. Those were the only junk bonds. Now there are many more gradations of bonds. Some are much more speculative than others, but they are priced accordingly.

Tally breaks the categories down into four groups:

Companies Whose Best Choice Is To Take on More Leverage. Multimedia, the company that owns the Phil Donahue show as well as many newspapers and television stations, is controlled by the family who started it, which owns about 45% of the stock. Every year, the company produces excess cash flow, so it has bought back its shares in the marketplace and leveraged itself. Its other choices would be: to raise dividends, which are taxed twice; to retain the money in the corporation, which would only invest the cash at a lower return in treasury bills; or to buy broadcasting companies, which, today, are expensive. Multimedia's shareholders enjoy the benefits of leverage, without double taxation of their dividends. CBS, on the other hand, also generates cash flow but has spent its money on often expensive acquisitions. Multimedia has a much worse credit rating than CBS does, but it is a better-managed company.

Teledyne and Litton are two other companies that use their cash flow to buy back shares because they think it is the best use of cash. Although these companies are leveraged, their operations and size are stable, and their bonds are referred to as plain vanilla junk bonds. When I asked Embry to define this term, he said it means a bond that can be rated triple, double or single A but has great liquidity.

A Middle Range of Companies. These companies show more volatility in economic swings or are inherently leveraged, such as home-builders. Airlines could be included in this category because they have operating and financial leverage. Much of American business falls into this category, companies with good operations and ordinary leverage that have to pay a premium for money because they are not household names.

Special Situations. This category would include, first of all, companies that are having a terrible time in their industry, such as Ideal Basic Industries, whose bonds are yielding 20% at big discounts; then small, troubled companies and leveraged buyouts where a great deal of senior debt has to be paid off. Last would come issues whose structure appears more complicated. Often, such issues carry debt-delayed coupons that make it difficult to calculate their return, although they may offer good opportunities.

The Bankrupt Company. In at least 95% of these cases, there is value in the enterprise, either in its assets or its tax losses. All the creditors of the company divvy up the leftovers and redistribute the debt in common stock, so that the bondholders end up being major shareholders. Penn Central is the most famous company that followed this path.

Many believe that all bonds are bad long-term investments. Anyone who is old enough to remember when triple A bonds yielded about 2½% in 1948 knows that, until recently, this was true. Some people have even referred to long-term bonds as certificates of confiscation. But bond yields will not again increase six times, as they did when they went from 2½% to 15%, and today's rates make bonds a valid investment. A million dollars invested at 2.8% for twenty years only became $1.7 million. At 16%, $1 million becomes $19.4 million.

Here are some of Tally Embry's thoughts on buying inelegant investments.

Rule 1:   There is no natural buyer for a bankrupt security.

The tendency in institutions is to sell a bond that has dropped below investment grade. All brokers and investment advisers will swap bonds for their clients rather than be held responsible for the debt of a troubled corporation. But sophisticated buyers will risk their money if the return is high enough.

Rule 2:   Bankruptcies create opportunities.

Defaulted bonds are where Gus Levy, David J. Greene and Charlie Allen made their first killings. They examined the railroads and utilities, and said, "If I buy a first mortgage bond, the court will uphold it, and I will eventually get the property."

Rule 3:   The big risk in any bond is to make a mistake in evaluating the assets of the company.

If Caterpillar Tractor can't make a profit, everyone who owns its bonds has to anticipate a default and watch his investment go down the tubes. If the company defaults, everything rests on the fundamental valuation: What are the assets worth, the value of the trademark or brand name, franchise or license? It is vital to assess the intangibles. The asset value of the *Wall Street Journal* may be as low as a million dollars, but its stream of earnings is worth much more; its long-term viability does not depend on book value alone.

Rule 4:   Sticking to big companies is the easiest way to guard against fraud.

A fraudulent company is difficult to spot. Even evaluating the board of directors isn't foolproof, as some of the principals are often the culprits. Embry believes the best way to avoid the problem is to buy large companies, because they can afford to lose $5 million without jeopardizing their credit. The bigger the company, the harder it is to put it out of business. Their assets have been on their books for a long time, they have more layers of management, more overview by the Securities and Exchange Commission and by lawyers and accountants. There is no reason ever to buy a small company, Embry said; it can be dependent on one person and if he's a bad egg, he can take a significant portion of the company assets, or significantly misrepresent them.

Rule 5: Estimates of assets must be adjusted to fit the industry.

In the oil and gas industry, figures for a discounted stream of future net revenues depend on variables that no one really knows. They represent a hole in the ground that goes down 15,000 feet, and a reservoir that an engineer guesses will yield $10 million over five years. But he would be the last person to put a lot of money on that guess.

If the assets are volatile, timing is difficult. If Braniff goes under in the middle of a recession, its lenders' planes drop in value from $8 million to $4 million. Assets of computer-leasing companies shrink when their IBM machines are outmoded with the introduction of another model.

In buying Metromedia bonds, the only concern about assets is, will there be any mechanism that can broadcast advertising to supplant television over the next five or ten years? If there is, then Metromedia's bonds could be in trouble.

Rule 6: A bond is just an instrument of a company. Before buying one, study the company's products.

Tally Embry recommended buying stock in companies whose products are familiar and reliable, as he said his grandmother did. If MCI provides good long-distance telephone service, its bond may be a good buy and pay a higher premium than a government bond does.

Rule 7: Bankrupt companies must work out their difficulties, and waiting for their bonds to appreciate can be a long and boring experience.

Embry owned $5 million of Continental Airlines bonds and they sat at 43 for an entire year before moving up in price. Tally says that investors have to understand what the company must do, as well as the overall stumbling blocks of investing in inelegant investments. Continental Airlines, when it went bankrupt, could have liquidated all of its assets and had money left over for the shareholders; if he had held on to the bonds, the company would have made them completely good by paying all the back interest and reinstating them. Or they would have given 100 cents on the dollar or 80 cents worth of a package of securities. Embry only had to wait the process out, which often can take over two years. A buyer less patient might not profit.

Rule 8: The stock market affects the valuation of assets and the estimate of potential returns from a bond investment.

If the stock market is doing well, assets are worth more money. If it's doing badly, asset values are compressed. Bonds will reflect this fluctuation, since they're dependent on asset valuation.

Rule 9: A bond becomes more attractive when smart investors start buying equity in the company.

If Carl Lindner is a shareholder, he will get his money after the bondholders get theirs. In the case of Itel, its preferred stock started accumulating income in January of 1986. Sam Zell is a very good investor, and he owned

20% of the equity. The preferred was good sooner than his common.

Rule 10:   When interest rates are going up, investors can hold cash, buy some short-term securities or search for attractive bankruptcies and buy their debt.

Embry says this is what he did in 1978, when long bonds were not paying well; inflation, short debt and long bonds were all 9%. Bankruptcies usually have a two-year workout, so again an investor has to be patient.

A recent purchase that had all the ingredients Embry likes to see in such inelegants was Muse Air 16⅞% equipment trust certificates, secured by three MV80 aircraft. There is a strong forward book of orders on the aircraft, and at 86½% on the dollar, they yield 19½% currently—a fabulous return. Harold Simmons just bought $16 million worth of the common stock. The airline is losing money, but this instrument is the equipment trust certificate where the company rents the planes for the investor and its assets (the planes) are worth more than the value of the bond issue. When the bond moves up with improvement in Muse Air's credit, Embry will sell it and find something else. He said, "You just do that over and over again. It's fun."

Rule 11:   Read the paper for ideas.

When a company, whether it is Western Union or Consumers Power or Chrysler, is going out of business, look at the company closely to see if there's something attractive in its debt structure or capitalization that can be bought cheaply. Ninety-nine percent of the other investors in the world will look at that paper and, instead of making an informal judgment, they will call their brokers and say, "Sell it, I don't want to be involved with that problem." Most people do not like inelegant investments; they prefer elegant ones, like Apple Computer, even though no one knows how Apple Computer will be doing eighteen months from now.

Rule 12: The more senior a buyer's investment in the capital structure, the better off he is.

In a first mortgage bond, no one comes between the holder and the property. He owns the property first, what is left covers the second mortgage bonds and after that, it goes to the preferred stock and then the common. Senior bonds are the best to buy.

Rule 13: If an investor plans to sell a bond when it is downgraded, he should act immediately.

Often, professional money managers have to wait to get approval at a portfolio strategy meeting before they can sell a security. But the more time passes, the more uncomfortable investors become. Each wave of selling pushes the security lower.

Rule 14: Generally, the right time to buy a bond in a troubled company is just before it files for bankruptcy.

Most of the time, the plans are known, and the securities are already trading at a bankruptcy level. In fact, often they trade up on the announced news.

Rule 15: In spite of its reputation, the dividends on preferred stock are not secure.

There is no demand on a company to pay them, although some interesting issues come out of leveraged buyouts. Preferreds had always been attractive for a rich individual who owns the company, because 85% of the dividend was excluded from taxes. (Now with the new tax law an owner will have an 80% exclusion, making preferreds still attractive). But outside buyers are better off in a large company with secure income. Preferreds have little value in either a small company or a bankrupt one.

Rule 16: **Investors considering the purchase of a new junk bond should find answers to these questions:**

What Type of Business Is It? Companies like Chrysler and International Harvester have many assets and a great number of constituents—suppliers, labor, the banks, bondholders, state governments—who care about the company and will work to keep the enterprise sound. Companies like airlines or fertilizer producers are operationally leveraged (competition determines their prices, and small changes in volume make large changes in profits and losses). Combining this operational instability with financial leverage can make a dangerous mix.

How Competent Is Management? It is important to remember that one person can make a major difference in a company. Investors should check the competence of management, and see if there is a movement afoot to make changes. International Harvester did far better after McCardell left, Chrysler boomed after Iacocca took over, and so did RCA when Thornton Bradshaw came in.

How Will the Company Be Operated? As a business, Caesars World is in better shape than Golden Nugget, but Steve Winn of Golden Nugget is a much better operator and a more exciting businessman than the management group at Caesars World. Or an entrepreneur like Carl Lindner or Saul Steinberg has greater ability to follow through and turn things around than the chairman of Texaco, who has institutional but not entrepreneurial skills.

What Is the Value of the Business? Historical balance sheets often do not indicate true value, because trademarks like Oreo Cookies or Coca-Cola may be worth $10 million, or $20 million, or $40 million and are often carried on the books at nothing. An investor needs to know how much money is made in the business. A look at a company's return on its capital and sales can be a better indicator in dealing with valuable intangibles.

Are the assets stable and remarketable, or are they specialized? A casino may have value because it's on the Boardwalk in Atlantic City, but, since not everyone can buy it or run a casino, there may be a limited market for resale. A stretched 747sp airplane, which is the transatlantic version of the 747, is less valuable on the resale market than a plain old 747, because only a few carriers can use it.

How Has the Common Stock Performed? This is the easiest thing to look at because the value of the business is reflected in its common stock price, regardless of what appears on the balance sheet, and shows the real equity market value of the company. U.S. Steel trades at only one third of its book value, but then it has some plants that are worthless, while cBs trades at 2½ times book because it has licenses that are worth a great deal more than what they cost.

Rule 17: When a company's debt is downgraded, there are often wonderful buying opportunities.

Back in 1982, because the financial arms of Chrysler and International Harvester were doing badly, investors grew worried about the finance subsidiaries of manufacturing companies. Because of their concern, Ford Motor bonds were downgraded, as were those of Montgomery Ward. These securities went from a 16½% yield to a 19½% yield in the two weeks when every insurance company and bank wanted to trade out of them. The same thing happened when investors said that all the nuclear utilities were going bankrupt. The yields for these ongoing enterprises were much higher than they should have been and made very attractive investments.

Rule 18: **To ensure that they are exposed only to the risk they think they are taking, investors should see if they can get into a corporation's senior capital structure.**

Are there sinking funds or restrictive covenants that would protect the bond issue from prior claims? The most valuable piece of paper is the biggest thorn in the side of the company.

Rule 19: **If an investor wants to sell a position in a small bond issue (only $5 million or $10 million in debt outstanding), he will have to find his own buyer and get a reasonably good-size premium as the original owner, just in case no third person is interested.**

Tally Embry highlighted the bonds of bankrupt companies, so I asked him what would be a usual percentage of each kind of junk bond in his portfolio. He said, "It really depends on the period of time. You don't want to buy bankrupt companies necessarily at the bottom of the market because they have their own individual time frames. Special situations are always attractive because of the high yields that they offer. For instance," he went on, "the issue that Union Carbide will offer next week of junk bonds looks attractive. It's a large multibillion-dollar package, to finance their stock purchase of fifty-three percent of the outstanding shares to avoid being taken over by GAF. It's a big company and the yields will vary between fourteen percent and fifteen percent."

A year ago Embry bought some of the bonds offered by John Kluge to refinance the bank debt of his leveraged buyout of Metromedia. The investor, then, had a few choices:

- a five-year zero-coupon

- a seven-year zero-coupon

- 15¼% senior subordinated debt

- a 13½% coupon that became a 17% coupon in five years, with the right to receive a percentage increase in the cash flow from Metromedia (the total yield would approximate 21%)

Tally bought the 15¼s because they were safe, and because with the high coupons, they could be resold easily. A competitor of the investment banker raising the money, Drexel Burnham, issued a report saying that the deal would never work and the company would either have to declare bankruptcy or be restructured outside of bankruptcy. This took place before Metromedia and Rupert Murdoch offered $625 million for the stock of the broadcasting subsidiaries that were generally valued at zero. The Metromedia zero-coupon bonds were selling at 32; a year later, they sold for 64. The Metromedia deal turned out well because assets that have a residual life of their own are often undervalued. Embry bought the bonds because his analysis showed that, at worst, he would be a shareholder in all those broadcasting properties, which did not seem bad. The value of the business would be extra.

The returns on Tally Embry's $250 million portfolio averaged 16.5% for the last five years, returns, he feels, that come with reasonable certainty. Only the best people in the equity market over a ten-year period have done better than 15%; most people make much less. The Lehman bond index over the same period averaged 12.5%; A. G. Becker's range of professional managers ran from 11% to 12.5%. There is still that same historic spread if you can step up to the plate and buy those high-yielding but inelegant investments.

VENTURES

The classification ventures is a broad one, including venture capital, leveraged buyouts and any other hybrid investment that, like the first two, is illiquid. While most investors are rarely included in private placements in the financial community, the field is expanding as brokerage firms compete in developing many lines of products.

Any investment that cannot be sold the next day should be considered much more closely than one that trades in the market and that does not lock in the buyer for a specific number of years. This rule should be applied not only to brokers or investment advisers, but to friends offering a share in their companies. There, not only money is at risk, but sometimes even more dangerous, friendship. This happened to close friends who were bombarded by their mutual friend to invest in his embryonic venture. Despite a negative analysis of the future of the product, they went ahead. Six months later, the friend no longer telephoned and the status of the company was vague. The prognosis for the investment and the friendships? Both negative.

Recently, a venture-capital investor at my beach club, searching for investment money to save one of his drowning infant firms, approached me for $50,000. (After our meeting, I began calling him "Rambo Livingston," and every club member knows what "Rambo Livingston" should look like.) As we started to talk, I asked some rudimentary questions about the company, its business, management and prospects, since it was so close to bankruptcy. When I asked for the financials, Rambo smiled and said, "You don't need them. If you join us, I'll put you on the board and you'll love it. The board is made up of the most attractive men, they're all men you'd love to have kiss you on the lips and pat you on the fanny." These, of course, were the same men who had instituted an earlier, disastrous business strategy. Politely, I insisted on the figures, seemingly undisturbed by Rambo's remarks. After reading them, I politely refused the deal. But Rambo couldn't accept my refusal gracefully. He remarked, "It's luck for us, because the deal is firm," naming a famous investor who had been smart enough to accept. Oddly enough, none of his behavior bothered me; in fact, I found his sales approach normal. Rambo fell right into the "club" character that I described in my opening chapter. The deal, an illiquid one, was too risky for me, and that, not his comments, was the bottom line.

There is always the secret belief, though, that perhaps we're missing out on a lifetime opportunity when we first hear about a new venture. The only answer to that is to try to do the homework, knowing that there is probably no way to judge a start-up company. Professional venture capitalists admit privately that they haven't the slightest idea which of the investments they choose for their portfolios will be a winner. That is why venture pools make sense, not only to spread risk but to spread the opportunity for success. In one of Alan Patricof's venture capital pools, an original $300,000 investment in Apple Computer netted $12 million, but he could not have singled out Apple at its start-up as his number-one prospect.

Two discussions brought this point home to me, one with a man who had worked at Rothschild/New Court for twenty years. I asked him how well he had done in the venture deals that the firm had offered employees an interest in over the years, and he smiled. He had bought whatever was available when he had money and passed when he was broke. His Russian roulette strategy proved disappointing, as the deals he had passed on turned out to be the great successes. The arbitrageurs' principle also applies here: Venture-capital investors must participate in a great many deals to spread their risks and opportunities. Another conversation, with Gerry Tsai, confirmed the chance aspect of venture investment and the fun of doing it. One day, Harold Geneen was visiting Gerry's office and insisted that Gerry buy an interest in a small private company that he knew: Data 100. Gerry bought some shares for his wife without knowing anything about the company, saying to me as he recounted the story, "Believe it or not, that's the only company that I really made big money in as an outside investor" (distinct from his stock positions in companies where he has worked).

There are some similarities between venture-capital and leveraged-buyout investing. Pat Cloherty, one of the few female venture capitalists, described both as bookends, or two stages of a company's development. The intentions are the same: to capitalize on an increase in market valuation. The principal objective of a venture capitalist is to produce a company worthy of being an independent, publicly owned enterprise, because that is where the investor maximizes his return. The venture investor can, of course, sell companies to third parties or recapitalize to get his money out, but the real objective is the creation of a public company. In a leveraged buyout, a public company is taken private, recapitalized heavily with debt, with the same basic intention of maximizing profits by later taking it public again. By suddenly giving management some equity interest (what privately owned companies are all about), a sleepy vehicle is suddenly made more attractive and profitable. Peter Gerry, president of Citicorp's Venture Capital Ltd., feels that, as investments, venture-capital opportunities and leveraged buyouts complement and balance each other in a portfolio. Citicorp invests in both vehicles, and Gerry's investment observations follow:

1. There is no perfect model for a leveraged buyout, but successful ones have certain characteristics. An investor looks for sufficient values to allow the transaction to provide a chance for a high enough return to management, the new equity holders. The keystone to a successful deal is to start with a company that has predictable operating income. Gerry said that one of Citicorp's first LBOs (leveraged buyouts) was for a company in the steel barrel and drum manufacturing business, and there are fewer such businesses today than when Citicorp made that investment. Competition can then become sloppy, leading to quick losses of market share. In a successful model, Gerry would like to see earnings growing at 5% to 10% annually, with only brief interruptions over the last ten years, and with the expectation that these earnings will continue. Predictable cash flows and limited needs for capital, plus assets that can be sold are other good attributes in LBO investments. Often, the actual proposals are for

companies in mature markets, that have a noncyclical product line with limited risk of technological change. Good opportunities for LBOs depend on the market; it can be feast or famine. Citicorp did only one in 1984 and six in 1985.

2. An investor wants to create value and later liquidate it in both LBOs and venture capital. The strategy covers a five- to ten-year period to make the most of the invested dollars. Gerry expects 20% to 25% annual returns from leveraged buyouts, the same rate as from a successful venture-capital portfolio, with less risk.

3. To achieve those returns in venture capital, an investor has to accept the fact that, during any ten years, there will be swings of performance from marvelous to discouraging. He must have an absolute commitment to the long term, and patience. But the first requirement is a vibrant market for venture capital, and that means a complementary tax policy. It took the Steiger Amendment to the Tax Act of 1978, the Capital Gains Resolution Act, to stimulate capital formation after a bleak period for start-up companies.

4. Invariably, all problems and disappointments can be traced to the management of a venture-capital company. They may start with the wrong strategy. I asked Gerry what clues to such problems he looked for when he was on the phone with one of his companies. "I don't like to hear the espousal of philosophies," he said, "that show how we're going to grow a huge organization to accomplish a task." Empire-building frequently is adopted by an individual entrepreneur, but a venture capitalist prefers to see a company go slowly and develop piece by piece. It's a continuing balancing act. A venture capitalist does not want to become a permanent investor in an illiquid enterprise that benefits only the officers and employees of the company.

5. The second-greatest cause of discontent, disappointment and failure in venture-capital-backed enterprises is

that they have made big mistakes in marketing. Any radical change there is usually a reflection of either crisis administration or an uninformed strategy doomed to failure. Another thing that Gerry has become more cautious of is the kind of business planning that puts the marketing organization before the product. Marketing and sales organizations are clearly a cost. They will either be investments well spent or they will have absolutely no recovery value. "If you look," Gerry said, "at the vast majority of troubled venture-capital-backed companies in the technology arena today, I would say that you will find common to most of them a wasting of capital [by] building marketing organizations that either did not have a product or service to sell or were trying to sell a 'me too' product in a crowded marketplace."

6. A successful start-up company can do handsomely for an investor when it goes public, as well as in the aftermarket. A $3 million investment in Federal Express was valued at $12 million when the company went public, but that same position is worth $150 million to $200 million today.

7. Research suggests that successful companies have generally been among the first three entrants in their markets. Moreover, that market was potentially huge. There is always some risk in being a pioneer in wistful solitude. But early entrants that can sustain their advantage in a large potential market, like Federal Express, have the ability to grow into major companies.

8. Venture capitalists must be skeptical of the projections of research organizations, the so-called crystal-ballers who analyze the size of a potential market.

9. A venture capital pool, Gerry says, functions best as a partnership that has worked well over a period of time. A consummate venture capitalist has financial skills, knowledge and market sense, and could, if he had to, manage any function of any company that he has ever

invested in. It takes years to develop those talents, as well as the leadership qualities.

10. Venture-capital investments are sequential, and most individual investors are used to a binary investment policy, buy and sell. In venture capital, it is buy, buy, buy, and hope later to sell. The sequence requires more money each time, and individual investors often balk at providing it. "This aspect of financing is a misunderstood characteristic of our business," Peter said. Frequently, it coincides with business milestones and therefore should be expected.

11. There are milestones for every company. The early milestones are the easiest because they are cheap: the development of a product. The next is bringing the product to commercial standards, and often this happens ahead of schedule and under budget. Gerry said some of his group's most gnawing failures have come in ahead of time, under budget. There is always the converse, too, those that are over budget and considerably delayed. Next comes the real task of rolling the product into the marketplace, and that is when more money is needed. Financing is needed here to provide facts that will combat the building of castles in the air and declarations that the product will sell like hotcakes. "This is where 'the rubber meets the road' in a company's progress," added Peter, and where he has found much capital wasted, abused and lost.

12. There are specific stages in the life cycle of a product or service: first, the development stage; then, the commercialization stage, to penetrate new markets and achieve market share; third, competition, with cost reductions to fund new products or services that will maintain a business base. Some companies stumble at this third milestone, and revenues will stagnate. Don Clifford of McKinsey has done the most work on definable thresholds in the creation and building of an enterprise. Peter Gerry has found his research to be accurate; the number of companies Gerry has seen trip precisely at the $20 million revenue

level is mind-boggling. This threshold dictates certain organizational changes.

Other bits of wisdom from professional venture capitalists:

- Betting on the wrong people is the biggest mistake. It's better to be with a grade A person and a grade B idea. Entrepreneurs must be resourceful and able to switch in midstream if an idea does not work, so strong leadership and technical competence are necessities.

- A board of directors can be helpful, particularly when a company stubs its toe.

- No professional in the venture-capital world would make an investment without seeing the people involved. (So there, Rambo, take that.)

- Problems surface faster than good news.

- There is never a perfect time to harvest an investment.

- Anyone achieving 25% returns in venture capital is doing a creditable job.

- The ground rules have changed. Technology moves fast, so management must move with it.

- Anyone in the field has to be optimistic, but optimism must be tempered with realism.

All this advice assumes that a perfect venture capital deal will come our way. Of the $16 billion in venture pools, about 40% is focused on leveraged buyouts. The money in the pools is professionally managed and mostly institutional, not from individuals. But this $16 billion is a small part of venture investing, a field that claims a minimum of $120 billion, based on a rough estimate of incorporations. The odds are that a good friend will approach us one day with his venture, and that is when an investor needs to know the risks involved.

7

SIGNS
AND PORTENTS
*The Important Indicators
That Influence
Decision-making Today*

A FAVORITE MEMORY FROM MY EARLY WALL Street years concerns a man who came to the Dreyfus Corporation office every week. Short and nondescript, he would wait outside Howard Stein's office until beckoned in. Only when Howard would ask him, "How do things look?" did he brighten up, changing his drab appearance as surprisingly as a chameleon does. Out of his left-inside pocket, a small black notebook would appear and Howard would listen thoughtfully as his weekly visitor presented each item and statistic. I watched this ritual for months before I understood what was going on. That little black book carried records of important stock market trends and patterns that this visitor had interpreted carefully over the years, signs that might reflect the trend of the market and that therefore were important to anyone making investment decisions. Ever since then, I have wished for my own secret black book that told the future trend of the stock market. I still do not have it. Yet, if I kept such a notebook today, it would include:

Buying-power Trends

"Optimism, by itself, can't put a stock market up. Only purchasing power can put a stock market up. Pessimism, by itself, can't put a stock market down, only selling power can." This statement comes from an ad Jack Dreyfus wrote thirty years ago to explain that it was the irresponsible use of credit that caused the market's heights in 1929 and the depths that followed. Most of the billions lost in the crash were made in 1927, 1928 and 1929. Margins ranged in 1929 downward from 25% to 10%, and often, if an individual's credit was good, no initial margin was required at all. Dreyfus used an example of margin arithmetic that shows the source of the tremendous purchasing power that carried securities to those heights and depths. A speculator operating on 10% margin could have started with $1,000 and invested it in a stock selling at 10 to the fullest extent his margin allowed. If the stock went to 60 and the speculator pyramided every 10 points, investing the excess purchasing power at 20, 30, 40, 50, this is what the figures would look like when the stock reached 60:

Margin	Price of Stock	Appreciation on Ten-Point Move	Equity	Buying Power	No. of Shares Held
10%	$10		$1,000	$10,000	1,000
	20	$10,000	11,000	110,000	5,500
	30	55,000	66,000	660,000	22,000
	40	220,000	286,000	2,860,000	71,500
	50	715,000	1,001,000	10,010,000	200,200
	60	2,002,000	3,003,000	30,030,000	500,500
50%	$10		$1,000	$2,000	200
	20	$2,000	3,000	6,000	300
	30	3,000	6,000	12,000	400
	40	4,000	10,000	20,000	500
	50	5,000	15,000	30,000	600
	60	6,000	21,000	42,000	700

Margin	Price of Stock	Appreciation on Ten-Point Move	Equity	Buying Power	No. of Shares Held
60%	$10		$1,000	$1,666.70	166.7
	20	$1,667	2,667	4,445.00	222.2
	30	2,222	4,889	8,148.30	271.6
	40	2,716	7,605	12,675.00	316.9
	50	3,169	10,774	17,956.70	359.1
	60	3,591	14,365	23,941.70	399.0
70%	$10		$1,000.00	$1,428.60	142.86
	20	$1,428.60	2,428.60	3,469.50	173.5
	30	1,735.00	4,163.60	5,948.10	198.3
	40	1,983.00	6,146.60	8,781.00	219.5
	50	2,195.00	8,341.60	11,916.80	238.3
	60	2,383.00	10,724.60	15,321.20	255.4

When I first saw these figures I could not believe them. The chances of a 10% speculator's being wiped out, Jack noted in the copy, were far greater than the 50% or 60% margin speculator.

No wonder, then, that Dreyfus in the Fifties carefully watched his margin accounts to see whether buying power or selling power was stronger. Speculators accounted for a large percent of what moved the market in those long-gone 2-million-share days. They were the ones with margin investments who checked prices hourly, often moving in concert and making it important to watch what they were doing. When the speculators talked about how good the market was, it was a sign that they were fully invested. As Dreyfus said, "You don't go around saying the market's going to go up when you've got cash in your account." Sensing what they were doing, plus watching the margin accounts, made Jack careful when the speculators got bullish. On the downside, they produced what Dreyfus called the bowling ball effect. The accounts that are forced to sell put pressure on the next group of margins, and their selling brings on the next. When investors would not touch the market with a ten-foot pole, it was usually sold out.

Another indicator of market trends that Dreyfus followed were the short interest figures. He divided the players in the market into two groups, and though investors outnumbered speculators, the latter influenced market fluctuations. To Dreyfus, speculators were Wall Street Jeb Stuarts (of Confederate fame), who moved in and out to strike fast. Thus speculators often went short, selling a stock they would have to buy later to cover their original move. Dreyfus was one of the first to see that such speculation was a manifestation of future strength in the market: Increasing short sales meant backed-up buying power.

Market students still study the short figures and margin accounts, but they are not such accurate indicators today, since the institutions have replaced those Jeb Stuart speculators in influencing market fluctuations. But, according to Dreyfus, investors have to keep thinking and studying conditions, not using yesterday's yardsticks. Always try to estimate buying and selling power.

An investor who follows buying power with great sophistication is John Templeton. He looks first at how much cash is available in the United States (investments that will mature in eighteen months). In late 1985, he estimated there was $2.4 trillion, more cash than the $1.9 trillion value of American stocks. Buying power was great, even before funds from abroad were added in. Then the pension funds, now $1.1 trillion, Templeton estimates at $4 trillion by 1995. He calculates that if half of that goes into common stocks, that $2 trillion is more than the total value of stocks available. Then, what about individual retirement accounts and 401K plans? Everybody ought to have one—if they are eligible. But suppose 25% of American workers have IRAs: That's over 25 million people at $2,000 a year, or $50 billion a year available for investments. The normal supply of new stocks issued averages only about $20 billion.

"We are talking," says Templeton, "about really fabulous quantities of cash that are available for investment." Though an average of $20 billion of new stocks come out each year, in 1985 $90 billion worth of stocks were retired by corporations through takeovers and acquisitions, resulting in a net $70 billion reduction in one year. Therefore, in the long run, perhaps twenty-five years from now, there could be a shortage of stocks, concluded Templeton.

> **Madelon's note:** **Templeton's buying power thesis is every investor's dream.**

THE INSIDERS—WHAT ARE THEY DOING?

Corporate Insiders

One of the most reliable predictors of future common stock performance is the trading activity of corporate officers, directors and other major shareholders within a company. More buying is a bullish sign; more selling, bearish. A publication called *The Insiders,* published by the Institute for Economic Research in Fort Lauderdale, Florida, gives details of these trends. In each issue they publish many statistics on individual companies, but I always look at their "Insiders Index," plotted against Standard and Poor's, which has been accurate in tracking market trends. Look at it closely. In November 1985, with the market under 1400, there were three insiders buying for each one selling, while in late January 1986, with the market over 1500, "Insiders" saw two sellers for every buyer.

Not everyone can play golf with a corporate insider or stop by at the club after work to share a drink and information. But by observing what insiders are doing rather than what they're saying, an investor can profit handsomely.

> **Madelon's note:** **They're not always right, remember, just about four out of five times.**

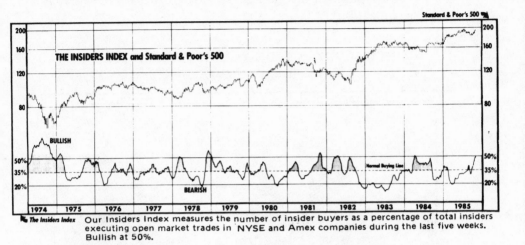

The Insiders Index Our Insiders Index measures the number of insider buyers as a percentage of total insiders executing open market trades in NYSE and Amex companies during the last five weeks. Bullish at 50%.

Wall Street Insiders

The specialists on the New York Stock Exchange have always been considered savvy investors, sterling indicators of which way the market is moving. As businessmen, specialists may be said to have a license to steal: No one questions their ability to make money for themselves. So I would like to be aware of what the specialists are up to—despite the belief that, as an indicator, their activity is not as reliable as it was before the introduction of options.

EMERGING GROWTH STOCKS

A good indicator of speculation and excesses in the market is the valuation of small growth companies. When they sell at multiples greatly in excess of Standard and Poor's, that can often be the top of the market. A good proxy for this market is the New Horizons Fund managed by T. Rowe Price. It's a $1 billion fund in high-quality, small growth companies (more than 150 of them), with a twenty-five-year history. When the New Horizons Fund price-earnings ratio is more than two times the ratio of Standard and Poor's, then small companies are overvalued, as in 1968, 1972 and mid-1983 (Dennis G. Sherva of Morgan

Stanley publishes these figures as does the T. Rowe Price organization).

NEW HORIZONS FUND P/E RATIO RELATIVE TO THE S&P 500 P/E RATIO

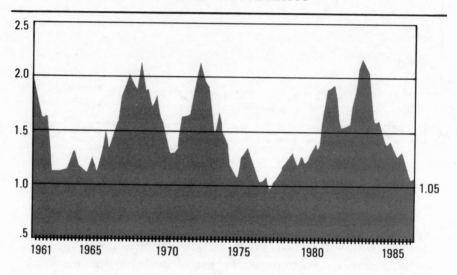

This chart is intended to show the history of the average (unweighted) P/E ratio of the Fund's portfolio companies compared with the P/E ratio of the S&P 500 index. Earnings per share are estimated by the Fund's Investment Advisor at each quarter end.

INTEREST RATES

Serious investors try to follow interest rates by keeping track of the "M" figures (the treasury purchasing programs). It is a hopeless endeavor, because the figures are sometimes distorted by new technicalities and are therefore deceptive. More important is any significant news from the government on changes in policy that could affect interest rates in the future. One example was the meeting of the Group of Five when the members decided to intervene in currency trading in order to lower the value of the dollar. This policy change influenced interest rates because the dollar cannot be lowered against other countries' currencies if American interest rates move higher. Foreigners would move more of their capital into dollars, preventing their decline. Treasury financings also can reveal the appetite of buyers for large government debt. And entrail watchers analyze whether successive sales are at lower or higher prices.

Two "musts" for every investor in tracking interest rates and monetary policy are to read *The Bank Credit Analyst* monthly, and then to list briefly in the black book their four or five observations. Another must is periodically to calculate the spread between treasury bills and treasury bonds by dividing the bill rate into the bond rate. A sample calculation would be:

$$\frac{9.4\% \text{ Treasury bonds}}{7\% \text{ Treasury bills}} = 1.38$$

Anything over 1.2 is clear sailing. The markets seem to get in trouble when the indicator moves below 1.2, which means that short-term interest rates are moving up faster than long rates, pressures are building in the economy and an inverse yield curve is developing. Such signs are warnings.

ECONOMIC NEWS AND INDICATORS

No economic theory has ever disproved that a business cycle exists in the United States. Periods of growth are followed by contractions. Luckily, the growth periods have been longer. Market timers often watch a variety of economic statistics to identify important changes in the wind. Unfortunately, few have succeeded regularly in spotting the subtle shifts. I would keep a list in my black book that would remind me of the trends to look for:

	Bull Markets Start	**Bear Markets Start**
investor attitude	negative— everyone wants to hold cash	euphoric
values	extraordinary, if you look	most stocks are overvalued
interest rates	high and start down as Federal Reserve loosens monetary policy	start to climb dramatically as Federal Reserve tightens monetary policy
inflation	has been high, but starts down, often reflected in breaking of commodity prices	starts to accelerate as shortages develop
consumer	liquid	illiquid
unemployment	high	low
government fiscal policy	stimulative with a tax cut or creation of new jobs	taxes increased
country	stable	unstable

Since the stock market often behaves like Jack Dreyfus's backwards analysis, this little chart helps me to focus and to put many figures into perspective.

Interest Rates

U.S. Treasury bill rates, set bimonthly, can show signs of a trend, as these rates are the most sensitive, responding immediately to changes in Federal Reserve policy.

Inflation

Wage settlements often set the rate of future inflation as new labor contracts are negotiated. If the percentages are increasing, these figures may reflect a tightening labor market and potential increases in the costs of goods and services.

Future Consumer Spending Patterns

Many analysts watch the number of employees on company payrolls to see whether it is increasing or decreasing. The confidence indexes are also good indicators: Consumer confidence in the future weakens concurrently with slowdowns in spending patterns. Often, the inventory-to-sales ratio increases as consumers curtail their buying. A change, say, from 1.3 to 1 to 1.6 to 1 shows an inventory buildup as sales slow.

Unemployment Figures

In January of 1986, the stock market in one day dropped just under 40 points when these figures came out. They revealed that unemployment was down only $\frac{1}{10}$ of a percent in the past month. Larry Klein, the Nobel prize-winning Wharton economist, said that what had been more revealing in the issued figures was a $\frac{3}{10}$ increase in the working week to 41 hours. Analysts were looking for proof positive that the economy was strengthening and found such a hint in these figures. Klein says that durable goods orders are followed closely for weakness or strength and he has observed that investors do not like quarterly reports of excessive growth in gross national revenues, or, in fact, of anything extreme.

GOVERNMENTAL ATTITUDE

When I asked Bob Wilson, a successful private investor, what indicator was important to him in predicting a stock market trend, he responded that there was no single indicator. But he admitted that the strongest predictor of where the stock market was heading was the attitude and policies of the government. In the early Seventies, Bob developed a reputation for shorting stocks that he thought were overvalued. Although he made money by shorting then, he doesn't believe that people who are negative can really do well in the market over the long term. Wilson had been negative then on government policy, feeling that it mimicked that of England, whose politics of envy and redistribution had been disastrous. Only when Congress in 1978 passed the Steiger Amendment and capital gains taxes were lowered did Wilson change his investment policy. That was the first step in a change of government attitude towards capital formation. Since then, Bob has been bullish, buying long.

To show what lowering the capital gains rate meant to the entrepreneurial sector of the economy alone:

- In 1983, $10 billion was raised for 304 companies that went public, whereas only about $300 million was raised for fourteen initial public companies combined, in the three years before 1978.

- Four billion dollars in venture-capital money was raised in 1983, 200 times more than the average year in the early Seventies.

- New business incorporations in the same period doubled to over 600,000 from 280,000 in 1978.

- At least 10 million new jobs came from those small companies, while employment declined in the large companies.

Lowering the capital gains rate was essential in the creation of many new and rapidly growing small companies and again shows why the attitude of government toward capital formation is one of the important market indicators.

PSYCHOLOGICAL VIBES

Market watchers can't explain these feelings but they somehow know that a change is about to take place. Sometimes they grow wary, and the change is negative; sometimes they are expectant, and the change is positive. Tom Griffen of GT Management in London calls these psychological stirrings commonsense vibration indicators, while my brother, Ray DeVoe of Legg Mason, calls them the shark-in-the-water syndrome.

To Griffen, commonsense vibes come from past experience. He is suddenly aware that something is out of kilter. And he offered these examples:

1. The English market at the end of 1974 was selling at 42% of its book value, the same as the American market in the Thirties. On Christmas Eve, Burmah Oil went bankrupt. Something is usually done in democracies to improve economic conditions when a big bankruptcy takes place. For instance, he said that any time a bank gets into trouble, people see the specter of the Thirties and increase the money supply. The English government had to do something about this news; Burmah Oil's predicament was tantamount to the bell going off, signaling that the stock market would turn. (Money was loosened.)

2. Another case he recalled concerned one of their analysts who went to a conference in Helsinki on the Finnish stock market. GT had already made investments in Finland, but on arriving, the analyst saw a group of a hundred American analysts and portfolio managers in the lobby. He never checked into his hotel. The bloom, he thought, had to be off the rose.

3. Griffen and another compatriot at GT became cautious about Hanson Trust stock. At a past underwriting, 50% of the stock was left in the hands of the underwriters. A broker placed the loose stock above the market, but then it weakened.

These sensations, whether wary or anticipatory, are the result, I think, of past experience and commonsense analysis. Ray DeVoe says such feelings are the same as those that occur while scuba diving—a tingling that means something else is out there, an eerie sensation of helplessness and instinctive fear. The late Ben Goodspeed, Ray explained, called it inferential overload: The intuitive right side of the brain piles up information that logic has rejected, causing the sensation that something is about to happen. DeVoe thinks that after twenty years in the securities business, no one indicator triggers this feeling. It comes from a certain sensitivity about the market. "What affects me," he said, "is a confluence of events that seems to say something is out of sync here, that people are not seeing what I see. Sometimes it's an economic event, but most often it's an excess in investor psychology." In the second quarter of 1983, investors were buying any high-tech stock available without reasoning, and issuing crazy statements about the stock's prospects. Sometimes suspicion looms when a company offers an analyst tickets to a hot Broadway show after a visit: Perhaps in that company, things are not quite what they seem.

THE SMALL INVESTORS—
WHAT ARE THEY DOING?

It used to be popular to try to spot what the small investor was doing, and then to do the opposite. A few favorite monthly reports like the odd-lot figures and the short positions were devoured by analysts. But these, along with New York Stock Exchange member shorts and the specialist figures, have become pointless because of the availability of options. They are now too volatile to interpret. Richard Eakle, Morgan Stanley's market technician, feels that the most reliable indicator of investor sentiment is the put-call ratio (puts divided by calls). This ratio shows institutional sentiment the way the odd-lot figure showed individuals'. Since options are used by both institutions and individual investors, this ratio is a better barometer today. The higher the ratio, the more positive an investor should become. As in the old days, the idea is to do the opposite of what other investors are doing.

Eakle follows the action on the Chicago Board Options Exchange (because that's the option equivalent of the big board) every day in the newspaper. The day we talked, January 24, 1986, with the market over 1500, calls were 330,029 and puts were 215,319.

$$\frac{215{,}319 \text{ puts}}{330{,}029 \text{ calls}} = 0.65$$

On August 17, 1985, with the Dow Jones average at 1312, the ratio was 1.15, puts exceeded calls dramatically, and that was bullish (more people were betting that stocks would go down than go up).

In 1985, the individual investor surprised the hungry Wall Street brokers. While the stock market had a sensational return of over 30%, one of the best years ever, 70% of the money invested went into fixed income instruments. In spite of anticipation that individuals would be back soon to purchase stocks through brokers, investors continued to use intermediaries such as mutual funds for their purchasing. As yields on money market instruments tumbled, investors moved to lock up longer-term rates, joining rather than competing with the institutional investment community. The institutionalization of individual investors seemed inevitable after their positive experience in liquid-asset funds, and they have been influenced by today's broker, who is more comfortable selling products than individual ideas. The small investor is alive and active. And if this group's activity was an indicator to invest in the opposite way, then the contrarian should have bought equities one on one, with a broker rather than through a fund.

TECHNICAL TRENDS

Eakle likes to play the trend in the market. Such a strategy still works and can offset the influence of the options market. By doing this, he does not quite get in at the bottom but he can get 75% to 80% of the move, and no one does better. To evaluate the trend, it is necessary first

to: (1) decide: Is the direction of the market up or down?
(2) determine what the message is: Why is this happening?
(3) concentrate on all the facets of the capital markets,
commodities as well as bonds and stocks. (Rick compared
the market to a plane. If one engine fails, he may be able
to land, but he will surely have a rocky trip.) The Dow
Jones commodity futures index appears in the paper
every day and can be tracked. As we talked, this index had
been moving up strongly, an indicator that merited watch-
ful concern to him.

Some other warning signals of market weakness to
Eakle are:

• The ratio of the New York Stock Exchange's advanc-
ing to declining volume. He also uses a ten-week moving
average and considers the stock market overbought whenever this series rises above 1.40.

• Fewer new weekly highs on the New York Stock Exchange.

• A dropping percentage of New York Stock Exchange
issues trading above their 200-day moving averages.

• Rising speculation. He measures the ratio of over-the-
counter volume to NYSE volume. Is the ratio close or is the
OTC volume exceeding NYSE volume? If so, that's a warning signal.

• Is the yield curve flattening? (Are long rates declining
while short rates are held?—a traditional indicator of a
more restrictive monetary policy.)

OPTIONS EXPIRATIONS

A recent introduction to the weekly television program,
Adam Smith's Money World, showed Dorothy, from *The Wiz-
ard of Oz,* being caught in a tornado. This image illustrated
the extreme frustration in the stock market caused by
professional traders on certain days, particularly at the
end of the day that options expire. Like Dorothy, an individual investor in Kansas City could get caught innocently

in the ensuing market whiplash. A market savant described the built-up pressure this way: If a stock moves from 35 to 40 and an option's strike price is 40, investors in the last half hour of trading will try to push the stock through 40, while others try to hold the line, all in the interest of their underlying option positions. Options, this savant said, were created to hedge positions, but in doing so, they have speeded up the horse race, and many people are abusing the system. Computer programs have made these strategies possible, and the number of investment houses active in buy programs has, through sheer force, created a tidal wave. The programs are activated and switched fast, as the participating "quants" (people good with numbers and computers) work against sophisticated formulas.

There is potential vulnerability for these investment sophisticates. Someday, a lady in Des Moines or Kansas City will place an order to sell IBM in the morning at 140. The investment firm handling her order knows it has a computer program, to be activated that day, that says the firm will buy IBM up to 142. Someday that investor will sue, saying, "You should have told me."

Until then, the only protection is to tell your broker to let you know if you are placing an order on a "tornado day" and to be aware of the option expiration dates. The first method is the safer because, as the option market grows, there will be more days ahead with swirling black clouds in the sky, and your broker will certainly see them before you do.

FINDING THE DATA

Investors look not only at broad indicators to estimate the market's direction, but also at specific series and data to follow individual stocks.

Stock Splits

These are not always a negative sign, but a warning chime: Seasoned investors pay attention to stock splits.

Roy Neuberger mentioned them as a "yellow light"; Richard Eakle watches the technical pattern of a stock more carefully after a company announces a stock split. He says that if a stock is selling above 100, it is more likely to go down, and if the split is a large one, 4 for 1 or 3 for 1, the price suffers. In 1980–81, Dome Petroleum split 5 for 1, and that was the peak of its cycle. In 1983, AMP, Motorola and National Cash Register all split 3 for 1 or 4 for 1, and they came down hard.

Reading the Newspaper

Reading the newspaper religiously helps to keep abreast of trends, as well as to closely follow a company and its industry. John Levin (another member of the Class of 1985) says it is the one imperative activity for every investor. In fact, many of his own investing ideas have come from the morning papers. He saw there that the biogenetic companies had successful new products. Boeing became more attractive to him when he read that they had lost Hughes to General Motors. Levin also uses the newspaper each morning to check his portfolio against the market. Though he was bullish, he had no entries on the buy side of his sheet. On the sell side, there were a few prospects. Some had gone long term and others he was watching because he thought something might be wrong.

Scanning Value Line

Both John Templeton and Warren Buffett said that they use the Value Line investment survey. Neither uses this survey for its investment opinion, but as a quick way to get information or to scan for a new idea. It is the quickest way to get an immediate view of a company, the source of a hundred things that a security analyst wants and needs to know. Standard and Poor's used to be used extensively by financial analysts, but Templeton thinks now that Value Line's data are more helpful, offering more information as well as percentage changes of a company's financial data, and even better, all on a single page.

Investment Newsletters

There are two newsletters that I would like to track: One, called *New Issues* from Fort Lauderdale, Florida, follows small companies that are going public, and the other, the *Morse Investment Report,* publishes a list of companies that are healthy, yet vulnerable to negative surprises. In short, a newsletter that highlights what is new and attractive, and another to remind me of significant changes that I may not be aware of.

The Tape

If a stock is not acting right on the tape, in spite of good fundamental news, then the market is confused about something. Gerry Tsai, a former portfolio star, and I once agreed that if the wind is blowing in the wrong direction with an investment, action is necessary. This rule he learned early in his career at Fidelity from its founder, Edward C. Johnson II, who used to tell him, "Gerry, don't say you love a stock, the stock doesn't know you at all." This rule, he found, is a difficult one to follow and Gerry mentioned the way IBM was acting then. The company's prospects were excellent and he had not sold a share as its price fell. Billy Salomon, the former managing director of Salomon Brothers, believes strongly that the direction of the market and of individual stocks is all there on the tape. The problem, he thinks, is that it is very difficult to sell securities. There are few good sellers or people who make money on the short side. "When you analyze it," he said, "it shouldn't make any difference. You should be making the same amount of money." Stocks and bonds to him are not like buildings. A building has floors that rent, it stands on the ground and it goes up and down in worth but never trades. It's an investment. When it comes to securities, though, today's investment can be tomorrow's loss. The saying that an investor's first loss is his smallest one, he thinks, is a pretty good one. Too many people don't watch the tape and keep trying to prove that they are much smarter than the market.

I would like to know what happened and how the tape acted during the past week from an objective participant. I want to know as clearly as I can what stocks and groups were strong and which were weak.

Ideally, a black-book list should be flexible. Signs and portents should always be updated and supplemented. Frankly, I look forward to the day my own chameleonlike gnome waits outside my door with all this information packed into his black notebook.

8

MAKING A PLAN
*Applying the Rules Learned
and How to Maximize
Your Money in the Market*

INVESTORS LIKE THOSE IN THIS BOOK, WHO DO
well year in and year out, share one common attribute:
passion. A passion for the business of Wall Street. Making
money. And their passion is unlike the kind that first
comes to mind, the passion of crazed, radical students, of
wild, young lovers. Instead, investors seem the opposite of
emotional, with their deceptively steady and controlled
coolness. Yet, underneath that, their desire to compete
and win the treasure perpetually flames, quietly fueled by
memories of their past successes. To suggest that there is
anything average about their investment performance is
one way to cause their flame to rise visibly. So the first rule
to make in building a plan for yourself is to decide that
you will care enough in the structuring of your financial
assets to become better than average. Jack Dreyfus expressed it well: "The average person is going to get average results, whatever he does." Certainly being only
average cannot be acceptable when financial security is at
stake. Be average at something else.

Yet John Templeton cautions that it would be rare,

although not impossible, for someone who is not a professional at security analysis to come out with a superior long-term record, especially if that person is trying to do it part time. So I asked him about Lord Keynes: "Didn't he do well in the market once he retired and worked in bed on his portfolio for a few hours every morning while reading the newspapers?" Templeton did not think so. Keynes's economic theories were great, Templeton believes, but his investment record was not that sensational. Nonetheless, I still like the image of Keynes playing "Financial Pursuit" over breakfast in bed. Perhaps we should aim merely to be very good at investing, at that stage between average and sensational, which is indeed possible for the individual investor. (A *"très bien"* in my Convent of the Sacred Heart days was considered our aim then. "Excellents" were rarely won.)

Ted Ashford, of the Class of 1985, when asked by associates what they should invest in, tells them first to invest in themselves through education, both formal and informal, then to invest in what they know best and finally to find a good adviser whom they trust. Ted's three suggestions combined will help you to become better than the average investor. Educate yourself continually, concentrate on what you know best and feel comfortable with, and then find an adviser, whether it's a broker or investment counselor, who understands your interests and whom you can trust.

As it happens, my sister-in-law, Helen Haskell Sampson, has followed Ted Ashford's recipe for success without ever being aware of its existence. Helen has educated herself financially by reading business newspapers and magazines and by talking to knowledgeable people, and she has bought stocks of companies that she understood best. She has also, over the last thirty years, worked closely with brokers.

Helen's story began back in 1958. After returning home one afternoon from the Monmouth Park racetrack, she decided, along with three friends, to buy a race horse. Innocently, she called what was then the National Newark and Essex Bank for a small loan. Even with collateral, the answer was an emphatic no. Horses were considered a poor risk in those days, and, as businesses, horse racing and racetracks were too "different," in fact, exotic. (Today, that same New Jersey bank, larger and renamed the Midlantic Bank, is lending to horse owners as well as to farm owners. Now they are all considered big business.) In 1958, though, Helen thought about how she was going to make enough money to pay for her share in a race horse, and she chose the stock market. For one thing, she did not want to travel to New York City from Red Bank, New Jersey, every day. "I had two small sons at the time," she explained, "and I didn't want to get up and go out of the house to work. So I thought of the stock market as a place to make money and still be able to work at home." Moreover, the market was attractive because it was liquid. She could buy and then sell immediately if she changed her mind; she could also know every day where she stood. If she worried about losing everything, she could put a stop-loss order on her stock, so that if it went down she could still retain most of her invested capital, while if it continued up, she could stay with it. So her thoughts ran.

Helen's first financial information network and school was the *Wall Street Journal.* (In those days, the *New York Times* financial section was not nearly as good.) Later on, as she became more interested, she added *Forbes* and *Fortune* to her reading list. She mentioned how often people find themselves waiting, a perfect time to read through the business publications, whether in a doctor's office or at home and even more so in the country, during one of those marathon waits for a repairman to come or goods to be delivered. The area that Helen Sampson lived in, near Rumson and Middleton, New Jersey, with its easy commute to Wall Street and lower Manhattan, attracted many brokers and financial participants. "People," she said, "love to talk about their own business so, in my area, you're always discussing stocks and the stock market." Thus Helen's choice of investing as a way to make money seemed natural to her. In reviewing her investing experiences over the last thirty years, she insisted that it is necessary to have one's own rules and regulations and to stick to them. The few times she did not, she got burned— usually because she bought a controversial company too soon, before its problems were over. So she believes that it is far better to wait until such a turnaround company is on its way back to health and its vital signs are clearer. Set up your own standards and follow them, she repeated. Some of hers follow:

Rule 1:   Invest in timely subjects.

A million ideas are timely and a curious and intuitive investor takes advantage of them. Several obvious examples of such new and interesting products that she noticed were:

- slot machines, before Atlantic City opened for gambling
- hamburgers available on every corner at a reasonable price
- a new cure for baldness
- a face cream that takes years off your complexion
- home care for the growing aging population

(You can even go further and make a list of human needs that should be met. Then tell that list to your broker and be on the lookout with him or her for products that meet these needs.)

"Find out," says Helen, "if any of these ideas are represented by a tangible stock. If so, buy a little. You can always buy more if it looks good and you can always buy on the way up as you get more information." With her strategy in place, she started out with a broker, Charlie Hutchinson, who was also just beginning, so they shared a learning curve. "I've been with him ever since. I discuss my ideas, intuitions and timely subjects with him and he tries to find a company that matches each one, that would be a good investment." Two stocks that they owned jointly were:

1. *Westec* (Western Gold and Uranium Equities). This company had run into difficulty after a mammoth acquisition binge. Helen and Charlie bought it at around 4 a share in 1963 because they expected the price of gold to rise, and sold it at 45 a share two years later. The stock eventually moved to the low 60s, but then broke.

2. *Cordis.* The idea of pacemakers, a new product that would help a great many people, seemed timely. Only two companies were in it and Cordis was one of them. Helen and Charlie purchased Cordis before it went public in 1967, averaging 3 a share and sold their investment in 1971 at 28 a share. The Cordis company still exists, but Helen likes to take long-term profits and does not believe in being greedy.

Helen also believes in having two investing pools of money, a conservative one that is held for preservation and income, and a more speculative one for greater risks and to buy the stocks of companies that are not established, to allow some large capital gains appreciation. But, Helen adds, investors must not go into risky situations until they have learned the basic game in their preservation portfolios. As she built up her profits in her conservative pool, Helen began to move money into private placements, buying an interest in a company like Cordis in its early stages. Another company that caught her eye was Radiophone, started by a man in her area in what was then the new field of personal pagers. She said that there were a number of hospitals in the Red Bank area, and she first noticed that doctors were carrying these new pagers. The shares she bought in the late Seventies averaged about 1¾ a share and she cashed in the same shares at 26 a share in 1986 when the company was bought by Metromedia.

Helen Sampson has developed a few other rules that have aided her in accumulating capital:

Rule 2: If an investment doubles, take the original capital out and put it into another company.

Rule 3: Keep good records.

Not only is this necessary for tax purposes but knowing the inventory enables an investor on any given day to know where he stands.

Rule 4: Invest the same dollar amounts in each stock.

Most people think of buying a certain number of shares. If you decide the amount you will invest is $10,000, that means buying 1,000 shares of a $10 stock or buying 10,000 shares of a $1 stock. This method allows you to make the big score. At least, at the start, you want your positions to be about equal. Later on, they will get out of proportion as they go up or down.

Rule 5: Don't overextend in the stock market.

Investing is for extra money, not the mortgage payment.

Rule 6: Don't be greedy.

Easy to say, but hard to apply. Sell and get out if growth in the company slows or falters.

Helen thinks, too, that investors can be overbrokered. She will listen if brokers call on the telephone, although she hates cold calling (by brokers who don't know her but have her name on a list of possible new clients) at dinnertime. Yet she will always ask them to send her material. If she likes the idea, she will buy some of the stock. If the investment goes well, they may work together in the future. "My theory," says Helen, "is that brokers will only cold-call with an idea they think is super. They know they won't keep you if they give you a bummer, so I do listen."

Helen also inherited a large position in a company, Rowan Industries, where her first husband, Amory Haskell, Jr., had worked. On his untimely death in an airplane crash in 1970, the stock moved down from $6 a share to 25 cents a share, that is, if you could find a market. She held the stock for sixteen years, believing it was "a heritage" and confident, knowing the cast of characters still in the company, that something would come of it. The company, renamed DeTomasa Industries (after her brother-in-law), is now selling at $27 a share because of a series of joint projects it has undertaken with Chrysler and Lee Iacocca. (Ben Graham would have cited this as a perfect example of a person close to a company who could hold the stock through the company's vicissitudes.)

Today Helen owns ten race horses and feels that investing is challenging and satisfying, admitting that she has done well at it. She remarked, "It's been profitable and that's why I began."

After reading this far, you should easily spot some familiar strategies and patterns in Helen's success. They represent some of the same rules that other, more famous investors have used. As you will see:

1. Stick to your own rules and regulations—shades of Warren Buffett and April Walstad.
2. Buy a small position and add as you get more conviction—George Soros.
3. Take long-term profits, and don't be greedy—Roy Neuberger and John Templeton.
4. Have two investment pools, one more conservative than the other—Jack Dreyfus.
5. Long-term investing is the way to ensure profits, and it is easier to do when you know a company well—Everyone.

Investing doesn't have to be a loser's game. Indeed, it's unlikely to be if you begin by assimilating the thoughts and procedures that winning investors have followed. Remember, too, that inertia and complacency can join to become a comfortable prison. Keep on questioning. I'm always glad when people ask, in one form or another, "Tell us the truth, we often feel that we're being given the runaround by our investment adviser. How can we do better with our investments?" And I say that the first thing to do is decide who they are going to work with and how they are going to make their investments. The possibilities, along with their pluses and minuses, are:

Make Your Own Stock Selection

Buy your choices at a discount brokerage firm. The plus, often repeated, is that you'll pay less in commissions. This is true, but you will get no helpful feedback or information. So this suggestion is only good to follow if you have your own resources and research network.

Using a Broker

The old-fashioned term "broker" has evolved, first changing to "RR" (a registered representative) and now to an account executive or financial consultant. There are many varieties of brokers to choose from. The large wire houses like Merrill Lynch or Shearson are multifaceted, and any broker will have a wide variety of products to sell. In fact, they have so many varieties of tax shelters, real estate pools and mutual funds that, unless you are talking to a seasoned pro, he will find it difficult to come up with a great stock for you. The firms have excellent research, but it becomes a superhuman undertaking to sort through all the investing choices. Many people believe that the rush of individuals to mutual funds in 1985 came not only when they submitted to the institutionalization of the market, but after they were trained by all those financial consultants promoting in-house funds. True, those consultants acted for reasons of efficiency, but also because their compensation from fund sales had become more attractive than from an individual equity trade.

Investment banking firms like Bear Stearns, Goldman Sachs and Morgan Stanley have fewer products to sell than their supermarket competitors. As a result, their brokers can, like convenience stores, provide personal attention as well as stock picks. (The average wire-house broker grosses approximately $150,000, whereas the average retail banker in an investment banking firm grosses between $300,000 and $400,000. The latter usually deals with a more sophisticated person who has been in the market for many years and has a minimum net worth of at least $1 million.) Most consumers like both the supermarket and convenience store approaches so one possible answer would be to have two different financial consultants.

An Advisory Account

In the past, money management firms shunned small accounts, setting their minimums at $500,000 to $1 million. This often precluded minor investors from access to individual portfolio structuring for a fee, usually 1% of the assets managed. But once again, the small investor is being favored, as firms realize the promise of such volume. The future will see new ways to develop products for this market. The advantages are that most advisory management firms have a longer-term horizon for their investment recommendations that promotes the investor's interest, net profits after taxes. Brokers whose earnings depend on trades done and commissions earned always have a conflict of interest with the long-term welfare of their clients.

Mutual Funds

These continue to be an attractive and efficient means to invest in the financial markets. They offer good money managers as well as instant liquidity if you need the money or change your investing objectives. To be able to switch money from one fund to another without penalties in the family of fund complexes is extremely enticing. On the negative side: if you need hand-holding and feel that it should come with your commitment of assets, you will not find much satisfaction investing this way.

Trust Departments of Banks

A trust department of a bank was usually chosen for you by a family member who had designated you as a beneficiary of his or her estate. Not so today. Now many banks, like Harris Trust Company in Chicago, are selected by individuals as the best custodian of their assets.

SELECTING AN ADVISER

Often, investors are selected rather than doing the selecting. A friend suggests an idea, or you listen to one of those cold calls and the next day you find yourself writing a check. When I asked John Templeton how he would suggest finding a good adviser, he began by saying that finding a good investment counselor was far easier than finding a good doctor, lawyer or accountant. For one thing, an investment adviser has a documented record, whereas the other recommendations are based on subjective rather than objective assessment. "Look at the investment counselor's record," he advised.

Benjamin Graham once noted that securities investment is unique among businesses. The investor asks someone else for advice on how to make a profit. "Businessmen," he added, "seek professional advice, but they do not expect to be told how to make a profit." (This anomaly may be the chief cause of the problems between investors and advisers.)

In *Vogue's* financial column, I once listed the qualities to look for in any search. Since such articles must fit the space assigned, their points are compressed, but such brevity helps thinking. So here, briefly, are my views on the subject:

If you're looking for a broker or investment adviser, take the time to meet him. You should be looking for the following qualities, but only the first two are measurable. The other eight are intuitive and intangible. Go with your feelings on them.

1. *Satisfied Clients.* Ask for four or five client (investor) references and call them. This is a *must!* Ask if they're happy, if they made money with their adviser. Ask for and weigh any negatives.

2. *Experience.* Five years' experience should be the minimum. You want your adviser to be seasoned by a down market, but, if possible, not with your money.

3. *A Feeling of Trust.* If you don't have confidence in your adviser, you're in trouble.

4. *Responsibility.* Do you consider this person prudent in his everyday dealings?

5. *Flexibility.* Successful investors are flexible. Stubborn, dogmatic people are to be avoided.

6. *Balanced Ego.* You want someone who will admit mistakes and try to avoid them the next time around.

7. *Curiosity.* Intelligence is too difficult to measure. Curiosity is more evident. And a person who is curious will find good investment ideas.

8. *Judgment.* Does he exhibit a sense of care and concern?

9. *Patience.* It takes time to make money. And you want an adviser who will also be patient with you and explain what he's doing for you without being arrogant.

10. *Unselfishness.* Has he a reputation for putting his clients' interests first?

My recommendation, to trust your impressions after you review this checklist, makes even more sense to me now that I have visited with some of the living legends. And Helen Sampson's experience with a broker just starting out also confirms the value of intuition in the whole selection process.

WORKING WITH A BROKER

I was amused at Helen Sampson's receptivity to telephone calls from unknown brokers. I remembered the last such call I received on my telephone machine. The voice said, "Good afternoon, Mr. and Mrs. Talley, I'm an account executive with Dean Witter. I'm calling you about a triple-tax-exempt bond at 9¼%. Top of the line. Please give me a call." Frankly, I am so used to my husband's cutting off such calls abruptly when we are dining that I had not considered their success rate until I interviewed a young broker, Clare Gold. Some of the things she told me made me admire the idea, and especially the tenacity of anyone who chooses sales as a career.

A disciplined new broker, she said, works on a formula. The one she uses is: Sixty cold calls a day from a qualified list should lead to ten prospects, of which two or three should become clients within two weeks of hearing the pitch. The average ticket gross should be $250, which is approximately a $10,000 order. If she can open fifteen new accounts a month and plan on three to five trades with each client over the course of the year, then she can gross $180,000 a year.

4 trades per client = $1,000 gross
15 new accounts a month × 12 months = 180 new clients
180 new clients × 4 trades per client = $180,000 gross

These numbers are for stock business; some clients provide other business.

Clare started as a broker at Merrill Lynch, but fortunately, over the years she has developed a book of business clients that moves with her. The compensation is excellent, she says, and the business enhances her ego. There is tremendous personal satisfaction in opening a new account. "You don't make a killing on your first trade, but still, it makes your day. You just sit back and feel tickled pink about it. That's the life and juice and the love of the industry." Moreover, such personal motivation also encourages brokers to try to open more accounts and keep their business growing. They need positive attitudes, because their daily environment is filled with confrontation: the internal stress of protecting their books of business from their peers, who are like hungry piranhas; the need to survive the politics of their firm, as well as its satellite offices; and in addition, the confrontation with clients. "Some people are brutal," Clare remarked. "They seem to love to insult and beat up their broker." Surprisingly, they continue nonetheless to work with that broker and it takes time to get used to their insults. (Another woman broker has a client in Europe who loves to call and tell her about his latest sexual adventures, to, as they say, "talk dirty" to her. Although she can't complain and hates those calls, she simply charges him higher commissions, taking the attitude, "If I have to listen, then he has to pay for it." Client X is not perturbed. Perhaps he's familiar with paying for his merchandise.)

The economics of continually looking for new business and worrying about the total commission can put great pressure on an individual broker, and also can motivate her to stay at the telephone. Some get frightened when they realize it is the end of the month and they have not covered their food bills, but clients notice when the broker overtrades their accounts. "The heat is on," says Clare, "when your boss calls you into his office and says, looking at your numbers, 'What's going on? You're doing a horrible job, you're obviously not working.' Fear is tremendously motivating; it quickly gets brokers back to their desks to work. When they decide you can't make it, the knife is quick and cold. A handshake, a few words. 'We're sorry we hired you, it was a mistake,' then 'good luck.' "

So the next time the telephone rings and there's a stranger at the other end, be kind. The best solicitors are well prepared to sell you an idea and Clare says that many people want to buy, giving encouraging hints that mean "keep going." Next to her desk she has a folder of sales hints that she had gathered in an earlier job in an investment bank. One of these aids is a memo on power phrases to use with clients. Laughing with her, I read through the list:

1. We never advertise. Our reputation is based on word-of-mouth for only one reason—investment success in good and bad times.

2. The chapter in the book I sent you called us the "Money Magicians." It's a reputation we've earned in 130 years of investment success.

3. Don't deny yourself the opportunity to deal with us.

4. You know this is the right investment and that you should be making it.

5. We want to have you as a long-term client. Not just as a one-time investor in a thousand shares of _____. Every investment is important, but the first one is absolutely crucial. We're confident that if you start your relationship with us by taking a position in _____, we'll have laid the most important cornerstone for a life-long relationship.

6. We're not interested in the number of shares you buy now. We can always buy more on the way up. What we are interested in is having you begin a relationship with us with an investment in _____.

7. Our single most important asset is our reputation—the fact that wealthy people in America have trusted us for over 130 years. While we are aggressive with some of our capital from time to time, we never gamble with our reputation. Before we come to you, we spend months and hundreds of thousands of dollars to analyse the recommendation.

8. Everyone likes to make his own decisions. We're investment professionals. I would take your advice on (health, law, insurance, etc.).

"Do you really use these phrases?" I asked Clare.
"Absolutely," she responded. "When I get on the phone my introduction is short.
" 'My name is Clare Gold and I'm a vice president at

_____. I want to introduce myself and the firm to you. We are working more with retail accounts than with institutional clients. With your permission, I'd like to call you three or four times over the course of the year when we have an interesting idea that has helped us and our reputation in the past. Fine. Now I have to ask a few questions.

" 'Can you commit at least $10,000 to an idea?'

"And then, 'Fine, I'll send you my card, and some background information, and the next time I call, it will be to show you our idea,' so they know that the next call is not a free lunch."

When she calls again to try to open a new account, she searches for a blue chip name that most people are familiar with and is not too volatile. It could be a good idea but it is usually one that is not going to get the broker in trouble, not necessarily their best idea, as Helen Sampson had felt, because if you lose money for a client on the first trade, he will not trade with you again. Trust and confidence disappear. That is called "burning a book."

Later on, says Clare, you suggest stocks with more sizzle. In fact, she was embarrassed to hear a co-worker talking with a client whose account he had just opened during the past month and with whom he had done four trades. The client reminded the broker that originally he had said he would only call three or four times during the year. Clare heard the broker reply:

"I know, but I can't help it. I have so many great ideas," and then in a whispered tone, "Mr. Client, look, you're not going to build a wing on your house and name it after me because I had you buy that Santa Fe stock. You'll do well in it over time, but this one is a knockout!" As he hung up, the broker was beaming with another order in his pocket.

In her handy file by her desk, Clare also keeps a list of objections that clients use most of the time, with ways to handle those objections. The usual ones fall into the categories of "I don't have any money," "I'll have to check with my wife, send me some material" and "I want to think about it overnight." What do you say, I asked her, when they say they don't have any money?

"I don't believe a man in your position has no money. Of course you have the money. My job is to show you the idea. Your job is to get the money. (Then you discuss buying on margin.)"

To "I have to talk to my wife"?

"I say, 'I'm a spouse, I have a spouse. I didn't call him to ask him if I should call you. I'm asking you to make a business decision.' They often laugh at this, which I interpret as their way of saying 'Keep it up, I'd like to buy.' "

To "I'd like to think about it overnight"?

"I say, 'Thinking about it is not going to make you money or me money. I called you today because the price is right today, the timing is right today, you're a busy man, you're not going to take my call tomorrow. Make a business decision while the facts are fresh in your mind, now.' "

To "Send me some material"?

"Well, I won't do it. Then I start selling the firm again and how we've done all the homework and that our major institutional clients are buying this. You have to create urgency," says Clare. " 'I've talked to management analysts on Wall Street. There is nothing that you're going to be able to find out that we don't already know and haven't already considered, so the research report will just sit on your desk for a few weeks.' If you then lower your voice and add some urgency, even better," says Clare. " 'There's going to be an announcement soon' or 'I've heard that another brokerage firm is about to recommend it' or 'So-and-so is adding to their position.' "

People like to be told what to do and they respond to a forceful opinion, as well as to a forceful salesperson. A strong buy, sell or hold is always seductive. What kind of broker are you going to have and how are you going to work with him? Is he going to make the decisions, are you going to make them, or is it going to be a joint effort? I like the idea of developing a good working relationship with a broker, or even with two, as I have suggested. One who works on special ideas with you and another in a large

firm that has access to a large number of products. Whatever you choose, the following thoughts should be helpful:

1. If a new broker calls you and you want to listen, ask
as many questions as possible about his idea. Go so far as
to ask, "Is this your best idea? Would you buy it for your
mother's account?" (Remember Jack Dreyfus's theory.)
"What is the potential for this stock over what period of
time?" Question, and don't be pressured.

2. If you are going on vacation, tell your regular broker
where you will be or give him discretion in selling for you.
Once, when I was in Beirut, my broker called to advise me
to cover a short. It would have been better if I had given
him my proxy before I left.

3. Be willing to hear feedback on any stock you have
ordered to be bought. Often people hesitate to comment
on another's choice, afraid to sound critical.

4. Most customers complain about inappropriate investments. Yet, on this subject, the client should be fair,
and not discuss his friends' great hits in speculative stocks
if he wants a conservative portfolio. No matter what a
client says, he usually wants activity, and even if the adviser
has done well with the account, will call up to ask why he
has not been in any takeover stocks for instance. He does
not want a quiet portfolio when the market has been
strong, so the broker walks a fine line in deciding between
what the client says he wants and what he really wants.
"They say one thing," says Clare, "but they often mean
another."

5. Brokers would prefer to sell stocks between $10 and
$20 because they do not use up all the client's money, so
some will be available for their next idea. The investor
often can make a larger percentage return in cheaper-
priced stocks.

6. Insist on knowing your return at the end of the year
and how it compares with the market. Naturally, you can-

not be annoyed if it is below par when you called all the shots.

7. Don't be afraid to ask questions. If your adviser is rude, find another.

As Helen Sampson said, "Working with a broker and doing well is fun and challenging—and it can be profitable." Some investors are intimidated by the process, preferring to concentrate their assets in mutual funds, but, even here, there are choices to be made that are worth the commissions paid to have the advice of a financial consultant, rather than risk selecting a no-load fund. The whole mutual fund industry has changed dramatically since the time twenty-five years ago, when funds encompassed only stocks. Now equity funds represent only about 26% of a $440 billion industry. It is a much more complex world. There are funds for bonds, short-term assets, tax-exempts and currencies. And if you were in one of these at the right time, you would have made substantial money. When I asked Mike Lipper, the president of Lipper Analytical Services, what the individual should do in selecting mutual funds, he said that, first of all, somebody reads a book like this, reads, and that makes him rare. He is willing to do some work. "With that in mind," he said, "it is my view that even somebody with modest means should have a portfolio of funds." He prefers five, although he thinks it could be done with three, and they should be different types of funds. A money market fund is a given for everyone to park cash in, to await opportunities or to accumulate if there are none. Another fund might address the inflation-deflation question, as a necessary hedge, such as a gold fund, natural resource fund or, conceivably, a bond fund. The choice between them is based on your expectations for inflation and deflation. The third fund, says Mike, should be a "Mom and apple pie" fund—basic American—and that would be a growth or growth-and-income fund. A fourth could be a fund that specializes in small companies, because job formation is one of their functions and this must become the key issue in the future for democracies. The fifth should be either an international fund or some other specialty that you are interested in. Lipper believes that at the very minimum, an investor should have 50% of his money in equities, that history has proven the inability of people to time the market, but in spite of this, percentages can be changed and moved around. If you buy a fund, he advises, try to find two or three others of a similar nature so that you can track the group's performance.

Roughly half the mutual fund industry has a sales charge and with the introduction of 12B1 funds (funds that spread the sales charge over the life of the investment), that portion is growing again. Lipper noted that we are in a country where people choose to be economically illiterate. It's too much effort even to read the financial pages of a local paper. It's work, it's dull and it does not provide answers. Instead, it raises the anxiety level with more questions. That is the reality and people do not like it. If you can put off decisions, great. Moreover, all forms and applications are difficult to fill out. "There is an economic value to having a broker for people who don't want to do their own work and use funds sold to them by a broker," Lipper said. "A good broker can nag you into buying or not buying at the right time. They're more skilled at the details of filling out those forms, dividend collection and the 1099 form proxies. But remember that most brokers are still trying to maximize their income in the shortest time and they will tend to sell people funds that are performing well now, so it would be far better to have a schematic investing plan of your own."

Yes, inertia seems safe. The easiest thing to do in investing is to go with the crowd. The hardest is to think independently. Even if you work with an investment adviser or a bank's trust department, you must work if your financial affairs are going to do better than average. Susan Davis, vice president of marketing at the Harris Bank in Chicago, believes that the most significant thing any investor can do is first to step back and have a serious conversation with himself about his life and then to become more adventure-some about the options he considers. Finance is just a piece of your life. You need to set general as well as financial goals. Davis says that most people simply put out fires day to day and do not focus on any long-range plan. A sensitive counselor can help to sort out priorities and values. Some people may resent such an intimate conversation, while others are pleased. It can take two or three goal-setting meetings with a counselor to get the under-pinning right.

Some people, intimidated because of their insecurities about finance, feel inadequate and out of control. This makes them defensive. Clients like this, says Davis, are hopeless. They need education and support. "We can't perform for them because they didn't even have expectations that we could perform to."

Then I asked Davis, "What, from your observations, are the mistakes most people make in choosing an investment adviser?"

A Lack of Knowing. The financial world is so complex that people sometimes prefer to wait at the edge of the pond when they should be out there swimming.

Unrealistic Expectations. People keep looking for the "white knight," just as girls sometimes look to marriage as the solution to their problems. They want a person to take charge, to be perfect. They want to delegate responsibility. But any investment counselor you find is only human. So no one measures up.

You have to take charge of your own affairs.

"Most of the people in the financial service business make their money," adds Susan, "by selling whatever they've got and you can get burned, burned, burned." Even a trust department that sells on a fee basis will do the normal fiduciary average for you, unless you get involved and know what you want. Even the best trust department that takes full responsibility can do a much better job when officers are close to the client rather than managing to some simplified standard. "If someone's attitude is 'hands off,' we do a good job, but we'll do much better when we're in touch with and close to a client."

Investing well can be a profitable adventure, but only if you make it happen, if you become what Benjamin Graham called an "enterprising investor" rather than a passive one. The willingness to take charge of your affairs and assume responsibility for their success or failure is the beginning of the voyage.

NOTES

Page

5 "The 400 Richest People in America," *Forbes* magazine, October 1984, October 1986.

18 "Arithmetic Can Kill a Ghost," Dreyfus & Co., advertisement, 1955.

19 Bernard M. Baruch, *My Own Story* (New York: Henry Holt & Co., 1957), pp. 64–66.

19–20 Martin Gilbert, *Winston S. Churchill*, vol. 5, 1922–1939 (London: Heinemann, 1976), p. 350.

22 Baruch, *My Own Story*, p. 243.

22 Benjamin Graham, *The Intelligent Investor*, 4th ed. rev. (New York: Harper & Row, 1973), p. 125.

22 Baruch, *My Own Story*, p. 105, 130.

23 John Maynard Keynes, *The Collected Writings of John Maynard Keynes*, vol. 12, ed. Donald Moggridge (Cambridge: The University Press, 1983), p. 109

23 Baruch, *My Own Story*, pp. 55, 107, 130.

29–30 Baruch, *My Own Story*, pp. 254–256.

31–32 Lawrence Minard, "The Original Contrarian," *Forbes*, September 1983, pp. 42–52.

50–51 Keynes, *Collected Writings*, pp. 17–18.

33 Keynes, *Collected Writings,* pp. 38, 39.

33, 34 Keynes, *Collected Writings,* pp. 51, 64.

34 Keynes, *Collected Writings,* p. 81.

34–35 Keynes, *Collected Writings,* p. 106.

35 Keynes, *Collected Writings,* p. 55.

38 Hartman T. Butter, "An Hour with Mr. Graham," from *Benjamin Graham: The Father of Financial Analysts* by Irving Kahn and Robert D. Milne (Charlottesville, Virginia: The Financial Analysts Research Foundation, 1977), p. 33.

40 Graham, *Intelligent Investor,* p. viii.

41 Graham, *Intelligent Investor,* p. 40.

43 Graham, *Intelligent Investor,* p. 36.

48 Berkshire Hathaway, Inc., annual report, March 4, 1986, p. 4.

49 John Train, *The Money Masters* (New York: Harper & Row, 1980), p. 10.

50 Roy Neuberger, "Roy Neuberger's Almanac," *Money* magazine, cover page.

60 Jack Dreyfus, *A Remarkable Medicine Has Been Overlooked* (New York: Simon & Schuster, 1970), pp. 29–30.

63 Marshall Smith, "Chaser of Lost Dogs and Boss of a Red-Hot Fund," *Life* magazine, February 11, 1966, p. 72.

74 Bernice Kanner, "Aw Shucks It's Warren Buffett," *New York* magazine, April 22, 1985, pp. 52–65.

74 Berkshire Hathaway, Inc., annual report, March 4, 1986.

79 Berkshire Hathaway, Inc., annual report, March 4, 1986, p. 7.

79 Kanner, "Aw Shucks It's Warren Buffett."

79 Train, *The Money Masters,* p. 215.

86 *Institutional Investor* cover, George Soros, June 1981.

88 Lord Victor Rothschild, *Random Variables* (London: William Collins & Sons and Co. Ltd. 1984), p. 135.

89 Anka Muhlstein, *Baron James: The Rise of the French Rothschilds* (New York: The Vendome Press, 1982), p. 35.

89 Muhlstein, *Baron James*, p. 107.

89 Baron Guy de Rothschild, *Contre Bonne Fortune* (Paris: Belford, 1983).

90 "Jacob Rothschild, London's New Financial Whiz," *Business Week* magazine, April 23, 1984, pp. 64–72.

106 "Funds Over Time," *Barron's*, August 11, 1986. Lipper Analytical Services—Ten year returns (June 30, 1976– June 30, 1986).

114 John Brooks, *The Go-Go Years* (New York: Weybright & Talley, 1973).

116–117 "Selection and Opinion," *Value Line*, July 25, 1986.

118 Adam Smith, *The Money Game* (New York: Random House, 1967), pp. 223–231.

122 Warren Buffett, in a speech delivered at Columbia University, New York, May 17, 1984.

146 Martin Mayer, *A New Breed on Wall Street* (London: MacMillan Co., 1969).

161 "John Slade's $9 Million Killing," *Institutional Investor*, November 1983.

181 James Sterngold, "Boesky Builds One Billion Dollar War Chest," *New York Times*, March 13, 1986, p. D1.

183 Barton Biggs, "Morgan Stanley Investment Perspectives," April 24, 1984.

207–208 "Arithmetic Can Kill a Ghost," Dreyfus & Co., advertisement, 1955.

234 Graham, *Intelligent Investor*, p. 131.

235 Madelon Talley, *Vogue* magazine, July 1985.

BIBLIOGRAPHY

Baruch, Bernard M. *My Own Story*. New York: Henry Holt & Co., 1957.

Brooks, John. *The Go-Go Years*. New York: Weybright & Talley, 1973.

———. *Once in Golconda*. New York: E. P. Dutton, 1985.

Dreyfus, Jack. *A Remarkable Medicine Has Been Overlooked*. New York: Simon & Schuster, 1970.

Grant, James. *Bernard Baruch: The Adventures of a Wall Street Legend*. New York: Simon & Schuster, 1983.

Kahn, Irving, and Milne, Robert D. *Benjamin Graham: The Father of Financial Analysis*. Charlottesville, Virginia: The Financial Analysts Research Foundation, 1977.

MacKay, Charles. *Extraordinary Popular Delusions and the Madness of Crowds*. New York: The Noonday Press, 1932.

Mayer, Martin. *A New Breed on Wall Street*. London: MacMillan Company, 1969.

Moggridge, Donald, ed. *The Collected Writings of John Maynard Keynes*. vol. 12. The Royal Economic Society. Cambridge: The University Press, 1983.

Muhlstein, Anka. *Baron James: The Rise of the French Rothschilds*. New York: The Vendome Press, 1982.

Proctor, William. *Templeton Prizes.* Garden City, New York: Doubleday & Co., 1983.

Rothschild, Lord Victor. *Random Variables.* London: William Collins & Sons and Co. Ltd., 1984.

Smith, Adam. *The Money Game.* New York: Random House, 1967.

Train, John. *The Money Masters.* New York: Harper & Row, 1980.

INDEX